Welcome to Uncertainty !

FROM THE SAME AUTHOR:

A Manager's Guide to Disruptive Innovation: Why Great Companies Fail in the Face of Disruption and How to Make Sure Your Company Doesn't (Diateino, 2018).

Constructing Cassandra: Reframing intelligence failures at the CIA, 1947-2001, with Milo Jones (Stanford University Press, 2013)

The balancing act of innovation, with Walter Van Dyck (Lannoo, 2011)

ISBN: 9798859042838

Cover photo from CDC on Pexels

Welcome to Uncertainty !

Surviving and Thriving in a World of Surprises

Philippe Silberzahn

"I don't know where I'm going from here,
but I promise it won't be boring."

David Bowie

Contents

Introduction: A World of Surprises

In October 1971, the Shah of Iran celebrated the 2,500th anniversary of the founding of the Persian Empire. The event was held at the archaeological site of Persepolis, the capital of the Achaemenid Empire, built in 521 BC by Darius I and Xerxes I, and destroyed two hundred years later by Alexander the Great. Dozens of heads of state were in attendance. The celebration was both a tribute to the founding of the Persian Empire by Cyrus the Great and an extravagant demonstration of the country's socio-economic development under the Shah. It was an event of excess: a royal feast, a huge camp set up in the middle of the desert, three days of lavish festivities, 250 limousines, and more. The Iranian people, kept on the sidelines, were furious. Ayatollah Khomeini, a highly respected yet little-known cleric, called the event "the devil's banquet", but who cared?

Four years later, the monthly National Geographic published a lengthy feature on Iran. Titled "Miracle of the Desert", it described a nation on the verge of modernization, led by a visionary and protective Shah. It spoke of oil, industrial development, computers, dynamic ministers, a powerful modern army, a peaceful and proud country able to reconcile tradition and modernization, and a fighter pilot crown prince. Iran was the great regional power, a key partner of the United States in a Middle East that had become increasingly complicated after the 1973 Yom Kippur War. Four years later, in January 1979, after an autumn of unrest, the Shah went into exile, never to return. The Islamic Republic was installed, upsetting the geopolitical balance in the Middle East, and depriving the United States of a key ally, an event whose consequences are still being felt today. The obscene celebrations at Persepolis, intended as a show of strength, were in fact the swan song of a blind, megalomaniacal monarch. Was the Iranian Revolution a thunderclap in a serene sky, an event predicted by nothing? On the contrary. Beginning in the 1960s, piety - until then the preserve of the poorly educated - began to spread among the middle class, which was emerging thanks to economic growth, as evidenced by the boom in mosque construction.

The Shah's modernization efforts met with growing resistance from an increasingly conservative population, among whom Khomeini, despised by the Tehran elite, enjoyed great prestige. The signs of the regime's growing fragility were there for all to see.

A different time, a different context. On January 9, 2007, Apple introduced the iPhone, a smartphone with a touchscreen interface that would revolutionize the mobile phone market. But according to the experts, it was nothing more than a gadget that would never represent more than a few percent of the market. In May 2008, more than a year after its launch and with the iPhone's success growing, market leader Nokia briefed financial analysts on its strategy. The company was at the top of its game, dubbed the "The cell phone King" by Forbes magazine. Not once during the briefing was the word "iPhone" mentioned, either by Nokia or by the analysts in the room. Despite its considerable resources, the leader proved completely incapable of recognizing the danger it was facing as his descent into the abyss was about to begin. Five years later, in September 2013, Apple had triumphed, and Nokia was a shadow of itself; it ended up being acquired by Microsoft for a few billion dollars, a sum that was completely written off a year later, so incapable was the fallen leader of generating any value.

A different context. On November 8, 2016, Donald Trump was elected President of the United States. It came as a considerable shock. The announcement of his candidacy in March 2015 had been met with derision, so much so that it seemed to be nothing more than a rich fool's fantasy. In primary after primary, however, Trump scored points, but the pundits continued to believe he had no chance. The seeming amateurishness of his campaign, chaotically managed in contrast to that of his opponent, Hillary Clinton, at the head of a veritable war machine, only reinforced the idea that he couldn't become president. Trump continued to win primaries and inched closer to the nomination, but the feeling remained the same: good performance, the pundits said, but it's time for a "real" candidate to take over - this is a presidential election, after all! Then he won the nomination, which would have been unthinkable a few months earlier, but nothing changed: he had no chance of winning. Just two weeks before the election, the Washington Post headlined: "Trump's chances of winning approach zero." The rest is history: he won an unwinnable election, defying just about every prediction made by the best American intelligentsia and political pundits over the past two years.

Finally, of course, Covid-19. When the first reports of a coronavirus epidemic came out of China in late 2019, it was in a little-known region and seemed to affect only the elderly. Who was worried? A coronavirus epidemic was nothing new: there had been SARS in 2003, but it had remained localized in Asia and was quickly contained. Moreover, the WHO initially reassured people, based on Chinese expert reports, that the virus could not be transmitted from person to person. This was not true, however, and the epidemic continued to spread. On January 23, the city of Wuhan, with a population of eleven million, was completely sealed off. The world showed little concern. By the end of February, however, the epidemic had spread to Europe. Italy was the first country to be affected, and on February 21 it introduced containment measures in several municipalities in the north of the country.

France remained unconcerned. On February 28, in a statement that will go down in the annals of blindness, Dr. Éric Caumes, head of the infectious diseases department at the Pitié-Salpêtrière hospital in Paris, declared that people should fear influenza, which kills up to 10,000 people a year in France, rather than the coronavirus. The comparison was unfortunate because the situation was rapidly deteriorating. On March 8, the Italian containment zone was extended to the entire north, affecting nearly sixteen million people, and just two days later the containment zone became national. Aware of the situation, French President Emmanuel Macron was equally reassuring. He even went ostensibly to the theater with his wife on March 6 to encourage the French to go out despite the epidemic: "Life goes on. There's no reason, except for vulnerable populations, to change our habits when it comes to going out", he declared.

A few days later, the world witnessed the martyrdom of the city of Bergamo, with its 120,000 inhabitants, which had become the epicenter of the epidemic: the number of deaths skyrocketed, and the health system was brought to its knees. Images of processions of military trucks taking away coffins at night, so as not to frighten the population, went around the world. Then the epidemic reached France. Less than ten days after inviting the French to go out, Emmanuel Macron backtracked and finally declared a national lockdown. This came as a quite a shock to people, who suddenly realized that we had entered a new era.

The Iranian revolution, the iPhone, Donald Trump, and Covid-19: four very different examples that illustrate the difficulty of predicting how the world will evolve, sometimes with catastrophic consequences. And there are many more in recent times: the collapse of Lehman Brothers and the

2008 crisis, the Arab Spring, the emergence of Daech, the war in Syria, mass emigration in Europe, Brexit, the return of the Taliban to power in 2021, the invasion of Ukraine in 2022 - the list goes on and on of events that we have been unable to anticipate despite clear signals, so difficult is it to see the future in the fog of the present. In the face of such uncertainty, the considerable arsenal of technical and human resources we deploy seems laughable and useless, with its mediocre results and catastrophic consequences.

Surprises are nothing new in human history, especially in wars or in the world of finance and economics. But we are most helpless in the face of the unprecedented, that is, the completely new. In war, an attack like the German invasion of Poland in 1939 often comes as a surprise, but it can be nothing new. Similarly, the arrival of a competitor may come as a surprise, but that's business. Novelty brings an additional difficulty. It has never happened before, which makes it hard to imagine that it is even possible. What's special about the unprecedented event is that its main effect is to render obsolete the assumptions on which predictions were made, and even our mental models, those big beliefs we've built up about the world. For example, the launch of the Sputnik satellite by Russia in 1957 was a major shock to America, which discovered that its main adversary, whom it had thought to be far behind, was in fact leading the space race.

The consequences of an unprecedented event are sometimes considerable, often painful, as in the case of Nokia, or even dramatic, as in the case of Covid-19, which officially killed about 4.4 million people at the time of this writing (certainly many more in reality). It's the navel-gazing hotel industry that doesn't see Airbnb coming. It's the taxi companies that, after years of comfortable monopoly, suddenly see Uber and Lyft coming out of nowhere. It's the retail industry, which is slowly waking up to Amazon's growing strength after years of underestimating it. France is stunned to discover the Islamist insurgency in Africa that has been brewing for years. None of this had been predicted by the armies of analysts maintained at great expense by giants - companies, states - who have discovered that they are blind.

So, analysts be damned? Forecasters be damned? What if, instead, the problem was with the very idea of forecasting? The world is changing radically, becoming increasingly uncertain. In such a world, it is not possible to predict the future, and those who base their actions on predictions sooner or later expose themselves to catastrophe. Predictions inevitably fall victim, sooner or later, to the unprecedented event that renders them obsolete. And yet the decision-making tools we use have not changed. They are based on a predictive paradigm. Most of them date back to the 1970s and are rooted in the civilization of the Industrial Revolution that began one hundred and fifty years ago. It's high time we completely rethought them for the new world.

For almost twenty years now, I've been defending the idea of the impossibility of prediction in my lectures to students, corporate executives, and public officials, and I've always noticed how difficult it is for my participants to accept it. The rhetorical technique I use, I confess, is relatively crude: it consists of listing ad nauseam examples of false predictions that have cost dearly to those who believed them. The exercise isn't difficult; you can easily find hundreds of them, famous or not. After a while, the message seems to sink in, and doubt begins to creep into the minds of the participants, or at least some of them. That's usually when the retort comes: "Fine, but what do you suggest instead?" This question always reminds me of the following anecdote: I am walking in the countryside with a friend after a heavy storm, and we see an electrical cable lying on the ground. My friend reaches out to grab it, but I suggest that he shouldn't touch it because it's dangerous. He turns to me and replies, "Fine, but what do you suggest instead?" Well, nothing. All I offer is that you won't die, which is enough, and in principle I don't owe you anything more. The same goes for prediction. If you use it, sooner or later you will be exposed to disaster. That's why this book suggests above all that you don't. It follows the adage of the philosopher Gaston Berger, who wrote: "Life is always a gamble; let's at least avoid absurd ones". The point, then, is to avoid the absurd gamble of making predictions in an uncertain and therefore unpredictable environment. In practice, of course, it's a bit more complicated; not having an accident is not enough to guide a strategy, but it's a good place to start.

But to eliminate the absurdity of prediction, you must show why it's absurd. Is that enough? Not really, no. We'd like to share the optimism of economist Ludwig von Mises who wrote: "In fact, rational businessmen are fully aware of the uncertainty of the future. They understand that economists cannot provide reliable information about what will happen, and that all they offer are interpretations of statistical data from the past. For capitalists and entrepreneurs, economists' opinions about the future count only as dubious guesses. They are skeptical and not easily fooled". But the reality is that as soon as they leave the room, my participants return to their forecasting habits.

Whatever the argument, whatever the number of examples, each more striking than the last, whatever the understanding of the problem, it does indeed seem impossible to bring about a change in management practices. It's come to this: you can't predict it. My participants hear it, they learn it, they understand it... and they choose to ignore it. So the central question we need to answer is: Why do intelligent people who know their approach is dangerous continue to use it despite clear evidence of the disasters it brings? Part of the answer lies in human psychology, part in the training we've received, and part in the fact that prediction is an institutional reality in most organizations. It is so widespread that its costs are shared. We can't hope to reduce its use without addressing the cultural dimension of its universality. Prediction is a cultural practice and an ideology; it cannot be swept away simply by showing that it doesn't work.

What if we can't predict? It's not a matter of replacing one method with another. The very nature of uncertainty makes the idea of a method, in the sense of a recipe that guarantees a result, impossible.

The thesis of this book is that to propose new tools and approaches, we must first clarify our understanding of the environment. If the way we see and understand the world is wrong, then everything that flows from it, including management methods and principles, is wrong and will lead to disaster. To deal with an uncertain world, therefore, we need to clarify three issues: first, the nature of the world and how it is evolving; second, how we can obtain valid information about the world in order to act; and third, how the various actors involved in decision making under uncertainty interact. This is what this book proposes. On this basis, it provides decision-makers and those who advise them with a set of principles to help them understand, protect themselves from, and above all take advantage of uncertainty and the unpredictable.

In a sense, this book has a long history. The idea itself was born in 2016, when I was invited to give a course entitled "Anticipation and Action" to students in a specialized master's program "Operations and Crisis Management in Cyber Defense" at the Saint-Cyr military school in France. Its writing began in a very uncertain personal context, that of a serious health problem that immobilized me in a hospital room for a month. My interest in uncertainty, however, goes back a long way. As far back as I can remember, I've always seen time as a progression toward something new. Long before I knew this, I adopted Gaston Berger's position very early on: tomorrow will not be like today, it will be different. As a teenager, I read the monthly magazine *Science & Vie*, and each month I followed the scientific progress that was changing the world for the better. As an economics student, I was struck by the absurdity of neoclassical models, timeless and so far from reality. Later, as an entrepreneur, I was directly confronted with uncertainty: having to make decisions with virtually no tangible evidence, when every direction seems equally valid, and not knowing for a long time, often until it's too late, whether you've made the right ones. I suspected, again intuitively at the time, that uncertainty was a kind of dark matter in decision making: important but largely invisible in the management literature of which I was an avid reader. It was only with the discovery of effectuation, a theory of entrepreneurship developed by the Indian American researcher Saras Sarasvathy, that I realized that uncertainty is in fact the raw material of entrepreneurs, the stuff they feed on to create new products, new markets, and new organizations.

For entrepreneurs, innovators and, in a sense, all those excluded from the system, uncertainty is therefore an opportunity, because change can benefit them. It is the precondition for creative change. As such, it is interesting to note that it is a central concept in seemingly very different activities: politics, intelligence, entrepreneurship, large for-profit and not-for-profit organizations, public administrations, associations, and so on. And yet it strikes fear into the hearts of the managers of large organizations that I work with in my training seminars, and into the hearts of our fellow citizens. Faced with a world that is changing rapidly and profoundly, they are at a loss because the usual decision-making models no longer work.

What entrepreneurs feed on when they change the world is also what frightens politicians and decision-makers. For the established organization, which sometimes has much to lose in the face of change, uncertainty is experienced primarily negatively. Much of its work consists of protecting itself against the dangers of uncertainty: technological changes, disruptions in its environment, the emergence of new competitors, changes in regulations, etc.

But uncertainty is also the only source of opportunity for future growth. It is even more than that. It can be a source of happiness, the joy of mastering one's environment, of inventing and charting one's own course, for individuals and organizations alike. Why should what motivates and delights entrepreneurs necessarily frighten corporate decision-makers? Anxiety-inducing uncertainty is a perception that needs to be changed. A world without uncertainty would not only be boring; it would be inert and deadly. We'd be a colony of ants going about our physiological business for the rest of our lives. Instead, we can constantly invent the world around us and in which we live. In fact, it's a distinctly human trait to construct the world we live in through thought and action. It is this dual nature that gives rise to the attitude of this book: to protect ourselves from uncertainty when necessary, of course, but to take advantage of it as much as possible. So welcome to uncertainty!

PART 1: WELCOME TO UNCERTAINTY !

Ontology: The World as it is

"The world is but a perennial wobble"

Montaigne

How does the future come about? How is it determined? How does the world evolve over time? What are the factors behind this evolution? This is the ontological dimension of our problem, i.e., that which relates to the very nature of the world.

THE WORLD WE LIVE IN: A COMPLEX SYSTEM

Mechanical watches are complicated objects, usually made up of hundreds of parts. Nevertheless, the role of each part and the way it interacts with the others is well known to their designers. The watch's behavior is a direct result of these interactions. All the information needed to predict the system's operation is available (this is the watch's blueprint). There is no uncertainty: however complicated, the behavior of the "system" is perfectly predictable, barring a breakdown. This is true even of the most sophisticated watches, which can consist of up to a thousand parts.

Natural phenomena such as the weather, on the other hand, are considered complex. They contain so many components that it's impossible to list them all and know all their interactions. The degree of uncertainty is therefore very high. Since we don't have all the information about the system, unlike a mechanical watch, the only way to try to predict the evolution of such a system is to create a model with a very small number of parameters. Meteorologists create increasingly sophisticated models, but they're a simplification of reality, and there's always the risk that they'll miss the parameter that's critical to tomorrow's weather forecast for your city. Complex systems are inherently uncertain and therefore difficult to predict.

Another factor of uncertainty is related to time. Your mechanical watch does not evolve over time. The parts remain the same, and their operation remains the same (except for wear and tear). The same cannot be said of a complex system, in which not only its components change, but also their relative importance and the way in which they interact. In a world endowed with time, nothing is ever complete since time itself constantly brings about change through a flood of new facts. "New things", large and small, are constantly happening, and it is this stream of new things, most of which we don't know about, that time brings. Again, using the example of the weather, no ecosystem is stable over time. This is what is at stake in today's climate problem.

The systems that interest us in this book - nations, organizations, markets in particular - are also complex, but they have a particular nature. They are *social* systems, that is, they are made up of thinking people. The social nature of these systems gives them specific characteristics that are additional factors of uncertainty. Let's look at the main ones.[1]

Characteristics of Complex Social Systems

Openness

What are the drivers of oil prices? If you try to list them all, the list quickly gets longer: supply and demand, of course, but also geopolitics in the Middle East, growth in consuming countries, and the development of alternative energies, to name just a few. Each determinant is a complex system, influenced by thousands of other variables. What's more, we can't identify which of these variables are critical. This is why the best forecasters have been chipping away at their predictions for decades, as we show below. As historian John Gaddis notes: "In complex systems, you can never extract the critical variables in advance."[2] In other words, there is potentially no limit to the parameters that can be considered to describe their behavior.

---

[1] This section is based on Josh Kerbel, "Thinking Straight: Cognitive Bias in the US Debate about China", Studies in Intelligence 48, 2004.

[2] John Lewis Gaddis, *The Landscape of History* (New York: Oxford University Press, 2014).

Synergistic and non-additive

Since Descartes, the approach to understanding the world has been that of reductionism, a theory according to which knowledge of a whole is obtained by studying its component parts. An additive system is understood by breaking it down into subsystems, each of which is broken down into other subsystems, and so on. Once each component is understood, the overall behavior of the system is simply the sum of the individual behaviors of each of the subsystems thus identified. But this method doesn't work for a complex system. It's non-additive: you can't cut such a system into pieces to understand it. What's more, the system is synergistic: its components interact, so the whole doesn't simply behave like the sum of its parts. The pieces are interdependent, and most importantly, they can't be easily disassembled. If you're an officer fighting the Taliban in Afghanistan, should you let the Afghan tribes grow poppies because that's the price you have to pay for their help? This is where the "fight the Taliban" component interacts with another component that a priori has nothing to do with it, the "fight drugs" component. This component in turn interacts with a "relations with local tribes" component. All this, and no doubt dozens of other components that another observer would see differently, make up a system that could be called "the situation in Afghanistan". Here we see the danger of the word "analysis", which comes from the Greek word "to cut up"; the logic of analysis is to break the problem down into sub-problems, solve each of them, and then put them back together again. For a complicated system like a watch, this works well. For a complex system, however, it's not possible because the links that prevent this decomposition create their own dynamics. So, we have to maintain a synthetic vision. To take Afghanistan as an example, to understand the situation in that country, you can't analyze the political system, the drug trade, and the religious phenomena separately.

Moreover, the breakdown of a complex human system will differ from observer to observer and may itself be the subject of disagreement. Ultimately, it is largely defined by our values: to take the Afghan example again, should we defend women's rights at the risk of alienating the support of tribal leaders? Should the conflict be defined as democratizing the country or fighting terrorism? After all, if the Americans hadn't intervened in 2001, maybe there wouldn't be an Afghan "problem" and the country would be living its life quietly (or not).

Unknown Cause-Effect Relationship Between Parameters

What caused the collapse of the USSR in 1991? Many Americans attribute it to the actions of Ronald Reagan, an ardent anti-communist, beginning in 1980. Catholics point to the role of Pope John Paul II in Poland. Soviet scholar Hélène Carrère d'Encausse emphasized the ethnic tensions within the system. Others note that the Soviet system showed signs of economic weakness as early as the 1960s. Still others believe that it was never viable and that only the Second World War gave it a respite. The debate is endless and will never be settled. The multiplicity of parameters in such a complex system makes it impossible to establish a clear cause-and-effect relationship.

What is difficult for the historical observer is even more difficult for the decision-maker who must try to influence a system. If cause-and-effect relationships are not clear, how can we act? Managing complex systems is often frustrating and can lead to feelings of powerlessness. Take French urban policy, for example: what explains the difficulties in the suburbs? In part, it is the very large presence of foreign populations who have difficulty assimilating. Why is it difficult for them to assimilate? In part, it has to do with the closed nature of the French economic system and the crisis it has been experiencing for years, which limits opportunities for poorly educated workers. The city's problems are also rooted in architectural issues, with the design of new cities in the 1960s recognized as problematic: neighborhoods are isolated, closed in on themselves. The possible causes quickly multiply, without any real certainty about their effects.

Impossible to Repeat Behavior

Could we "try" a revolution in Tibet to test how the Chinese regime would react, and call it off if things went badly? Difficult, of course, because it would change the world, and not necessarily for the better. At the end of the experiment, we wouldn't be able to put our pipettes away and go home.

One of the fundamentals of developing scientific knowledge is to propose a hypothesis and conduct an experiment to test it. If the experiment is positive, the conjecture can be maintained. If not, it is disproved and a new one must be proposed. The same experiment (e.g., mixing two chemicals) can be repeated dozens or even hundreds of times, with perfect control over the test conditions. The result will always be the same. This repeatability is the hallmark of the so-called "hard" sciences: mainly physics, chemistry, and biology.

Complex systems, especially social systems, are not repeatable. The Vietnam War was seen by Americans as a repetition of the Korean War, which had just ended a few years earlier, even though the two situations were completely different. There is only one Vietnam War, with its historical, religious, political, ethnic, and geographical peculiarities, and any future war will necessarily be different. There's only one nuclear accident like Fukushima in 2011, very different from Chernobyl and Three Miles Island. And so on.

This unprecedented character of each system has a direct implication: it limits the lessons that can be learned from a precedent. Ben Bernanke, chairman of the US Federal Reserve, was a specialist in the 1929 crisis, the subject of his doctoral thesis, but this knowledge was of little use, if not counterproductive, because the 2008 crisis was so different: it was a debt crisis, whereas the 1929 crisis was a crisis of overproduction and speculation. As a result, there were few lessons that could be drawn from it to anticipate the 2008 crisis. This unrepeatability means that we must be very careful with analogies. During the Suez Canal crisis in 1956, the unfortunate Franco-British intervention was justified by comparing the Egyptian dictator Nasser to Hitler. We couldn't make the mistake of appeasing a dictator again without risking the same consequences. It was forgotten that Nasser, certainly an aggressive nationalist, was not about to invade Belgium, exterminate the Jews, or declare war on the whole world. A flawed analogy led the French and the British to attach an exaggerated importance to a relatively local, albeit serious, incident, which proved counterproductive. Similarly, as mentioned at the beginning of the book, Covid-19 was initially mistaken for influenza, which delayed the response to the epidemic.

Mismatch between input and output

On December 1, 1955, in Montgomery, Alabama, Rosa Parks, who was black, refused to give up her seat on a bus to a white passenger, as required by law. She was arrested. A 26-year-old black minister, Martin Luther King, decided to support her and launched a campaign of boycotts and demonstrations against the bus company that quickly gained a national and even international audience. On November 13, 1956, the U.S. Supreme Court finally declared segregated busing unconstitutional, the first step in the restoration of civil rights in the 1960s. It all started with a denied seat on a bus.

This story illustrates another characteristic of complex systems: the mismatch between input and output. In other words, small causes can lead to large effects. Rosa Parks alone is not the cause of desegregation. She is merely the straw that broke the camel's back, the final element at the end of a long chain of invisible events - or events we don't want to see - that suddenly reveal the non-linearity of the system. This brings us to Malcolm Gladwell's notion of "tipping point" and the concepts developed in catastrophe theory.[3] Conversely, massive inputs may have no effect at all, or their effect may diminish rapidly: for example, the massive injections of liquidity into the global monetary system after 2008 had virtually no impact on the recovery. This mismatch between input and output is another reason why it is so difficult to manage these systems and predict their evolution. We never know what our efforts will produce. This is particularly frustrating for those in positions of power who have considerable resources at their disposal and who believe that all they have to do is apply them to get what they want out of a system.

Researchers Chia and Holt show that the massive Western aid that Southeast Asia received in the immediate aftermath of the 2004 tsunami was useful in saving lives in the first few hours, but quickly proved counterproductive, clogging airports, and saturating local infrastructure. In the end, it had little impact on helping residents rebuild their lives.[4] This mismatch between input and output makes it extremely difficult to predict the behavior of a complex system. We can't know in advance how it will react, especially since it's unlikely to react in the same way twice. Remember, every system evolves over time.

Volatility and non-linearity

Until December 2010, most observers praised Tunisia's political stability, which had lasted since independence and especially since President Ben Ali came to power in 1987. The sudden explosion that revealed the extreme volatility of the country's political situation belied all this. Volatility is a characteristic of a complex system. It represents the tendency of a parameter to deviate from its mean value over a given period. A volatile system is one that can develop relatively moderately (values close to the mean) and then suddenly change abruptly with a sharp change in relative value.

---

[3] Malcolm Gladwell, *The Tipping Point: How Little Things Can Make a Big Difference* (Back Bay Books, 2002). The term "catastrophe" refers to the point at which a function abruptly changes form.

[4] Robert C. H. Chia & Robin Holt, *Strategy without Design: The Silent Efficacy of Indirect Action* (Cambridge, UK: Cambridge University Press, 2009), 17.

This ability is very difficult to assess. There is a difference between volatility as an intrinsic characteristic of the system and volatility as it is expressed in reality. We confuse the absence of volatility with stability. By definition, a dictatorship tends to reduce volatility by banning political demonstrations, thus giving the appearance of stability. But in doing so, it may increase the risk of explosion. In fact, reducing volatility can be counterproductive. Since the 1980s, the goal of economic and financial policy has been to reduce market volatility to avoid booms and busts. In a 2004 speech, future Fed Chairman Ben Bernanke celebrated one such success: "One of the most striking features of the economic landscape over the past twenty years has been a substantial decline in macroeconomic volatility [...]. [This makes me optimistic about the future."[5] The speech was entitled "The Great Moderation", which is not without its irony given that it was delivered just four years before the 2008 crisis, which once again demonstrated the extreme volatility of the markets. His argument was that economists now had the tools to control volatility, but reality has shown this to be an illusion. Volatility had indeed been controlled for some time, but this had prevented imbalances from correcting themselves, thus gradually increasing overall risk.

Subjective Definition of the Question

Marijuana use is viewed differently by a Parisian policeman, a student from Marseilles, a Dutch manager, and a libertarian activist from Colorado. How the issue is defined has a significant impact on how it is dealt with (including the decision not to deal with it). Some will talk about "drug trafficking" and approach it from a criminal angle, while others will talk about "drug use" and approach it as a public health or recreational issue. Complex human systems are by definition human creations, so how they are defined is subjective. In the 1950s, the United States decided that Vietnam was a problem for them. They might have considered it a French colonial problem that didn't concern them, but they decided that this country was crucial in the fight against communism. It's often a question of values: whether to prioritize the fight against the Taliban, the development of Afghan women's rights, or the fight against drugs.

---

[5] https://www.federalreserve.gov/boarddocs/speeches/2004/20040220/

Ambiguity

Many young people in France want to start their own business. Entrepreneurship advocates rejoice, noting a profound shift in values and attitudes toward autonomy, business, and wealth creation. For many of these young people, who know entrepreneurship only from success stories on television, being an entrepreneur means living the good life, having no boss, and doing what you want. One of the conditions for human action is to interpret what we observe in our environment. It's a matter of making sense of it, and not everyone will give the same meaning to what they observe. Ambiguity characterizes that which is open to multiple interpretations.

We mentioned earlier the lavish celebrations at Persepolis organized by the Shah of Iran. Initially interpreted as a show of strength, they are now seen as his swan song. Similarly, in 1957, the USSR launched the first artificial satellite into orbit. This was a major shock to the United States, which had been traumatized by falling behind in the space race. The successful and highly publicized launch of the Sputnik satellite was interpreted at the time as proof of the dynamism of the Soviet regime, but this was highly misleading. Far from revealing the USSR's strength, we now know that it had mobilized its meager resources in a competition for prestige that is the hallmark of authoritarian systems. The USSR clearly chose between butter and satellites. We find the same attitude in North Korea today.

This approach to interpretation is closely linked to the identity of the actor: we interpret according to who we are. What is ambiguous for one actor may be clear for another, and two systems may be interpreted differently: for example, the Americans interpreted the Viet Minh insurgency as a communist plot, whereas they could have seen it as a nationalist movement using communism as a unifying language. The meaning we give to certain events, which is a matter of choice on our part, has a considerable influence on the importance we attach to them and therefore on the way we deal with them.

Unintended Consequences

A large city is stuck in traffic. The authorities decide to widen the main roads in and out of the city. When the work is completed, traffic flows smoothly. Newspapers proudly headline: "No more traffic jams, the road is open again!" The absence of traffic jams encourages motorists who had decided to use public transport to return to their cars. After a few months, the road surface is doubled, but the congestion returns - there are simply more cars, and therefore more pollution. The action may produce the desired result, at least initially, but it may also produce other, unintended, and undesired effects. This is obviously an enormous difficulty for the decision-maker, who, despite knowledge and resources, feels powerless and frustrated. The very sharp increase in the price of tobacco through taxation is intended to discourage consumption in the name of public health. But the unintended effects are immediate: faced with the very high price of a pack, an increasing number of consumers turn to smuggling, which is flourishing and whose growth mobilizes the police and the judiciary when their efforts could be more useful in other areas. Consumption does not decrease, but a population that initially wanted nothing more than to smoke quietly finds itself criminalized. Unintended effects are therefore an additional source of uncertainty that makes it difficult to predict the behavior of a complex system.

Reflexivity

Social systems are reflexive. They are made up of human actors who are aware that they are part of the system and can see themselves as objects. They therefore develop anticipations of the system and learn from its developments. If there's a rumor that we're going to run out of butter, I run to the supermarket and buy some. When many of us do the same, the butter runs out. Those who didn't initially believe the rumor also rush to buy, exacerbating the shortage.

Anticipation can thus be profoundly destabilizing. The system evolves not only on its own, but also according to how the players think it will evolve. The neat Cartesian separation between the system and its observer no longer works. You can't accumulate information about the system and then, once that information has been accumulated, act on the system without that information changing. A human system therefore also must deal with the thoughts of the individuals that make it up, which of course adds an incredible amount of uncertainty compared to complex natural systems like the weather, and therefore makes it difficult to predict its evolution.

The Manifestation of Non-linearity: Black Swans

Author Nassim Taleb wrote extensively about the non-linearity of our environment. In his eponymous book, he uses the term "black swan" to describe a low-probability, high-impact event[6]. The French Revolution, World War I, the Asian tsunami of December 2004, the financial crisis

---

[6] Nassim N. Taleb, *The Black Swan* (Random House, 2007)

of 2008, the launch of the iPhone, the Arab Spring, the election of Donald Trump as president of the United States, and of course the sudden outbreak of the Covid-19 epidemic in early 2020 and the invasion Ukraine are typical examples of black swans.

The term comes from a speculation that has puzzled generations of philosophers since the Greeks: all the swans we have observed since the dawn of time have been white. Does this mean that all swans are white? No. Until we are certain that we have observed absolutely every living swan in the world, we can't conclude that they are all this color. You can watch as many as you want, but you'll never know for sure. In fact, at the end of the 17th century, a traveler discovered a black swan in Australia, ending thousands of years of speculation and obliging anyone who spoke of a swan to specify whether it was white or black. The impact of this discovery was not great, but the expression stuck.

The black swan has a double nature: an objective nature, the sudden and very sharp variation in a parameter of the environment, and a subjective nature, the fact that this variation is not foreseen in our model of the world, whether explicit or implicit. The former refers to the volatility of the environment, while the latter refers to the model we build. We'll look at the latter in the next section. There are positive black swans (good surprises) and negative black swans (bad surprises). Some industries are more prone to one or the other. For example, movie studios are prone to positive black swans. A studio invests a certain amount of money in a movie. Whatever the outcome of the movie, it cannot lose more than this initial investment - the loss is limited. But if the movie is a huge success, the profit is far greater than that investment; in fact, it's potentially unlimited. For example, The Blair Witch Project, made in 1999 for only $60,000, was an unexpected success and has grossed about $260 million to date. Book publishing or venture capital are similar in their configuration, which makes them susceptible to positive black swans. While the ultimate profit and loss are unpredictable, the maximum loss is known with certainty from the outset, so the risk structure is inherently favorable.

Conversely, some industries are cursed with negative black swans. This is especially true of banking and insurance. For a given asset, especially derivatives and complex products, the losses are potentially enormous and often very difficult to assess when a black swan event occurs. This was the case during the subprime crisis of 2008: the first task of financial institutions was to mobilize their teams to estimate their potential losses. For example, in February 2008, the American insurance group AIG, which had initially estimated its losses after the crash at only $350 million, subsequently reassessed them and came up with a figure of $5.23 billion, a correction of almost 1,400%! In these industries, forecasting is particularly difficult. Despite the use of sophisticated tools, such as Value at Risk (VaR), designed to estimate maximum possible losses, banks and financial institutions have experienced losses far greater than their expectations. The reason is that the assumptions on which these tools are based (mainly that of a linear world with a normal distribution of events) are wrong. The financial sector is therefore particularly vulnerable to black swan events and is typical of a non-linear system. With $32 billion in assets, the 2008 collapse of mortgage lender IndyMac was one of the largest in the rich history of American finance. Let's look at its performance over the preceding years in Figure 1.

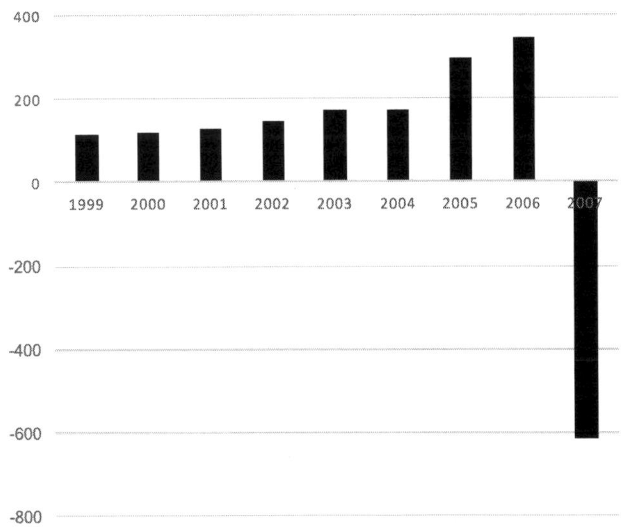

Figure 1 : IndyMac's net income in millions of dollars (source: EDGAR)

From 1998 to 2006, earnings moved in a linear fashion. It goes up a little bit, then it goes down, it goes up again, and it goes down again. We're talking about an evolution in the order of a few percent. Then, in 2007, everything changed: the profit became a loss of $614 million. It's a change of magnitude that reveals the non-linear nature of the financial institution's profit, which had previously been hidden. Not only do the pre-2007 figures in no way foreshadow what's to come, but the two years prior to that give cause for optimism. This is not the only time that current data is misleading when it comes to anticipating the future.

Let's look at another example, again in finance. The chart below shows the total change in a portfolio of derivatives exposed to UK interest rates over a twenty-year period, from 1988 to 2008 (Figure 2).

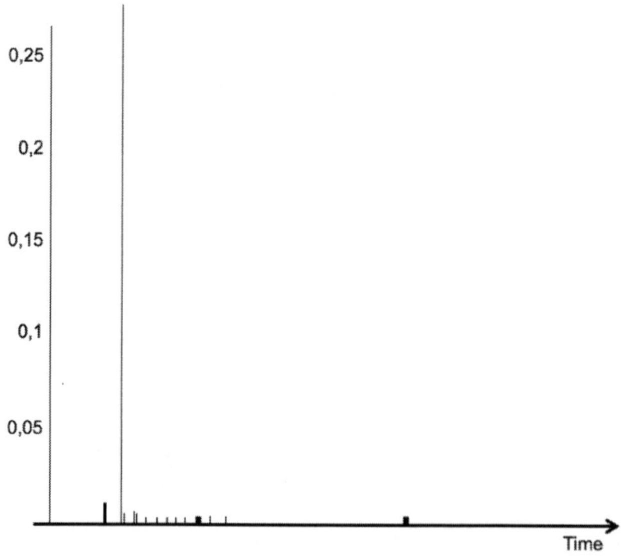

Figure 2: Total change in a portfolio of derivatives exposed to UK interest rates over a twenty-year period

More than 99% of this total variation comes from the portfolio variation that occurred on a single day (that's the long vertical line), September 17, 1992, when the British pound left the European Monetary Snake, the predecessor of the euro. In other words, the 7,300-day variation is insignificant compared to the single day variation, that famous September 17, 1992. This is a very good example of a totally non-linear system, with an extremely high degree of variation that changes the very scale of the system and its representation. No financial model built on the assumption of linearity can withstand such variation.

The financial world is the domain of non-linearity par excellence. But it is not the only one. Geopolitics, in the broadest sense, is also non-linear: just think of the Arab Spring, which came like a thunderclap in a serene sky and began in Tunisia, a country whose stability most observers praised just a few hours before the events began. Similarly, in November

2010, the government of Bahrain placed an advertisement in the prestigious magazine The Economist, extolling the quality of life the country offers expatriates. It stated: "In a study conducted for HSBC [a major international bank], Bahrain was ranked 5th best in the world for quality of life. A surprise only to those who don't know the Gulf's sweet centre." A few months later, Bahrain was in the grip of violent riots by its Shiite population which led to the intervention of troops from neighboring Saudi Arabia. From the "Gulf's sweet centre" to unrest, the wheel turned very quickly.

Let's take another example from a completely different field: the evolution of the number of breweries in the US, shown in Figure 3.

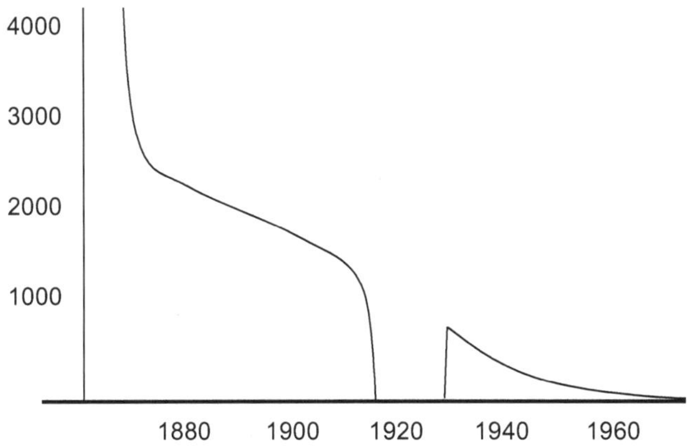

Figure 3: Number of brewers in the United States 1880-1980 (source: qz com/Brewers-association)

At the end of the 19th century, this number was very high. In the twentieth century, it gradually declined until the 1980s. A strategy analyst would easily find the explanation: it's a classic phenomenon of progressive concentration in a maturing industry. You start with a lot of entrepreneurs and end up with a few big players sharing the market. But the first hitch in this linear vision came with Prohibition. In 1919, the production and sale of alcohol was suddenly banned in the United States. There was a sudden, completely unexpected drop in the number of brewers (at least legal brewers). The women's virtue leagues behind the law had long fought to ban the sale of alcohol, which was wreaking havoc among their husbands, brothers, and sons, but no one really took them seriously. With the end of Prohibition in 1933, evolution resumed its linear course and concentration continued, allowing our strategic analyst to reassure himself and cling to his theoretical model after a (major) bump in the road.

In 1980, the analysis is simple: the industry is now mature. There are only a few big players left. It's a race to the bottom, and only the biggest will survive. No doubt the analyst's recommendation to one of his potential clients would be to merge or acquire to get even bigger and come out on top. But by the end of the 1980s, everything changed, as Figure 4 shows.

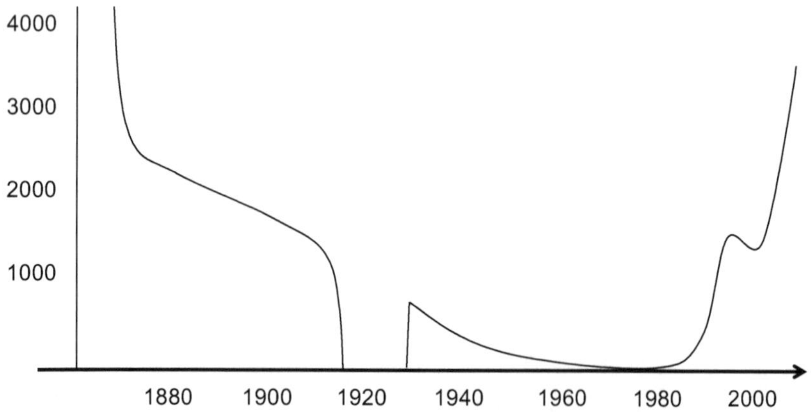

Figure 4: Number of brewers in the United States 1980-2010 (source: qz.com/Brewers-association)

The number of brewers increases dramatically and the game restarts. So, what happened? The emergence of microbreweries, small producers with a local, niche strategy, focusing on quality and personalization rather than mass production. Their arrival was completely unexpected. In just a few years, and even though their overall market share remains relatively small, they have completely redefined the beer market.

As a result, the strategic analysis carried out in 1980, based on a logic of continuity, once again completely missed the brutal evolution that was about to take place. This is the second time in this market that a totally unexpected discontinuity has ruined analysis and forecasting.

One could argue that in 120 years there have only been two accidents and that the rest of the time analysis has worked well. Don't laugh, I hear this argument all the time. But as Nassim Taleb points out, the problem is not how often you're right, but how often you're wrong. In other words, it's not the number of accidents that counts, but their significance. Captain Smith, commander of the Titanic, had only one accident in his 40-year career, but this rather flattering statistic in terms of the number of accidents pales into insignificance in the face of the enormous impact of the one he had.

The most recent example of massive non-linearity is the Covid epidemic. As soon as it broke out, many indicators changed abruptly: air traffic, hotel occupancy, and so on. One example among many is the evolution of unemployment in the United States in the first six months of the year 2020 (figure 5).

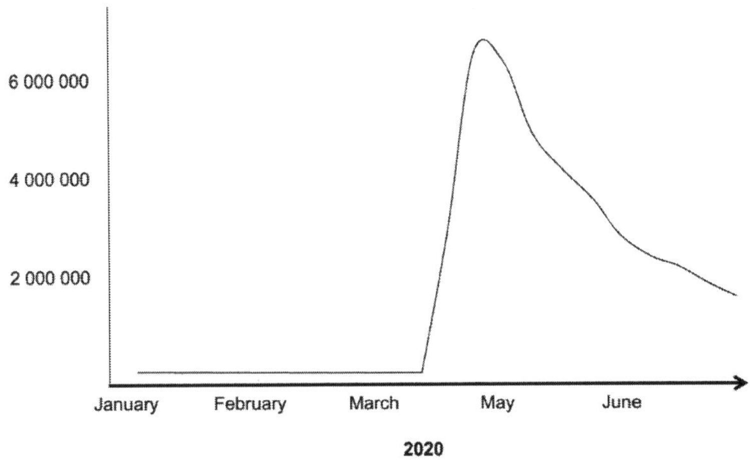

Figure 5: Impact of the Covid-19 pandemic on the number of unemployed in the United States (source: Fortune)

Before Covid, the trend is linear and relatively mild. Then comes the shock, with only a very gradual recovery.

A MORE UNCERTAIN WORLD THAN BEFORE?

The uncertainty of the world is evident to all. We live in a time of profound disruptions, and the only constant of our time is not only change, but its acceleration. Is this acceleration unique to our time? Some doubt it, pointing out that there's nothing new about it. Our world is more uncertain than before, but before what? Before 1989 and the fall of the Berlin Wall? We have a picture of a world in which a duopoly - America and its allies against the USSR and its allies - would have ensured stability throughout the postwar period. But this was not the case: the world before the fall of the wall was unstable: The Chinese Revolution in 1949, 30 years of wars of independence in Asia after World War II, the Korean War in 1950, several revolutions and wars in Africa, economic upheavals, terrorism from the 1960s on, the assassination of Kennedy in 1963, social unrest in 1968, the oil crisis in 1973, the civil war in Lebanon, until then known as the "Switzerland of the Middle East", from 1975 on, economic and social changes, and the Iranian Revolution in 1978, to name just a few. The American economist John Kenneth Galbraith captured this strong sense of uncertainty and instability in his 1977 book *The Age of Uncertainty*, which was later made into a major BBC documentary. Uncertainty, already!

Before the Second World War? But the interwar years revealed a Europe in which no less than three empires (German, Austro-Hungarian, and Ottoman) had suddenly and unexpectedly disappeared. The 1930s were marked by a profound economic, political, and moral crisis, great political and social instability, and, from 1936, war in Spain and then in China.

Perhaps our world was more unstable than it had been before 1914? Indeed, 1914 marked a major break in a European world that had enjoyed almost uninterrupted peace for a century, when the Congress of Vienna ended the Napoleonic wars and reorganized Europe. But before 1914, there had been the Franco-Prussian War of 1870, a major shock that left a lasting mark on the French psyche and unified Germany. There had also been the Second Industrial Revolution, which exploded in the 1880s. During this period, the world underwent considerable changes: the invention of electricity, the automobile, mass consumption, etc., but also social upheavals: the researcher Peter Drucker points out that around 1900, domestic servants were the second largest occupational category in the United States, after farmers. At that time, a household was defined as middle class if it had two or more servants. By the time of World War II, this group had almost completely disappeared, reflecting a social change of enormous proportions in a relatively short period of time that went almost unnoticed.[7]

Fifty million people visited the 1900 World's Fair in Paris and discovered a myriad of technological innovations that would rapidly transform their daily lives. The world was changing at a dizzying pace,

---

[7] Peter F. Drucker, "The Age of Social Transformation", *The Atlantic Monthly*, novembre 1994.

and people were quick to notice.[8] "The pace of time has completely changed," wrote French historian Jules Michelet in... 1872. "It has doubled its pace in a strange way. In a single human lifetime, I have seen two great revolutions, which in the past would perhaps have put two thousand years between them."[9] As early as 1826, the writer and politician Chateaubriand observed that what struck his contemporaries most was the feeling that time was accelerating and that we were losing our points of reference. He added: "The present is elusive, the future unpredictable, and the past itself becomes incomprehensible."[10] In the 19th century, France went from one regime to another at a dizzying pace before finally settling on a republic, almost by default and without much conviction at first, and only in 1875, after a lost war followed by a short, but brutal civil war.

And before 1815, there were the Napoleonic Wars, which devastated Europe and redrew its map: 2,500,000 military dead and missing, one million civilian deaths. Napoleon was the great disruption that shook the European monarchies, some of them thousands of years old. Before that, there was the French Revolution, which came as a surprise and changed the country, as well as the rest of the world.

The preceding periods were not smooth sailing, but it can be argued that in the centuries before the French Revolution, there were few changes in a man's life, and he was likely to live just like his father and grandfather. This is not to say that these eras were free of black swans and upheavals. The collapse of the Western Roman Empire in 476 was a major shock that ended centuries of stability - the famous Pax Romana - and reshuffled the cards of power on a global scale. Similarly, the Middle Ages were not without their innovations (e.g., eyeglasses), but they spread very slowly and generally affected very few people. The Copernican revolution between the sixteenth and eighteenth centuries, a profound change in the way the world was represented, was traumatic in its time. But again, it affected only a small number of intellectuals and had no real impact on people's lives. Even then, many were unaware of

---

[8] The American economist Robert Gordon even defends the idea, in a fascinating and well-researched book, that in the history of mankind, it is the period 1870-1920, and not the current one, that has seen the most profound changes. Robert J. Gordon, The Rise and Fall of American Growth: The U.S. Standard of Living Since the Civil War, Princeton University Press, 2016.

[9] Jules Michelet, *Histoire du XIXe siècle*, Marpon et Flammarion, 1880.

[10] François Hartog, *Régimes d'historicité : Présentisme et expériences du temps*, Points, 2015, p. 115.

the changes that were taking place. Historian Johan Huizinga writes: "The chroniclers of the 15th century were, almost all of them, the dupes of an absolute ignorance of their time, whose real moving forces escaped their attention."[11]

The religious wars of the 16th and 17th centuries, with their series of massacres, are another example of the political, social, and international upheavals that affected all of Europe. A real disruptive change was undoubtedly Gutenberg's invention of the printing press. Unlike previous innovations, this one had a immediate and massive impact, enabling the widespread distribution of books, which had until then been a luxury item, and thus the circulation of ideas, which in turn fueled change.

To say that uncertainty is peculiar to our time doesn't mean that it didn't exist in previous eras. Ours is different because it is marked by a much greater interconnectedness between different parts of the world. There's not much that happens anywhere that doesn't affect us. To return to our discussion of complex systems at the beginning of this chapter, the number of parameters that a decision maker must consider today is much greater than it was fifty or a hundred years ago. It is this number that is a factor of complexity, and therefore of increasing uncertainty.

---

[11] Johan Huizinga, *The Waning of the Middle Ages: A Study of the Forms of Life, Thought and Art in France and The Netherlands in the XIVth and XVth Centuries* (Normanby Press, 2016).

Epistemology: The Predictive Impasse

"You see, one thing is, I can live with doubt and uncertainty and not knowing. I think it's much more interesting to live not knowing than to have answers which might be wrong. I have approximate answers and possible beliefs and different degrees of certainty about different things, but I'm not absolutely sure of anything and there are many things I don't know anything about, such as whether it means anything to ask why we're here, and what the question might mean. I might think about it a little bit and if I can't figure it out, then I go on to something else, but I don't have to know an answer, I don't feel frightened by not knowing things, by being lost in a mysterious universe without having any purpose, which is the way it really is so far as I can tell. It doesn't frighten me."

Richard Feynman

In this chapter, we introduce the human actor (political, economic, social, industrial, or other) as a decision maker. The questions we want to ask are: what can we know about the world today, and to what extent can this knowledge enable us to anticipate its future evolution? To what extent can this anticipation enable us to make better decisions? This is the epistemological dimension of our problem, i.e., what defines how we can acquire knowledge and how we can know that this knowledge is correct. Only a solid epistemological foundation can enable us to confidently use the information we have to make decisions under uncertainty.

KNOWLEDGE AND DECISION: THE RATIONAL ACTOR MODEL

Why do we need to know our environment to make a decision? The question may seem far-fetched, but it's not all that obvious. As is often the case in our work, we rely on implicit assumptions, and it's important to make them explicit.

The standard decision model is the Rational Actor Model (RAM). It makes two assumptions. The first is that the decision made must be the best possible decision. The idea is that the more information available, the better the decision. The paradigm here is that of optimization, with a clear causal relationship between the quantity and quality of information and the quality of the decision. The second assumption is that the decision must succeed. The goal, of course, is to avoid failure. The model is said to be prudent in that it presents an agent who makes decisions while avoiding failure. Again, the quantity and quality of information is assumed to help avoid failure: the better informed you are before deciding, the less likely you are to make a mistake.

In this model, the decision maker is a calculator and an optimizer: he or she has all the necessary information and makes the best possible decision based on it. The decision made is objectively the best one, and another agent would have made the same decision. The rational actor assumption is used in most current economic and financial models. These models assume that economic agents are perfectly capable of anticipating the consequences of their decisions. This type of rational decision-making contrasts with the ancient Greek model in which a general would consult the oracle before going into battle. The oracle would slit the throat of a sheep to examine its entrails, or examine the shape of the clouds, and pronounce some profound word that would encourage or discourage the general in his adventure.

This type of decision making can be described as non-rational, since it is obvious that there is no causal relationship between the entrails of a sheep or the shape of the clouds and the outcome of a battle. A rational decision is one in which the agent relies on a plausible causality between the data he uses and the expected outcome. If I increase the advertising budget, I expect that my product will sell more because the causality between the advertising budget and the sales volume is plausible, even explicable. This does not mean that sales will necessarily increase. We're in the realm of the plausible, not the necessary, because we're not dealing with a law of physics.

The rational actor model has, of course, been much criticized for the unrealistic assumptions on which it is based. Among other things, the idea that the decision maker has all the necessary information is never true in practice, far from it. First, it is physically impossible to obtain all information on a given topic, since it is infinite. Economist and philosopher Friedrich Hayek observed that no single mind can ever have all the facts. Another economist, Kenneth Arrow, shows that to preserve the properties of the rational model under uncertainty, it is necessary to impose overwhelming and unrealistic demands on the information and computational capacities of economic agents.

Second, the information available is not always of good quality: it may be incorrect, incomplete, outdated, difficult to understand, ambiguous, and so on. In practice, a decision is always made on the basis of a set of information that represents only a small, highly imperfect subset of all potentially available information. This is why Herbert Simon, another economist, introduced the notion of *bounded rationality*. According to him, "agents encounter limits in formulating and solving complex problems and in processing [...] information". In bounded rationality, the decision is still made rationally, but based on insufficient information. This is a much more realistic position. Simon also notes that from then on, the decision becomes a localized process (we can no longer consider the entire universe, but only what is available to us) and path-dependent, i.e., we depend in stage n on what we did in stage n-1: I can only increase my production if I previously expanded my factory. Gathering information is costly and time consuming. When it comes to deciding, the decision maker must first decide whether to continue gathering information or to stop. Decision making is therefore a process, not an instant, and there is a trade-off to be made: more information might improve the quality of the decision (this is not always true), but it would delay the decision and possibly render it useless.

Herbert Simon moves away from a purely theoretical model to qualify the more realistic approach with the word *satisficing*, a neologism meaning that the decision is made once we have found a satisfactory solution, even if a better one might be found if we kept looking.

It's something we all do. If we want to buy a house, we won't visit every house in the world before we make our choice. We'll select a few in a region and visit only some of them, having eliminated the others with a phone call. It's rational not to consider all the information available, and besides, we'll only be able to choose from the houses that are for sale at that time. If we broaden our search and delay our decision, some will be sold and no longer available to us, while others will become available simply by waiting. In the end, the house we buy is not the optimal choice in absolute terms, but only in relation to the sample we were able to choose from at any given time. We simply don't have the means to consider all the information available.[12]

Contrary to the assumptions of the rational actor model, the actor cannot make the best decision, but rather chooses the first one that satisfies his criteria. Considering the cost of searching for a better solution and the risk of delaying the decision, this attitude is ultimately quite relevant and... rational.

PREDICTION, THE CORNERSTONE OF DECISION MODELS

Prediction as a Refusal of Fatalism

Historically, the need for prediction stems from a desire for emancipation. It reflects a desire to control one's life and a refusal to accept fatalism. The farmer who can predict tomorrow's rain will harvest today and save his crop. Paradoxically, before it became the basis of the dominant decision-making paradigm, prediction was long controversial. For Christianity, the future belongs to God, and humans must not interfere. For a long time, therefore, the church rejected all predictions, and, for example, weather forecasting was forbidden until the early 17th century. The Talmud forbids all techniques of predicting the future on the grounds that they are tantamount to denying the existence of freedom. The use of statistics, especially probability, was also slow to be accepted by religious authorities. It's no coincidence that Peter Bernstein's book on the history of risk, which evokes this reluctance, is called *Against the Gods*.[13]

With the Reformation, however, came the idea that man realizes God's grace through his actions. This was the first emancipation of time. Time becomes an object of mastery rather than of submission. Knowing the future can be useful, even if we can't change anything (it's going to rain this afternoon, so I'll postpone my trip until tomorrow). Anticipation can therefore be protective (protecting yourself as much as possible from an event you can't prevent), corrective (preventing an event or limiting its negative consequences), or even creative (taking advantage of an event you anticipate).

---

[12] Note that subsequent actions can improve the initial choice. For example, if I renovate my house to make it more valuable.

[13] Peter L Bernstein, *Against the gods: the remarkable story of risk* (New-York, NY: John Wiley & Sons, 1996).

Prediction to Build the "Data of the Future"

So what about the future? If it's contingent, it hasn't been written yet. It is a great factual void. The "facts" that characterize it have not yet happened. They are non-data or non-facts (or not-yet-facts). It is therefore a misnomer to speak of "future data", but we'll use it anyway for the sake of simplicity. The word *data* comes from the Latin *datum*, meaning "that which is given, that which exists". This is a very unfortunate choice indeed, because even when it comes to the past, this "data" is sometimes very difficult to obtain. We know only a tiny fraction of what has happened in history, and discoveries regularly challenge what we thought we knew, such as the origins of humanity.

Economist G.L.S. Shackle notes that "knowing the future" is a contradiction in terms. "We can't know the future because it hasn't happened yet."[14] We can imagine it, we can anticipate it, we can dream it, but we can neither know it nor explore it. The problem with the future is not that I can't discover the facts to come, but that they simply don't exist, and the data about them even less so. This is not a problem of knowledge, but an irreducible ontological problem.

The question is: if data about the future don't exist, how can an agent remain rational in his actions? Because if he reasons about the future without data, he is no longer rational: there is no plausible causality. He has data about the past, with the limitations we've mentioned, but no data about the future. The answer is simple: by artificially creating this data. The actor will create from scratch a set of "data" about the future. He will thus find himself in the situation required by the rational model: a set of (imperfect) data about the past and a set of (artificial) data about the future. The model can thus be maintained. This artificial future data set is obtained by means of prediction. Of course, since the actor is rational in the modern sense, this construction of the data set won't be done by slitting a sheep's throat, rolling a dice, or looking at the shape of the clouds. It's going to be done based on a set of hypotheses and using methods that make those predictions reasonable and plausible. In any case, we can justify them by mobilizing laws and rules that justify a certain causality. This need to remain within the model of the rational actor explains why forecasting is the foundation of modern decision-making methods, whether in strategy, marketing, logistics and production, entrepreneurship, or the military and political arts. It is based

---

[14] We can see the fundamental contradiction underpinning certain works that claim to be a "history of the future" when they're just exploring scenarios.

on Auguste Comte's famous adage that one must know to predict in order to act, which is the foundation of modern thinking.[15]

The Dismal Results of Prediction

Prediction is therefore the cornerstone of the dominant decision model. It relies entirely on it. But there's a problem: If history is any guide, the record of prediction is dismal, and we seem incapable of predicting correctly. Consider a few examples.

In 1876, William Orton, president of Western Union, America's leading telegraph company, joked about the newly invented telephone: "What use can such an electric toy be to us?"

Before 1914, the consensus was that war was impossible. When it broke out, everyone agreed that it would be short and that it would be "the war to end all wars". It turned out to be long, with 8 million dead, 6 million disabled and 8 million orphaned, not to mention the immense material and social damage. It was only a prelude to World War II, which caused even more death and destruction.

On Tuesday, October 29, 1929, after the stock market crash, the Wall Street Journal headlined "Market in Orderly Retreat: Continued Bank Pool Operations Prevent Repetition of Thursday's Hysteria." But that day, the market lost another 12% and became known as Black Tuesday.

In the 1950s, Americans flocked to Cuba. The island was ideal for investment because it was close to the United States and therefore politically safe. In 1959, Fidel Castro seized power and brought an abrupt end to the paradise for investors and vacationers.

In 1962, Decca Recording Co. refused to sign the Beatles, saying, "We don't like their sound, and the guitar is already outdated."

In 1959, the Haloid Company developed the Model 914, a revolutionary new photocopier that was simpler and faster, but more expensive, than existing ones. It commissioned a market study from Arthur D. Little, one of the most prestigious technology consulting firms of the time. The study concluded that there was no market for the 914. Fortunately, the company took no notice. It launched its product, renamed itself Xerox, and became one of the great multinationals of the 20th century.

"With more than 50 foreign models already on sale here, the Japanese auto industry is not about to get a share of the U.S. market," wrote

---

[15] On Auguste Comte, read H Martineau, *The Positive Philosophy of Auguste Comte* (Cambridge University Press, 2009).

Business Week magazine on August 2, 1968. Ten years later, Japanese automakers had captured 20 percent of the market, bringing American manufacturers to their knees.

In 1977, three years after the oil crisis, U.S. President Jimmy Carter declared: "Each new inventory of oil reserves is more alarming than the last. World production can probably continue to rise for another six to eight years. But sometime in the 1980s, it will stop. Demand will outstrip production. We have no choice." Production has continued to rise to this day, forty years later, and at the time of writing, reserves are still being discovered and the price of oil is at an all-time low in present value terms.

In 1989, Nobel Prize-winning economist Paul A. Samuelson wrote: "Contrary to what many skeptics have long believed, the Soviet economy is proof that a managed socialist economy can work and even succeed". Well, the skeptics were right: the Berlin Wall fell a few months later, and the socialist countries collapsed in an unprecedented moral and economic bankruptcy.

In 1994, market research for Nespresso, now one of Nestlé's most profitable products, was all negative. The customers surveyed saw absolutely no point in such a product. The same happened with Motorola's market research for mobile phones in 1989. They underestimated the market by a factor of 1,200. But mistakes can also be made in the other direction: in 2000, mobile phone operators tried to launch WAP, a technology for developing mobile applications in a mini-Web format. Despite a spectacular launch, it was a total flop. At the same time, the explosion of text messaging, a hitherto more or less hidden phone function, took the same operators completely by surprise.

Japanese GDP forecasts for the year 2000, made in 1995, were off by 24%. The country had been in recession since 1991, following the bursting of its financial bubble, but everyone agreed that it was only temporary. The American mutual fund company Fidelity advertised that now was the time to invest in the Japanese market, as it would soon rebound. Nevertheless, the stock market continued to fall.

In 1998, Paul Krugman, future Nobel Prize winner in economics, declared: "By 2005 or so, it will be clear that the Internet's impact on the economy will have been no greater than that of the fax machine."

In September 2007, Ad Age magazine, the benchmark of the advertising world, ranked Twitter 9th on its list of fads to avoid on the Web. It said: "What could be more annoying and less useful than a site where thousands of people have just 140 characters to tell you what they do every day?" Today, Twitter (Now "X") has about 450 million active users, 500 million tweets are produced every day, and the network has become indispensable in politics and business.

"The state of the macro-economy is good", wrote IMF chief economist Olivier Blanchard in August 2008, just two weeks before the collapse of Lehman Brothers and the start of the worst economic crisis since 1929. It's worth noting that Lehman's collapse was considered utterly impossible by all financial and political experts right up to the eve of the collapse. Never, so they thought, would the U.S. government allow such an important bank to fail.

On April 18, 2017, British Prime Minister Theresa May surprised everyone by announcing that she would call a general election for June 8. May, who was appointed after the surprise Brexit vote that led to the departure of her predecessor, David Cameron, was trying to end internal disagreement over Brexit ahead of tough negotiations with Brussels. Michael Thrasher, a renowned expert on British elections, agreed with most of his colleagues that she would win a majority of at least 140 MPs, based on his projections. He estimated that the number of Conservative MPs could rise from 331 to 395, while the number of Labour MPs could fall from 229 to 164. Labour's leader, Jeremy Corbin, an old-school Marxist, was unpopular and highly controversial even within his own party. He had no credibility as a political leader, let alone a possible Prime minister. As far as anyone was concerned, it was a done deal. And yet, on June 8, there was a surprise: only 318 Conservatives were elected. Labour, on the other hand, won 262 seats, a result unimaginable just a few weeks earlier. Another election, another complete upset.

Let's take a closer look at three examples of predictions. The first is the price of oil, shown in Figure 6. This is one of the most important forecasts for the global economy, and armies of experts around the world have been devoted to it for years. The chart below summarizes the price forecasts calculated by the U.S. Department of Energy over the period 1982-2008 and compares them to actual prices.

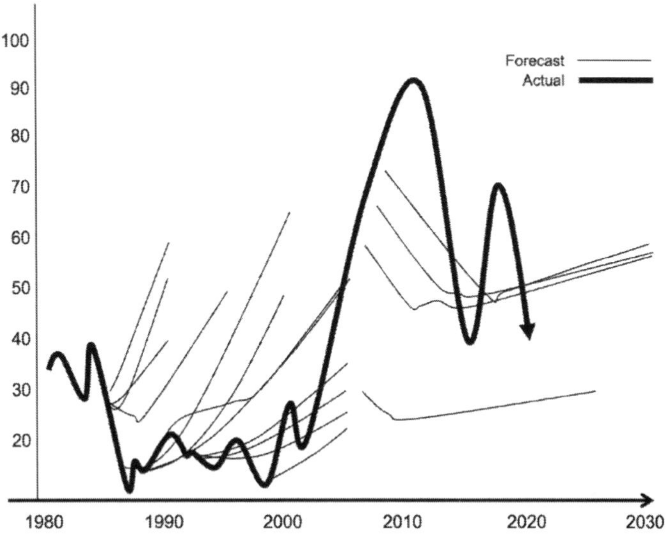

Figure 6: Forecast and actual oil prices in dollars per barrel (source: IEA)

It is striking to see how wrong the forecasts have been. It is also striking to see that these prices are almost systematically overestimated, with a very large amplitude. This undoubtedly reflects the prevalence of the "peak oil" hypothesis, i.e., the strongly held belief since the 1960s that we are on the verge of exhausting oil reserves and that the price will therefore rise. It's worth noting that, paradoxically, forecasters completely missed the price explosion in 2007, and missed its collapse shortly thereafter. Our forecasting systems are inherently linear and therefore ill-equipped to anticipate sudden changes.

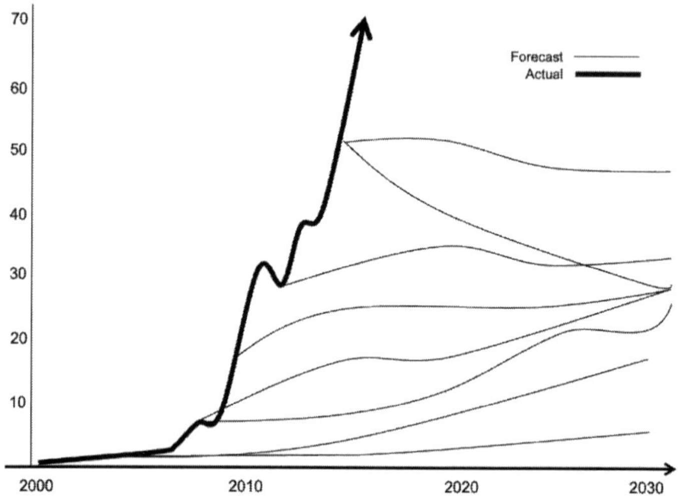

Figure 7: Photovoltaic capacity forecast in GW and historical values (source: Auke Hoekstra 2017)

Let's stay with energy, but this time with the photoelectric power predicted by the International Energy Agency (IEA), shown in Figure 7. The errors are massive; it's the very scale of these predictions that is wrong, to the point of absurdity.

The third example is the International Monetary Fund (IMF). The graph in Figure 8 shows its GDP forecasts.

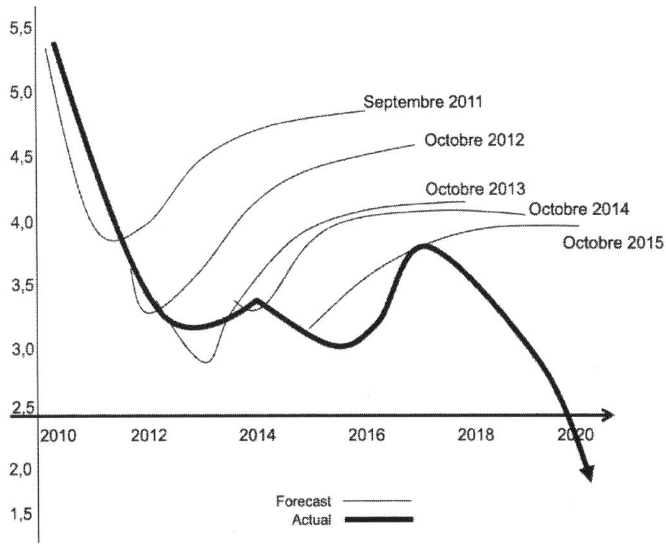

Figure 8: Global GDP forecast (source: IMF)

The forecast is for a relatively short period, 2010-2020. And yet the errors are huge. The error continues in 2016, when GDP growth was 3.1% and the forecast missed it by more than that. Finally, the error for 2020 is considerable, since the pandemic, an unprecedented event par excellence, reduces growth to -3.27%, which no forecast had anticipated. We could go on for pages illustrating catastrophically wrong predictions in every area of human activity made by intelligent, educated, informed people who are experts in their fields and know what they're talking about. We're very bad at this.

When I mention the many failures of prediction, one response inevitably comes: "Yes, but surely there are also examples of successful prediction?" Of course, there are, and if prediction widely used, it's not without reason. When a company launches a new product, it often has to configure its production line months or even years in advance. This requires a series of predictions about the product's evolution, final characteristics, production methods, expected volumes, specification variations, and so on. The same goes for distribution, which is sometimes organized well in advance for complex products such as airplanes. It would be inconceivable not to make these predictions, even though they are all likely to be wrong, with serious consequences. Under these conditions, prediction makes it possible to replace chance with error, which is progress. Nevertheless, error remains a possibility, with serious consequences. Can we be satisfied with this fatalism? On the other hand, a happy outcome can sometimes be very misleading: if you look hard enough, you can always find someone who predicted an event that surprised everyone.[16]

It's a ritual and a line of defense for those who maintain that predictions can be made, as long as they're done right. The evening news can't resist finding some little granny who predicted this or that, and trying to unravel her secret: she gets up at 5 a.m., she's been drinking green tea since she was a kid, etc. But this is like a clock: even if it breaks down, at least twice a day it gives the correct time. As Voltaire said, not even an astrologer can have the privilege of being wrong all the time. Since we all spend our time making predictions, it's not surprising that out of the billions made every day, with a little searching, we can't find an exact one as the product of a stroke of luck. The law of large numbers is at work. And after 2008, of course, we dug up this or that economist who "predicted" the crisis, but that's no use: how can I identify a priori and with certainty the one who will make the right prediction next time? It's impossible, of course, because once again it's a statistical game that only works for the past. Whoever was right in 2008 could be completely wrong in 2021.

The truth is that most of the economics profession has been completely taken in, because the ontological and epistemological foundations of their models are flawed. The same goes for forecasters and futurologists. In an inadvertent admission of the risks of his profession, the statistician and forecaster Nate Silver, about whom more later, subtitled his book "Why so many predictions fail, but not all of them." Why not all? Tentative answer: luck, perhaps? Alvin Toffler is one of the most famous futurists, and judging what he got right and what he didn't has become an international sport. Again, when you make so many predictions over such a long period of time, and you're as intelligent and cultured as he is, you can't help but have a few good ones. But the very existence of bad ones - and there are plenty of them - invalidates the method itself! In this regard, the economist Bernard Cazes refers to the important principle of *non-compensation*, according to which a forecaster's successes cannot compensate for his failures. Assuming that the same method has been used several times, it should produce results

[16] Add to this the fact that every good bureaucrat peppers his report with footnotes evoking alternative predictions so that, should one arise, he can credibly protest: "It's in my report!"

of comparable quality, while the presence of errors raises the question of whether the successes are not random.[17] Mostly, they are.

The discussion of each guru's "predictive performance" is therefore interesting, but in the end the argument boils down to this: a predictor's past success is in no way indicative of its future success, as investment product prospectuses are wont to remind us. You're not making statistics; you're thinking about your next decision. Knowing that the price of an error will be paid by you, are you willing to take the risk? How much are you willing to bet on a prediction by the great Toffler? He'll collect his fee immediately, while you risk your skin on his prediction. Are you sure you want to play? We'll stick to the line we took at the beginning of the book: please, avoid absurd bets!

Errors of Prediction: The Inevitable Japanese Domination that Never Happened

"Losing the war with Japan" is a report on Japan's economic power and its impact on the United States, broadcast by Frontline magazine in November 1991. It paints a very bleak picture of the situation at the time, drawing a parallel with the first Iraq war, which the United States had just won brilliantly in a matter of days. The point of the report is that while the US was fighting a real war in Iraq, the Japanese were destroying American industry through economic warfare. The introduction to the report ends with a researcher saying, "The Cold War is over, and Japan has won."

There are three fundamental forecasting errors in this report. The first concerns Japan's future as a leading economic power. Undeniably, its economic success since its military defeat in 1945 has been remarkable. Automobiles, iron and steel, electronics, watchmaking, etc. - the sectors dominated by Japanese companies are numerous. In 1991, Japan was a leading economic power, announcing ambitious plans for robotics and artificial intelligence that made other economic powers shudder. But just as the report noted this success and predicted Japan's inevitable dominance, its growth collapsed. The Tokyo stock market plummeted, and the country entered a long period of stagnation.

The second forecasting error concerns the future of the U.S. economy. Based on the prediction that Japan has won the economic war, pessimism about the American economy was widespread. The report

[17] Cazes, *Histoire des futurs* (L'Harmattan, 2008), p. 82.

used a rather crude narrative technique, drawing a parallel between the Iraq war, which allowed America to demonstrate its smart weapons, and the economic war that Japan somehow won behind its back. At the time, certain sectors of American industry were struggling to keep up with Japanese companies, particularly in steel, manufacturing, and, of course, the auto industry, with its depressing spectacle of layoffs and plant closings. America was in the midst of a recession that cost President George H. Bush his re-election. Meanwhile, the Japanese, buoyed by their success and stuffed with dollars, were buying up the jewels of the American economy: movie studios, prestigious buildings, and works of art at dizzying prices. The contrast was painful. It was the American system itself that seemed unable to keep up with the new challenges.

And yet, here again, at the very moment of this decline, the American economy was emerging from recession. Nobody knew it at the time, but it was on the cusp of a long period of growth that would last until 2008, when the subprime crisis erupted. At the very moment when the decline seemed obvious, the giants of the new period of innovation were born: the Internet revolution. AOL, founded in 1985, revolutionized what was then called the "information superhighway" by offering easy, low-cost access to the Internet. This was followed by the creation of Netscape and Amazon in 1994, Microsoft's introduction of Windows 95, which democratized computing, the beginning of Apple's resurgence in 1997, and the creation of Google in 1998. At the time of Frontline, none of this had had an impact; everything was microscopic. Only the factory closings of the old economy were visible, and so that's all we talked about (that's what we saw); but the next generation was on the way, and the United States, defying all the usual short-termist prognostications, was at the forefront of the new IT revolution, in hardware and software (that's what we didn't see). The report predicted an inevitable decline, but instead an industrial renaissance was underway. The margin of error was considerable.

But there's a third, perhaps equally important one. The report claimed to explain who has won the race for economic supremacy, pointing to Japan's success and America's stagnation. There was no doubt about it: the big winner was Japan. And not once did Frontline mention China! And yet, since Deng Xiaoping's reforms in the late 1970s, China had already undergone considerable economic development. It was still just a giant workshop, but its impact was beginning to be felt, there was no doubt that it was poised to play a major economic role, but not a word in the report. The error of prediction, this time by omission, is again considerable.

This report, which could be an isolated case of bad journalism, was in fact highly representative of the thinking of the time.[18] *For instance, in the United States, the book Japan as Number One, subtitled "Lessons for the United States," became a best-seller.*[19] *The inevitable rise of Japan and the decline of America (and the West in general) was widely shared at the time, demonstrating the importance of the "group effect" in the persistence of a belief. Many experts supported this call to adopt the characteristics of the Japanese model, or at least what they perceived, often superficially, to be its characteristics: an economy managed by an "enlightened" Ministry of Industry that avoided the "short-termism" of American capitalism.*

What these examples underscore is the extent to which foresight is based on hypotheses, some of which are more akin to false beliefs, reflecting identity and ideological prisms, if not simply the intellectual thoughtlessness of their authors. Only by making these assumptions and beliefs explicit can we avoid the most obvious shortcomings of the foresight exercise. But they also reflect a profound lack of understanding of the times. It's all very well for a few intellectuals to talk about a Japan they don't know and to make fanciful predictions, but it's harder to accept that they are incapable of understanding their country and their times. At the very least, one might have expected them to have a better sense of the real health of the American economy, noting the decline of an old economy and the simultaneous rise of a new one. This was nothing new; the process had been going on since the Industrial Revolution and was well described by the economist Joseph Schumpeter, who coined the term "creative destruction" to describe it.[20]

[18] As a student in London in 1995, this author, convinced like many others of Japan's power, once had a discussion with a Japanese classmate: "Tell me, Kazuo, Japan's economic difficulties are only temporary, aren't they? The country will bounce back quickly, won't it? - Think again," he replied. "Everything's rotten and we'll be here for a long time."

[19] Ezra Vogel, *Japan as Number One: Lessons for America* (First Tuttle edition, Harper Colophon, 1979).

[20] Joseph A. Schumpeter, *Capitalism, Socialism, and Democracy* (Harper Perennial Modern Classics; Third edition, 2008). The book itself is not a very successful exercise: the author predicts the failure of capitalism and the success of socialism.

In this case, the experts don't make mistakes in their forecasting work because the task is difficult, but because they don't do their job. This lack of understanding, the result of social isolation and intellectual laziness, is reflected in the fiasco of predicting the results of the 2016 US election.

THE CHALLENGE OF UNCERTAINTY

What is Uncertainty?

Uncertainty is the lack of objective information about a given environment. A non-deterministic environment develops through contingency. What can happen, not what must happen, happens. The constant accumulation of new facts means that it is never possible to have complete knowledge of the environment at any given time. As we have pointed out, uncertainty is not the result of our difficulty in acquiring information, but of the fact that this information does not exist or does not yet exist. As economist Frank Knight points out, it is our imperfect knowledge of the future - a consequence of change, not the change itself - that is crucial to understanding our problem.

Uncertainty is often associated with isotropy. Isotropy is a term introduced by philosopher Jerry Fodor to describe the fact that, when making decisions and taking actions with uncertain future consequences, it is not clear which information is worth paying attention to, which is relevant, and which is not.[21] This is the case with the very simple example of predicting the price of oil: there are thousands, even hundreds of thousands, of factors influencing its price. We never know where to stop: isotropy is the hallmark of open systems. We must look in all directions because everything is potentially relevant. This is, of course, an additional problem for Cartesian decision models: we don't even know what information is relevant or irrelevant to our decision!

Unlike Laplace, a 19th Century mathematician who saw the world as a machine whose secrets we would soon unlock, the development of science and technology has not brought greater certainty. On the contrary, in a way that may seem paradoxical, it has produced ever greater uncertainty and a sense that what we don't know is more important than what we do know. Just think of the controversies over global warming, nuclear energy, health, or GMOs. This is a far cry from

---

[21] Jerry Fodor, *The Modularity of the Mind: An Essay on the Psychology of the Faculties* (MIT Press, 1983).

the rational model, which assumes that the more we know about the environment, the less uncertainty there is.

This imperfect knowledge of today's world takes place in a dynamic situation: it's constantly evolving. In our race for complete information, we are always running behind, with no hope of catching up, because the flood of new facts never stops, while there always comes a time when we have to make a decision. Uncertainty thus intimately links information about the present world and the temporal dimension of decision making. This is especially true in the case of unprecedented events that create a shock of uncertainty. We can see this in the case of teleworking: before the pandemic, it was almost nonexistent. Then it suddenly became very popular, and the consensus was that it would become the norm. But as the initial containment period came to an end, organizations tried to get people back into the office, and they were reluctant. We know that the way we work will never be the same again, and we also know that the "everyone teleworks" version is a utopia; we are condemned to a very uncertain in-between that will take time to emerge.

Why does uncertainty make it impossible to predict? Precisely because of the ever-changing nature of the world. Prediction assumes that we can "freeze" the future at a given moment into a description that is complete enough to decide. But this is obviously impossible, because everything is constantly changing, and when a decision has to be made, a very large part of the necessary information lies in the future and is therefore still undetermined. No calculation, insofar as it would necessarily concern the past, can resolve this difficulty inherent in the existence of time. This link between uncertainty and the impossibility of prediction has long been recognized. The definition of uncertainty as "the character of the unpredictable" appears in French literature as early as 1559. More specifically, uncertainty makes it impossible to predict future states of the world, the impact of events or changes on a particular organization, and the likely consequences of a decision.

Uncertainty results in a fundamental indeterminacy of the future and a heterogeneity of events that may occur, which cannot be classified or categorized. It is the domain of the unprecedented. It is characteristic of revolutions, the emergence of new markets, and so on. It now plays a major role in quantum physics, which has overthrown Newtonian physics, which ignored it.

"The uncertainty of the future is already implicit in the very notion of action," remarks Mises, "for the man who acts, the future is hidden."[22] In economics, Richard Cantillon was the first to invoke uncertainty, noting that entrepreneurs make a trade-off between the present and the future: They spend time and money today (buying raw materials or machinery, hiring employees, etc.) to produce and sell products in the future. The expenditure, because it occurs today, is certain. The gain, because it occurs in the future, is uncertain: perhaps the entrepreneur will not succeed in creating the product; perhaps it won't sell at all; perhaps they will have to revise his price downward in order to sell the product; perhaps, on the contrary, the product will be so successful that the entrepreneur will have to build a new factory in a hurry. All these factors, and there are dozens more that determine the future situation of our entrepreneur's business, are unknown when he makes his investment and production decisions. Worse, they are unknowable. The difficulty for the entrepreneur is not to find this information, but that it doesn't exist yet. He must therefore make decisions in a situation of incomplete information. Uncertainty arises from this irreducible non-existence of information and is rooted in the uniqueness of the phenomenon: the development and launch of a new product that has never existed before.

Because of this uncertainty, the propositions studied by our entrepreneur are undecidable: he can't prove by calculation, for example, that his product will be a success at the price set. Nor can he prove the opposite. Only his actions can show this. So how does he decide which proposals to accept? Economist Frank Knight's contribution here is crucial because, in his landmark 1921 book *Risk, Uncertainty and Profit*, he showed that the entrepreneur uses judgment to decide. Judgment is the act of evaluating beings and circumstances to determine one's behavior. Uncertainty is therefore the area where calculation is not enough.

The Difference Between Risk and Uncertainty

Uncertainty is often confused with risk, but it's important to distinguish between the two. Let's recall Dr. Caumes' statement comparing Covid-19 to the flu at the beginning of the epidemic. It seemed like common sense, but the comparison was not legitimate. Influenza is a recurring, known event; it is a risk, i.e., one that can be managed by statistical observation. Covid-19 was unprecedented and its effects unpredictable. It was in the realm of uncertainty and therefore less easily managed. The simple fact that, more than a year after the epidemic began, experts

---

[22] Ludwig von Mises, *Human Action*, (Ludwig von Mises Institute, 2010).

continued to disagree on virtually every fundamental point about it was typical of an uncertain problem.

Frank Knight clarified the distinction between risk and uncertainty. Using the vocabulary of probability, he defined risk as a future whose distribution of possible states is known. In other words, we know what can happen and the probability of each possible event. For example, if we put three green balls and two red balls in an urn, we know the risk of drawing a green ball (3/5, or 60%). Uncertainty, on the other hand, corresponds to a future whose distribution of states is not only unknown, but impossible to know. We don't know the number of balls in the urn, let alone their color, and we don't even know what the urn contains.

Risk can therefore be calculated as a probability. This probability is either theoretical, as when we calculate the probability of getting a 5 when we throw a dice, or empirical (known a posteriori), as when we observe a historical series of repeated events without knowing their distribution law a priori. Statements like "I have a one in six chance of rolling a 5" or "Given the history of car theft in the XX region, the owner of a YY car model has an x% chance of having it stolen" therefore make sense. This is what Keynes emphasizes when he writes: "I must explain that by the expression 'uncertain' knowledge I do not mean simply to distinguish what is known with certainty from what is only probable. The game of roulette is not subject to uncertainty in this sense, nor is the prospect of drawing a good lottery number."[23] Keynes' point is essential: uncertainty is not reducible to calculation. There is one area where probabilities can be applied, and that's in the area of risk, where we have either theoretical (the roll of a dice) or empirical (the history of car thefts) knowledge of the phenomenon under consideration. But that's not the case with uncertainty. According to Pierre Massé: "Not only are the virtual states that constitute them part of a system of probabilities that is often difficult to estimate, but these virtual states themselves are difficult to count and define."[24] Knight shows that our environment consists of three types of systems: those governed by prediction (the distribution of events is known theoretically and a priori, as in the case of dice); those governed by risk (the distribution of events is known empirically, i.e., a posteriori, by observing draws over time, as in the case of car theft); and those governed by uncertainty (the nature of

---

[23] John Maynard Keynes, *The General Theory of Employment, Interest and Money* (Wordsworth Edition, 2017).

[24] Berger, Massé, and Bourbon-Busset, *De la prospective* (L'Harmattan, 2007)

the events is not known a priori, and therefore their distribution cannot be, as in the case of an emerging market or a revolution, and more generally of any unprecedented event). Knight's theoretical contribution is very important, not least because it finally makes it possible to distinguish risk from uncertainty. This distinction is crucial. And yet the two are often confused, even though they cover radically different areas. Much of what passes for risk management is really about uncertainty. Using a vocabulary of probabilities for a situation of uncertainty is therefore a mistake. It's like using a hammer to drive a screw. Uncertainty, the lack of information about a given environment, translates into an inability to predict.

Probability and New Events

An essential feature of an uncertain future, resulting from a constant stream of new facts, is the creation of unprecedented events. Keynes says of uncertainty: "The sense in which I use the term is that the prospect of a European war was uncertain, or the price of copper and the rate of interest twenty years hence, or the date of obsolescence of a new invention, or the position of private property owners in the social system of 1970. In these matters there is no scientific basis upon which we can authoritatively formulate any probabilistic reasoning whatsoever. We simply don't know."[25] Probabilities are useless for novel events because they only convey information about a future population, not about an event itself. This is a point that Shackle develops at length, and it's worth quoting in extenso: "It is natural to claim that a frequency distribution of the outcomes of a roll of two dice 'tells us something,' 'sheds light' on how the two dice are 'more likely' or 'less likely' to fall on an identified, particular, properly named face, all or nothing. But what light? What is the precise question that the properties of a frequency table answer about the outcome of a projected die? Does the frequency table answer the question, 'How many dots will appear on the top faces of this actual roll?' Obviously not. Does it answer the question, 'If we make, say, 36,000 throws, how many of them, approximately, will show a three, or how many a seven?' Suppose the experiments suggest that it can answer that question. What is the relevance of this answer if we are interested in a single identified roll?"[26] Answer: None, of course.

---

[25] Keynes, *General Theory*. Unfortunately, after this mention, Keynes does not develop the question of uncertainty any further in the book.

[26] George L S Shackle, *Imagination and the Nature of Choice* (Columbia University Press, 1979), p. 72.

Statistics give us information about a population, which is useless if we're looking for information about the event itself. That's the point of the unprecedented event.

Even in an exercise as simple as throwing a dice, we can't predict with any certainty what number will come up on any given roll. All that probability can tell us is that if a "large number" of throws are made, the resulting set of throws (the population) will be evenly distributed among the six sides of the die, assuming, of course, that the die is not loaded.

There are five conditions for the validity of the probabilistic approach: 1) we can make many draws; 2) the possible draws are perfectly identified and perfectly distinct (we know the categories); 3) these draws are strictly identical in their conditions and the system remains unchanged between two draws. If you change the die between two throws, the approach no longer works; 4) you need to obtain information about the resulting population, not about a particular throw; 5) you have perfect knowledge of all the parameters of the throw: the number of faces, the fact that they are equiprobable, that you know with certainty that the die is not tipped, and so on. In the case of the unprecedented event, none of these conditions are met. 1) there is only one "draw" (the event occurs only once); 2) the draws are not easy to identify, and we cannot immediately create categories, because the event does not recur, and because at best we can only find similar events; 3) the draws are unique, and the "system" changes considerably between two events, even if they are similar; 4) we need information at the level of the event itself, since information at the level of the "population" (which by definition does not exist) is meaningless and useless; 5) we have very limited knowledge of all the parameters of the event. We can see that even the probabilistic vocabulary poses a problem, forcing us to make contortions to fit the unique situation into this model, essentially because, again, it only works when there are many identically repeated events. After 9 rolls, it's possible to have a very unbalanced population (a majority of 6s, for example). Balance is restored only gradually. We don't do statistics on a small number of events[27] , and even less on a single event, because, as Daniel Kahneman observes, we are more likely to find extreme values (high or low) in small samples.[28]

[27] See Amos Tversky and Daniel Kahneman, "Belief in the law of small numbers", Psychological Bulletin 76, no. 2, 1971, pp. 105-110.

[28] Daniel Kahneman, *Thinking, Fast and Slow* (Farrar, Straus and Giroux; 1st edition, 2013).

So, saying that my car has a 2.4% chance of being stolen is useful to my insurer because it allows them to calculate the cost of my insurance. In effect, they aggregate many these events, and what they need is population-level information to anticipate his potential cost. The economic objective for them is achieved thanks to this number and they can make their decision. But it is of little use to me, who is at the level of the event itself, which for me will be binary: either my car will be stolen, or it won't. Even if the probability is only 2.4%, it doesn't really matter if it gets stolen. Saying there's a 15% chance of war is meaningless. It's not enough to decide. If we want to think about the uncertainty of the world and its evolution, we must get rid of the statistical vocabulary: nobody is able to calculate the probability of success of the electric car or of trips to Mars (there are an infinite number of infinite possibilities). The idea of a probability for such unprecedented events makes no sense.

Event Categorization

The use of statistics is based on our ability to classify the events we observe. When confronted with an event, our first reflex is to categorize it. Have I encountered this event before? If so, what did I call it? Can I associate it with other identical events and thus establish stable categories? Only a positive answer will keep us within the realm of probability. Indeed, as Knight observes, there are too many objects for a finite intelligence to deal with. Hence the fundamental role that categorization has always played in intelligence thought and theory. In other words, knowledge can only be built on the past, and only about events that are sufficiently similar to be categorizable.

But in life there are very few identical cases that can be clearly categorized. Even events that seem to recur frequently are in fact often unique. Such is the case with certain epidemics or elections. No two are ever the same. This is obvious, but it seems to elude forecasters. In fact, one of them, Nate Silver, whom we mentioned earlier, is known to have predicted with great accuracy the results of the 2012 American elections (senatorial and presidential). He was therefore the oracle of those of 2016, but he totally failed to anticipate the victory of Donald Trump. Once again, what seems to be a general and recurring case is in fact often only a special case.

The Hidden Uncertainty Behind Risk

The fact that we are using probabilistic tools to describe an uncertain reality is not the only difficulty. A second is related to the limits of

Knight's distinction between risk and uncertainty. We have seen that risk is well illustrated by car thefts: a very rich history that allows us to build statistics by model, by region, and so on. From these statistics, we can derive the probability of thefts. But this is not as trivial as it seems.

There is no guarantee that some event won't disrupt this history. Suddenly, a particular model may become fashionable, and thefts of that model may suddenly explode. This means that (historical) statistics can no longer be legitimately used to infer (future) probabilities. This explains the shocks that insurers regularly experience, even those with the best risk management services: they are actually managing uncertain situations that behave like risk "most of the time".

This is another example of how history-based forecasting works quite well as long as there is continuity but fails as soon as there is discontinuity. The problem, of course, is that the discontinuity is not recognized until after the fact, when the wrong prediction has been made and the consequences must be dealt with. This shows, as Knight observed, that it is not a matter of whether an environment is uncertain or not. In a sense, they all are. What matters is the judgment we make about our environment. Writes Knight: "We perceive the world before we react to it, and we react not to what we perceive but always to what we infer from it."[29] So there's a strong subjective dimension to assessing the degree of uncertainty in one's environment. An agent may be misled by a long history of continuity and infer that his environment is not uncertain. The opposite, thinking one's environment is uncertain when it isn't, is rarer and has fewer consequences.

WHY WE CAN'T PREDICT

We have already mentioned the sad record of prediction in the most diverse fields of human activity: industry, politics, war, music, scientific discovery, and so on. There is no field in which prediction has not repeatedly failed, sometimes with disastrous consequences. The economist Ezra Solomon used to say that the only function of economic forecasting is to make astrology respectable,[30] but this applies to forecasting in many other fields. Let's first look at the reasons why we can't predict.[31] Next, we'll review the main approaches to forecasting and discuss their limitations.

---

[29] Frank Knight, *Risk, uncertainty and profit*, Houghton Mifflin, 1921, p. 201.

[30] Susan Ratcliffe, *Oxford Essential Quotations*, Oxford University Press, 2016.

[31] When we look at the reasons why we cannot predict, we are not referring to

Novelty

The first source of indeterminacy is novelty, the continuous flow of new facts from the future into the present. This novelty can be small, like a piece of news, or large, like a great invention, a literary success, or the collapse of an empire. The future does not emerge from an extrapolation of the past but is (partly) constructed by our actions. As it is constructed, it is much more the result of imagination than of calculation. This is the difference between risk, which can be estimated by calculating historical data, and uncertainty, which concerns new and therefore unprecedented events. Novelty, which is the product of the flow of natural events and human actions, is therefore neither reducible to calculation nor induced by historical data. Take, for example, the case of an insurer developing new products to protect against cybercrime, solar storms, or global warming: the task is complex because we are dealing with events that are still very rare or have never occurred, and estimates of their potential impact are based on highly controversial scientific analyses, where they exist. Predicting such events is virtually impossible.

Similarly, if an investor in 1975 wanted to estimate the potential of the Internet, which had been invented ten years earlier, he would have no data: the network at that time was used by a few academics and in no way foreshadowed what it is today. The same was true in 1980 and again in 1991, when the Web protocol had just been invented: at the time, it was imagined that it would facilitate the creation of technical documentation, but little more. We know a lot more now, of course, but the invention of the Internet was a one-time thing. The next revolutionary invention, like cloning or space travel for everyone or something I can't imagine today, will be very different. If something new could be predicted today, it would by definition not be new. Novelty can be imagined, especially in science fiction, but it can't be predicted-that's an inherent limitation. The novelty factor therefore introduces a fundamental uncertainty into the environment, making it completely unpredictable. There's an important nuance here: with Taleb's black swan, we're still in the realm of risk, where the environment is nonlinear, but the events that occur are not in themselves novel. They are not a surprise; it is their occurrence that is the surprise. Everyone knows what a swan is, or a currency fluctuation, or a loan

---

technical errors made during the forecasting exercise. We are looking at the intrinsic reasons why it is not possible to predict. This is an ontological limitation, i.e., one related to the nature of our environment, not a technical or methodological one. No improvement in prediction techniques can solve it.

default - they've been around for centuries. In this case, the surprise comes from a modeling error or ignorance of the probabilities calculated by the model. Novelty, on the other hand, leads to the appearance of unprecedented phenomena that cannot be reduced to modeling.

Volatility

The second source of indeterminacy is the volatility of the environment. The continuous flow of new facts from the future into the present can sometimes correspond to a linear system. This is the case, for example, with the turnover of a grocer or a doctor. A consultation with a general practitioner costs 25 Euros. If the doctor works nine hours a day, 220 days a year, and spends 30 minutes with each patient, her annual turnover will be about $100,000. Sometimes she may earn a little more, sometimes a little less, but the variation will never be very large. But in most systems that we're interested in, the continuous flow of new facts corresponds to a nonlinear system in which we can have very large variations. Financial markets are typical of this kind of environment. The sudden 20% rise in the Swiss franc in January 2015, which took all financial experts by surprise, is a striking example, as this currency had been stable for a very long time. As we pointed out above, the sudden appreciation of a currency is nothing new, but foreign exchange markets are typical cases of volatile systems. Non-linearity can therefore exist without the slightest novelty or breakthrough innovation. The 2008 crisis abruptly ended fifteen years of steady American economic growth and saw bankers declaring that such an event was so rare that it could only occur once every ten thousand years, showing that they had failed to understand the non-linear nature - and therefore not reducible to a normal distribution curve - of the environment in which they operated. This shows how high the price can be for using the wrong epistemology in one's field of expertise.

A related problem with volatility is that short-term forecasting is not always more accurate than long-term forecasting. This is counter intuitive. Imagine an analyst hired by the French government to assess the political situation in Tunisia at the end of 2010. What does he do? He meets with officials. He also meets the opposition parties and civil society: business leaders, association leaders, trade unionists, religious leaders, and so on. He will also meet intellectuals and politicians. He also meets with intellectuals and academics. He makes sure that the overview is as broad as possible. He focuses on the main variables that make public opinion. He finished his report on December 15. The only person who really matters in his assessment, Mohamed Bouazizi, is a street vendor. Obviously, he didn't interview him. And even if he had, he would have told him about the daily humiliations that he, like other Tunisians, has endured for years in his business, which is constantly controlled by the police. The analyst would have taken note of his testimony and may have concluded that there was a general malaise, but nothing really new and therefore nothing to worry about. The next day, after another checkpoint, this time by a female police officer, Bouazizi snapped and set himself on fire, triggering the Arab Spring. Our analyst's prediction collapses. He made his prediction at the very moment of discontinuity.

In a linearly evolving environment, where the future becomes only a little different every day, a short-term forecast is "more likely" to be accurate than a long-term one; uncertainty is therefore a kind of cone that grows progressively over time in a continuous manner. Tomorrow the cone is very small, the day after tomorrow it will be a little larger, and a year from now it will be even larger. But in a nonlinear system, this is not accurate: in such a system, we're no more certain of our prediction for tomorrow than we are of our prediction for next year. Like our analyst, we may be on the cusp of a major discontinuity that will distort all our forecasts and make our "margin of error" null and void. But, of course, we don't know when such a discontinuity will occur. It could happen in years or in a few hours. Again, the difficulty is that this wheel can sometimes not turn for very long periods of time, which explains why so many predictions turn out to be correct. In other words, forecasting is an art that works very well... between two catastrophes.

Combination of Factors

One of the consequences of complex human systems, as we have seen, is that there is no limit to their definition, which means that the number of variables relevant to their evolution is potentially unlimited. To make a prediction, therefore, we must consider a very large number of variables. For each of them, we must make assumptions about its value over time to avoid combinatorial explosion. Ultimately, the forecast is based on this large number of assumptions and is therefore extremely fragile. Each variable has its own margin of error, and these combine in the model to produce gigantic ranges of possible error, to the point of rendering the result meaningless.

A good example of the difficulty of prediction associated with the combination of factors is the development of ultrasound. This ultrasound-based imaging technique has had and continues to have a significant positive impact on human and animal health, and not only in the reproductive field. It is also used in industry. Where does it come from? Not from the medical world at all! In fact, the first studies on ultrasound were applied to the detection of submarines, just before the First World War! In 1951, a doctor and an electronics engineer took up the idea and presented a new device to the medical community: the ultrasound scanner. They expected it to be used in the search for brain tumors, but they were wrong: from the early 1970s, it would make a career in obstetrics, then in other specialties where it is still used today. But the story doesn't end there. Simpler and cheaper, ultrasound is now used everywhere, including China and India. In these and other Asian countries, its use is considered directly responsible for the gender imbalance: ultrasound makes it possible to detect female fetuses for abortion, which is very practical in cultures that prefer boys over girls. In China, for example, 118 boys are born for every 103 girls, while the global average is between 103 and 107. As a result, some 25 million Chinese men will be unable to find wives in the coming years. So, first, an invention designed for anti-submarine warfare becomes a medical device in the field of obstetrics, bringing considerable progress in human health. In a second phase, this medical device is used for harmful purposes and becomes responsible for a great tragedy, with social and therefore political consequences that are still evolving and difficult to predict: the relaxation of immigration laws for women in the case of marriage, at best, human trafficking, at worst. If you're a French engineer fighting German submarines in 1911, you can't predict that you'll be indirectly killing millions of Chinese female fetuses a century later. The social and cultural context in which innovation develops has given rise to an unexpected use: fetal sex selection.

The democratization of technology does not have the same impact in all countries: only countries with a preference for boys have this use, underscoring the importance of values. In addition to the technical impossibility of anticipation, there is also a cultural and social impossibility. As Ariel Colonomos notes: "To make a statement about the future, we would have to predict the values, preferences and norms that will prevail in tomorrow's world."[32] But if predicting technological evolution is difficult, predicting the evolution of values is even more so. In France, abortion was punishable by death (for the woman) in 1945.

[32] Ariel Colonomos, The Politics of Oracles: Telling the Future Today, Albin Michel, 2014, p. 257.

Thirty years later, in 1975, it was legalized, then reimbursed by social security in 1982. In less than forty years, one generation, an act that was once criminal has become reimbursed by the state. The change in values underlying this radical evolution is profound, as evidenced by the violent climate in which the law was debated in 1974; it would have been totally unforeseeable in 1945. This impossibility of anticipating the use of a technical invention, because it mixes technical and social uncertainty, has been demonstrated in many other cases.

Reconciliation

A final reason we can't predict is that what happens in the world is the result of the simultaneous decisions of millions of people. This is well illustrated by the famous game of rock, paper, scissors, in which two players simultaneously choose one of three possible moves by symbolizing it with their hand: rock (closed fist), leaf (flat hand), or scissors (two fingers in a V-shape). The game is circular: each choice can only win against one of the other two. The rock blunts the scissors but is enveloped by the paper. The paper is cut by the scissors. When a player chooses, he doesn't know what his opponent will choose, because there is no surefire winning strategy. The outcome, when the choices are matched, is completely unpredictable because it depends on the choices of each player.

We can generalize this example to decisions: if I decide to take an action, I know that at the same moment thousands, even millions of other players are doing the same (or taking a nap or watching TV). I won't know their decision (if that's possible) until the "next turn," when everyone has acted and it's too late to change my decision. What will happen in the next shot will therefore be the combination of all these decisions (for those who made them), each of which was necessarily made in ignorance of the others. Again, this is an intrinsic limitation, not an inability to gather information, since the latter may not be available (most players can't indicate their decision until they've made it).

PREDICTIVE APPROACHES AND THEIR LIMITATIONS

Prediction is difficult because all predictive approaches have significant limitations. The following is an overview of the most important ones.

First Approach: Law of Physics

The ideal case for accurately predicting the occurrence of a phenomenon is when a deterministic law is known a priori. This is very often the case in science. For example, if I throw a stone in a certain way, I can accurately predict the trajectory it will follow and where it will fall. I can repeat the operation an infinite number of times, and if the conditions don't change (for example, a sudden storm), my prediction will always be accurate. Similarly, if I throw a six-sided die and know for sure that it's not rigged, I can predict with certainty that after a certain number of throws, the 4 will come up one-sixth of the time.[33] Strictly speaking, however, science cannot predict the future. It can only predict what will happen if certain actions are taken.

However, cases where laws of physics are available are extremely rare. They exist in the natural sciences (Newtonian physics, but not quantum physics, chemistry, electronics), but never in what is the subject of this book, social systems such as markets, societies, or political systems. A society is not a large clock whose components and interconnected mechanisms are known or even knowable.

It's interesting to note that most of the examples used in statistics textbooks are taken from dice or card draws, ideal situations for illustrating principles, but bearing no relation to the uncertain reality faced by decision makers. A great deal of intelligence is used to model situations that decision makers will never encounter in real life.

Second Approach: Learning and Induction

In the absence of a physical law known a priori, as in the case of dice, we can try to develop an empirical law, i.e., a law based on the observation of facts. This "law" is constructed by learning, a posteriori. Learning is not, strictly speaking, a method of prediction, but it can form the basis of one. It consists in observing the repetition of a phenomenon and deriving from it a law that allows us to anticipate the future, as we have seen in the example of car theft. If we observe that about 2% of a certain model of car is stolen every year in a certain region, we can estimate that such a model has a 2% chance of being stolen next year. This is the principle of induction, which consists in generalizing a reasoning or observation from analogous singular cases to derive a "law". In the case of prediction, this operation is extended to predict the future based on past events. It is, of course, an empirical law. We don't know why these 2% are being stolen, but we do know the fact. In

[33] In reality, I'm never *completely* sure that the die isn't loaded. I'm bound to trust someone on this point (the thrower, the manufacturer, etc.).

principle, the more we observe car thefts, the more this “law” is reinforced.

This empirical approach is probably the oldest predictive mechanism used by humans. We can imagine that long ago, on the savannah, some of our ancestors, more adventurous than others, dared to eat certain berries. If he died immediately after eating it, his fellow members would induce an empirical law: “The purple berry that grows on the deciduous tree is deadly.”

Learning can also be voluntarily induced in a controlled way, in the realm of experimentation. This has long been the case in the sciences, of course, but also in the field of entrepreneurship and innovation in new markets: since we don’t really know if a new product will work, we market it to a limited public to gauge reactions; we may modify it based on those reactions.

There are several conditions for learning to work. First, there must be enough observations. If our brave ancestor dies after eating the purple berry, the cause-and-effect relationship is not obvious. He might have had a heart attack that had nothing to do with the berry. We can’t make laws about rare events. However, if we observe that every time a member of the tribe eats it, he dies within two days, causality can be reasonably established. Thus, the condition for establishing an empirical law is that the event occurs a sufficient number of times.

The notion of regularity is important here, and points to a second condition: the event must be repeated identically for learning to work. For example, a terrorist kills people by driving his truck into a crowd in a popular place. Putting up concrete blocks to prevent future attacks doesn’t necessarily make sense, since these will surely take a different form, such as a knife attack, but it is reassuring. Learning is only possible based on repeated, categorizable events. This is what the insurance company does for car thefts, which are categorized by model, year, color, place of theft, etc. When a new car is stolen, the system learns. When a new car is stolen, we know exactly what category to put it in, and it immediately adds to our statistical knowledge of that event. This is impossible for new events, because each one is new.

A third condition is that cause and effect must be clearly linked. In the example of wild berries, learning can only work if death occurs quickly, otherwise it becomes more difficult to associate cause and effect. Similarly, if our ancestor eats several kinds of berries, eats fish, and mocks the gods, the exact cause of his death will be harder to determine.

We are faced with what researchers call causal ambiguity, the inability to attribute a result to a particular cause. This means that learning cannot work. We can immediately see the limit for complex social systems: as we indicated above, the number of variables to be considered is so large that causal ambiguity will be maximal.

However, there is a fundamental limitation to the learning-based model that we mentioned earlier, and that is that we can never be sure that what we have learned will remain valid, even after the phenomenon has occurred many times. Underlying causes that may have been stable for a long time can suddenly change. Historical statistics can no longer be used to infer probabilities of occurrence; we must start from scratch. The problem, of course, is that we never know in advance whether the learning conditions are still valid. Learning is therefore a poor strategy in an uncertain environment prone to black swan events.

The same goes for intuition, which is often presented as a good way to make decisions under uncertainty. According to the Webster dictionary, "Intuition is the power of knowing immediately and without conscious reasoning". It is based on tacit knowledge and suffers from the same limitations. It cannot be used in the absence of stable regularities in the environment.

There are, of course, domains where learning-based prediction works. This is the case in medicine, for example, with heart attacks. These are usually very difficult to predict. About half of all serious accidents involve people who were not previously identified as being at risk. You can use artificial intelligence to analyze the information contained in 300,000 patient records and be able to distinguish interesting signals. In the end, the system's predictions can prove far better than those of doctors, identifying more patients who went on to develop heart disease. Here, learning from a mass of data works because we're in a non-reflexive area of science, and causalities don't evolve over time. Note that learning is about correlations; there is no causal understanding. It can work because causalities don't change over time. The same cannot be said for social systems. The impressive successes achieved by combining artificial intelligence (machine learning) and big data in scientific fields should not give false hope to those dealing with social systems. The limits, indeed, the dangers of learning in uncertain situations are even greater today because, as we pointed out earlier, our times are changing more frequently and more profoundly. This is part of the sense that things are moving faster and that we live in a volatile environment. When change is more frequent, more profound, and more abrupt, learning strategies work even less well. The inferences that could be made in a stable world, such as the savannah, where everything stayed the same for hundreds of years, can no longer be made in a world of repeated political, technological, economic, and social upheaval. In such an environment, learning even becomes counterproductive, because we learn the wrong lessons from what we observe. This brings us to the limits of learning paradigms and the concept of the learning organization, which was very much in vogue in the 1990s.

The Limits of Induction: The Turkey

The limits of induction were illustrated by the philosopher Bertrand Russell with his chicken metaphor, recently taken up by Nassim Taleb with a turkey. Imagine a turkey. Every morning it watches in satisfaction as the farmer drops off a large bowl of delicious grains. Its weight increases, and so does its confidence in the future. This goes on for days and days. Then one morning the farmer comes, not with a bowl, but with a knife. It's late November, Thanksgiving is coming up, and the farmer cuts off its head. The question is, to what extent could the knowledge the turkey had accumulated day after day enable it to anticipate what was about to happen? None, of course. The accumulation of similar "farmer brings me food" events led to the induction of the empirical law "the farmer loves me and therefore will never harm me", which turned out to be false, with tragic consequences (for the turkey).

In other words, what the bird didn't know was more important than what it did know. Day after day, it accumulated data that was useless, even counterproductive, because it reinforced the idea that it knew its environment better and better and was therefore less and less likely to be surprised. Not only did the accumulation of data not improve its predictive ability, but it decreased it! Notice, too, that the turkey's sense of confidence and safety peaked precisely when the life-threatening risk was highest. Time is of the essence here. When the turkey first sees the farmer arrive, it is certainly a little suspicious. But this suspicion gradually disappears as the "evidence" of the farmer's good intentions accumulates day by day. As the process continues, with a new bowl of grain each day, the turkey becomes less suspicious and more trusting. In environments where "accidents" are rare, they tend to be more serious because the players expect them less. And the rarer they are, the less players expect them. Prediction ("The farmer loves me, so he'll bring me a nice bowl of grain tomorrow, just like every day before") works successfully, day after day, for a very long time. If the turkey saw a fellow turkey being slaughtered by the farmer every day, it would look at him differently. But the one time it sees it, it dies. The experience is said to be "destructive"; there is no learning possible for the turkey, for whom the event is unique. The one it developed led it to conceive a false empirical law; it literally misled it, while the one that counted could not develop. Note also that the event is asymmetrical: it's a surprise for the turkey, but not at all for the farmer, who knew the fatal outcome from the start.

Induction reveals the occurrence of a black swan because it tells us, in philosophical language, that the absence of proof (we have never seen a swan of any color other than white) is not proof of absence (no swan can be of any color other than white). In other words, just because an event has never happened doesn't mean it can't happen. Going from "never happened" to "cannot happen" is a huge logical fallacy. And yet we make it every day. I remember getting into a taxi a few years ago. The driver was obviously in a hurry and driving very fast. I worked up the courage to politely say that I wasn't in a hurry and that we could drive slowly. The driver's response? "Don't worry, I've been driving for nineteen years, and I've never had an accident." This is what I call the immortality argument (a misnomer in the taxi context). This author has been through fifty-six years without dying, fifty-six years of daily proof that I'm not dead (more than 120,000 observations neatly filed away in my Excel spreadsheet), and therefore I will never die. My driver had never been in an accident, so he concluded - wrongly, of course - that he never would. I've never felt so close to a turkey, but fortunately my time had not yet come. In the same way, you can observe only white swans for two thousand years and then one day discover a black one. That's why we use the phrase "tyranny of the singular event". It only takes one sighting of a black swan to ruin two thousand years of observing white swans. And if we continue to observe white swans, we can never be sure that we won't see a black one... someday.

Induction isn't just a turkey problem, unfortunately. In October 1962, the CIA discovered a major Soviet operation in Cuba. President Kennedy suspected Russia of secretly installing long-range missiles aimed at the United States. When questioned, however, the CIA was categorical: they could not be nuclear missiles, since Russia had never installed them outside its territory for security reasons; therefore, it was not possible for them to do so in Cuba. The reasoning is typical turkey, a continuity argument. Since it never happened, it's impossible. But on October 14, a U-2 spy plane flight over Cuba revealed the impossible: dozens of launch sites for intercontinental missiles capable of reaching the United States had been built.

This clearly shows the limits of induction: the fact that a phenomenon has occurred in no way guarantees that it will continue in the future. The fact that it has been going on for a very long time makes no difference. The only effect of duration is to increase our confidence in the false empirical law we have developed. Duration in no way reinforces the value of the law, which is false to begin with.

Extrapolation: All Empirical Laws are "grue"

The limits of induction and empirical laws are illustrated by a famous philosophical exercise known as the grue paradox. The paradox was described by the philosopher Nelson Goodman using an example based on emeralds, which are green minerals.[34] *Let's assume that all emeralds are green. This hypothesis is confirmed by countless observations of green emeralds, namely its positive instances. Now consider a rival hypothesis: all emeralds are grue. Here, grue is a new predicate defined as the property of being green before some date T - say, the year 2080 - and blue afterwards. Thus, this second hypothesis, that all emeralds are grue, is confirmed by any observation of a green emerald before the year 2080, because grue means to be green before 2080. Of course, since all available observations are from before 2080, they all confirm the grue hypothesis, just as they confirm the "green" hypothesis. Goodman then argues that if the observation of a green emerald supports the logical induction "all emeralds are green", it also supports the statement "all emeralds are grue". Surprisingly, we readily accept the first proposition, but not the second.*

This paradox can be used to be more careful with historical "laws" than is currently the case. Most of these laws are true... until they become false. For example, in its January 2016 forecast for the coming year, the Financial Times was adamant: Who will win the American election? Answer: Hillary Clinton, because "all elections are won in the middle."[35] *In fact, what is presented as an obvious fact, a law, is nothing more than*

[34] Nelson Goodman, *Fact, Fiction, and Forecast* (Harvard University Press; 4th edition, 1983).

[35] "Forecasting the world in 2016", Financial Times.

a historical fact. This law is true, in the manner of grue: it is true until a certain date, when it may become false. For the United States, that date happens to be November 2016. Instead, we should have said: "Until then, an election has always been won in the center," and then asked ourselves: will this historical fact remain valid in the case of this election? Without necessarily having the answer, the simple fact of asking the question opens new perspectives for anticipating an event that nevertheless seems totally impossible.

We mentioned above the CIA estimate that the Soviets would never install nuclear missiles in Cuba, for the good reason that they had never installed any outside their territory. The "law" that "the Soviets do not install nuclear missiles outside their territory" was in fact *grue*. It should have been rephrased as "The Soviets do not install nuclear missiles outside their territory until a date T; they do so from that date onward". Then consider whether T could be September 1962. It is therefore important to consider all historical "laws" as grue. Grue tells us that "never happened" should really mean "not yet happened, but possible". Everything that is not impossible, everything that is an "epistemic possibility", to use Shackle's phrase, is grue. The grue argument also works with prognosticators. This or that "expert" is highly regarded because he or she predicted the last three presidential elections? Grue! If you bet on his predictions for the next one, you could very well be the sucker, because, as is often the case, he's the one making the predictions, and you're the one paying the consequences.

Third Approach: Extrapolation

Extrapolation is based on the idea that tomorrow will somehow be a continuation of today. According to the Webster dictionary, extrapolation means "to project, extend, or expand (known data or experience) into an area not known or experienced so as to arrive at a usually conjectural knowledge of the unknown area". Specifically, it consists of extending a statistical series by introducing a new term that obeys the law of the series after a series of old terms.

For example, if we want to predict the market for children's rotisserie chicken for the next two years, we'll start with sales over the last five years, then make some assumptions about the growth factors to determine "future" values. If the market has been growing at 1.5% per year for the past five years, we can assume that it will continue to do so, and therefore we can assume that next year's consumption will be the same as this year's +1.5%. Why one forecast rather than another? The philosopher Hume replies that the prediction chosen is the one that is consistent with past regularity, because that regularity has established a habit.

It is assumed that there is no reason why this increase should not continue. Extrapolation is therefore based on a fundamental assumption: the continuity of the phenomenon, the linearity of the system whose evolution we are trying to predict. We assume that tomorrow will be like today, with a relatively "small" plus or minus variation. But there's nothing obvious about that. Forecasters know this well, so they come up with variations on the theme. For example, chicken consumption is growing faster and faster: +1% three years ago, +1.5% two years ago, +2% last year, so we can assume +2.5% next year. The extrapolation can be based on the increase, or the rate of increase, or any other variation. Additional factors can be brought into play, such as estimating that chicken consumption will increase more over three years because it tends to substitute for red meat. The technical arsenal is limitless. The important thing is to determine a "pattern" of evolution and then use that pattern to calculate future values based on past values.

The most cautious forecastors will frame their calculations by defining a low, medium, and high hypothesis of curve evolution, but what we call low, medium, and high is, of course, entirely subjective. Often, as Nassim Taleb points out, a high hypothesis is simply the highest we've seen so far. In Fukushima, the walls were built to a height of 5.20 meters because that was the height of the largest tidal wave ever seen. On March 11, 2011, the tsunami set a record at… 17 meters, with the consequences we all know. But there's more: because environmental evolution is non-linear, we can suddenly find ourselves with a very strong discontinuity and a complete change of scale. Chicken consumption may have been rising steadily for years, when suddenly a health scare causes it to plummet. Nelson Goodman comments on the fundamental limitation of extrapolation: "Predictions are about what has not yet been observed. And they cannot be logically deduced from what has been observed, because what has happened imposes no logical constraints on what will happen."[36] Again, this is the fundamental hyphenation between present and future. The assumption of environmental continuity, so necessary for extrapolation to work, is not verified in human systems. Using it therefore exposes us to catastrophe,

[36] Goodman, op. cit., p. 59.

sooner or later. The paper dress episode provides an excellent example of the limits of extrapolation in forecasting.

The Limits of Extrapolation: Paper Dresses

In March 1967, Time magazine published a rousing article about a new revolution, paper dresses.[37] *The article explains that paper has made so many technological advances that it can now achieve equal or superior performance to textiles in terms of strength, durability, solidity, etc., and can therefore begin to replace the latter because it is more practical: no need to wash, just throw it away! Several manufacturers have launched product lines (dresses, but also suits, curtains, tablecloths, etc.) that have been an immediate success. Many are even out of stock. Fashion designers are interested in the new material. The article concludes that paper fabrics are a sure success. And yet no one dresses in paper today. The market was a flash in the pan.*

Let's look at the journalist's reasoning. He bases his prediction on an extrapolation: he notes the very rapid rise in sales of paper dresses and concludes, based on the continuity argument, that this trend is bound to continue. But this is not the case. After a few months of enthusiasm, sales slowed and then collapsed. What could explain this?

First, the journalist uses the wrong analogy. He's writing about a time, the 1960s, when everything became disposable. It seemed obvious that clothes would become disposable, but that did not happen. A suit is not a razor or a glass of water; it's a much more sophisticated object, closely tied to the personality of the wearer. A very strong trend may apply in one area, but not at all in another.

Second, the journalist's thinking is narrow and technical. He relies solely on the technical performance of paper fabric to demonstrate its superiority over textile, thus predicting the success of the former at the expense of the latter. In doing so, he ignores the context in which it will spread, especially the social context. In this case, wearing a paper dress is hardly an attractive proposition, and despite manufacturers' assurances, there is a widespread fear that paper will catch fire or fall apart when soaked with water in the rain. The limitation of the analysis to purely technical aspects at the expense of social and anthropological aspects, which are more diffuse and harder to grasp, leads to a simplistic approach to anticipation.

[37] "Fashion: Real Live Paper Dolls", Time, March 17, 1967.

The journalist also ignores lack of knowledge: the diffuse fear mentioned above did not appear in market research, as is often the case with questions that respondents find embarrassing. The same goes for the fear that the use of paper clothing might create an unflattering image. Most of the data about the problem therefore remains invisible, despite the analytical arsenal at our disposal. Like Taleb's turkey, what the observer doesn't know about the problem turns out to be more important than what he does know. But he doesn't know what he doesn't know; he doesn't even try to identify it.

In addition, the journalist argues "all other things being equal". His argument, which predicts the success of paper, assumes that paper has an advantage over textile in terms of cost and technical possibilities. This might be true at the time the article was written. But at that time, the textile industry was engaged in a determined policy of cost reduction, especially by relocating to low-wage countries. Paper quickly lost its initial advantage. What's more, the textile industry was far from declining; it was constantly innovating by introducing new materials with ever more interesting properties, which in turn reduced paper's initial advantage. The "all things being equal" argument implicitly assumes that the rest of the world does not change as we move forward, which of course is rarely the case. Paper was competing with textiles, but the latter were constantly improving their offerings and costs, so the target was moving. This reasoning is often found in futurologists' studies, which explains their limitations. For example, the study published every five years by the CIA envisions all sorts of changes in the world over the next twenty-five years, but puts America unchanged into that world in one fell swoop, ignoring all the interactions that may have taken place over those twenty-five years.

Finally, nowhere in the article does our poor journalist raise the question of the likely reaction of the textile industry. And yet, it's hard to imagine that the major textile manufacturers would have remained unmoved by the paper manufacturers' determination to take their market away from them. Anticipation must always try to consider the reaction of the "other", the "opponent", even if this is often difficult.

Fourth Approach: Scenario Building

A scenario is a rich description of a plausible future. It's a kind of leap into the future. For example, we might imagine "Europe in 2080". We then study the implications of this plausible future, such as the price of a barrel of oil at $300 or $10. A scenario is not based on extrapolation but on the assignment of extreme values to certain variables carefully chosen for their significant impact on what we wish to study.

The advantage of a scenario is that, on the one hand, it allows us to broaden our horizons and, on the other, it prepares us to act if the scenario becomes reality. In this sense, a scenario is like a flight simulator used to train pilots: it creates artificial but plausible conditions and allows us to train ourselves to operate under these conditions.

The use of scenarios was initiated by the American researcher Herman Kahn in the 1950s in the context of nuclear warfare. It was then developed within the Shell oil group by several pioneers, including the researcher Pierre Wack.[38] One of their scenarios in the 1970s was based on oil at $300 a barrel. This work apparently enabled Shell to better manage the 1973 oil crisis, which no one had anticipated. Even today, the study of future scenarios remains a genre in its own right and is regularly published.[39]

A scenario is not conceptually different from a forecast. The only difference is that instead of one predicted future, there are several. Unlike a prediction, however, the creator of a scenario does not take a position on these futures and their likelihood of occurring, but simply considers them plausible.

Scenarios, however, quickly reach their limits: they are often based on the evolution of only one or two variables, without which the complexity of the whole becomes unmanageable. Scenario building is characterized by a paradox: the more detailed the scenario, the more attractive it is, but the less realistic and therefore less likely it is, hence the less useful. Conversely, the less detailed the scenario, the less useful it will be!

What's more, the further into the future you go, the more the number of possible variables explodes, and the more the scenario loses value. And this explosion happens very quickly - it's the very principle of uncertainty. We must include in the scenario futures that are very difficult to imagine and make many arbitrary choices to avoid multiplying the options. For example, if we still talk about the price of oil, to imagine its evolution we would have to include all the innovations

---

[38] Pierre Wack, "Scenarios: Uncharted Waters Ahead", Harvard Business Review, September 1985.

[39] See "Global Trends 2030" developed by the US intelligence community: https://www.dni.gov/files/documents/ GlobalTrends_2030.pdf.

in the energy field to give ourselves a chance to be realistic: fuel cells, nuclear, solar, wind, etc. Each of these fields is an ocean of uncertainty, even in the very short term. Then there's everything we can't even imagine yet (radical innovations, geopolitical upheavals, consumption patterns, new discoveries, etc.).[40] We would then have to take into account all political developments or, on the contrary, assume total political stability over the scenario horizon, which is obviously an unreasonable risk. This is one of the reasons why oil price forecasting is one of the areas where errors have been almost systematic and massive since 1973, as we saw above. It's a graveyard for forecasters, but that doesn't stop them from persisting.

Another limitation of scenarios is that judging a hypothesis to be plausible is not as simple as it seems. It's a value judgment. We may decide not to investigate a scenario that we find implausible, only to see it come true sometime later. You can choose to focus on this or that variable, leaving aside the one that really matters. Few governments have prepared for Brexit in this way. The analyst, say in the German government, who would have advised to prepare for it in spring 2016 would have been laughed at by his colleagues. Conversely, it is possible to study certain scenarios that we think are wrongly obvious. Taking oil as an example, the imminent exhaustion of our oil reserves (peak oil) has been accepted by almost everyone for at least sixty years. For sixty years now, it has been accepted that peak oil will occur in fifteen years! So while scenarios may present themselves as bold explorations of extreme futures, they often end up rooted in the current paradigm of their creators, and most often reflect disembodied, linear thinking and a positivist epistemology. That doesn't mean they're useless, but we need to be aware of their limitations.

Above all, the problem with scenarios is that they have not resolved their epistemological contradiction: as we have just recalled, in uncertainty we are faced with an infinite number of variables, and prediction is impossible. The entire scientific arsenal will never be sufficient to resolve this difficulty. The title of Peter Schwartz's seminal work on scenario planning, *The Art of the Long View: Planning for the Future in an Uncertain World*[41], is a striking illustration of this. The entire title is a

[40] The shale gas and horizontal drilling revolution in the United States in the early 2000s, which took the entire industry by surprise, is a typical case of an innovation that completely changed the economic, political, and strategic landscape of the gas market. All the predictions made by the best experts over many years have been rendered completely obsolete by this breakthrough.

contradiction in terms: "Long view," as we've pointed out, there's nothing to "see" in the future because it hasn't been written yet. "Planning for the future" is a vocabulary that reflects a predictive paradigm; planning in an uncertain world is impossible. The title is grandiloquent, but it reveals an epistemological confusion. It is not a problem of academic argumentation. It's a fundamental contradiction that renders the proposed method sterile and its application dangerous.

Possible Futures: The Artistic Contribution

Much more interesting exercises in "possible futures" can be found in literature. Utopians like Thomas More, and Plato before him, tried to imagine what they saw as the ideal city. Literature has also imagined dystopian futures, the opposite of utopia (indeed, one person's utopia is often another's dystopia). In *Brave New World*, written by Aldous Huxley and published in 1932, babies are made in factories, men take a pill every morning to make them happy, people are divided into five different castes and conditioned to be proud of the one they belong to, and they travel in flying cars. *1984*, written by George Orwell and published in 1949, anticipates a future in which people are monitored 24 hours a day by an omnipresent dictatorial state in the form of Big Brother.[42] In Philip K. Dick's *Minority Report*, the police have the means to predict crimes and act before they are committed. The works of Jules Verne, Ray Bradbury, James Ballard, and Isaac Asimov, among many others, are also rich in their exploration of human emotions and possible futures, and, even for some of them that are sometimes ancient, they sometimes resonate strangely with current events. Science fiction (also aptly called anticipatory literature) provides a rich source for imagining possible futures. At the end of 2019, the French Army launched a program called "Red Team", inviting science fiction authors and screenwriters to imagine potential conflicts on the horizon of 2030-2060.

Science fiction is useful not because it's predictive, but because it allows us to play with our view of the world. It creates a space where we can challenge our assumptions and mental models. Comics and video games,

---

[41] Peter Schwartz, *The Art of the Long View: Planning for the Future in an Uncertain World* (Currency, 1996)

[42] The value of 1984 and its ability to anticipate is evidenced by the fact that sales of the novel in the United States peaked in 2013, when the extent of the NSA's electronic surveillance program was revealed. In many ways, Orwellian fiction has been overtaken by reality.

thanks to their great creativity, are also powerful tools for exploring utopian or dystopian future universes. Art in general also explores possible futures, and even futures that never happened. Finally, the richness, boldness, quality, and diversity of the various artistic genres that imagine possible futures means that to understand the present and think about the future, it's often better to read a book, visit an avant-garde exhibition, or watch a science fiction movie than to read the report of an eminent futurologist. Similarly, artists are often far better able to sense their time than sociologists, and therefore better able to sense where it might be going; to understand Afghanistan, it's probably better to read Rudyard Kipling than a CIA report.

Fifth Approach: Foresight

Foresight is the ability to predict what will happen or be needed in the future. Foresight is a whole field, and we'll only touch on it briefly here. The founder of foresight is Gaston Berger, who wrote in the 1950s before he was killed in a car accident. In practice, it's very similar to scenarios and futures studies, but it's more action-oriented. That's how it should be judged.

Michel Godet, a leading contemporary futurologist, distinguishes three possible attitudes toward the future: reactivity, pre-activity, and proactivity. Reactivity means not anticipating events, but simply reacting to them. Pre-activity is about anticipating foreseeable changes in order to better prepare for and take advantage of them. This is the domain of scenarios and what the Anglo-Saxons call strategic foresight. With proactivity, we try to bring about the desired changes through concrete actions. There have been many foresight studies over the past sixty years, and the industry is flourishing. But is it useful? That's doubtful. According to Gaston Berger, foresight invites us to "see far ahead," but this choice of the word "see" is unfortunate: since the future is unwritten, there's nothing to see! We can imagine far, we can predict far, but we can't see far. He adds that "our civilization is like a car driving faster and faster on an unknown road as night falls. Its headlights must reach farther and farther if we are to avoid disaster."[43] But again, the choice of metaphor is unfortunate: with a car, the road exists; the future is unwritten, so there is no road to light! It's an epistemological impossibility that points to the inherent limitation of foresight work: it's intellectually fascinating, but futile. As soon as foresight attempts to be

[43] Berger, Massé, and Bourbon-Busset, De la prospective, op. cit.

more precise than the trend, it runs up against this impossibility of prediction in a non-deterministic environment. Similarly, foresight often works with "desired futures". But desired by whom? Who decides what is desirable and what is not? A committee of wise men or a committee of public salvation? The people? The market? Most changes are initially unwanted.

Did foresight drive the entrepreneurs who revolutionized our society? Not at all (Steve Case, founder of Internet pioneer AOL, claims to have been influenced by futurist Alvin Toffler, but we don't know how, and there aren't many). According to Berger, thanks to foresight, the future belongs to the realm of will, but for him that means above all the will of the State and its experts; and the State doesn't change the world, it merely regulates it, at best. Foresight therefore doesn't address the right actors, and these actors aren't interested in its work anyway. The future can only be created by entrepreneurs, in the broadest sense of the word. The entrepreneurial transformation of the world is the great dark matter of foresight. What's more, because they're not at the center of the action, futurists suffer from a great sensitivity to unprecedented events that they can't predict or even foresee. What's the point of planning if everything is called into question by the unprecedented?

Berger also writes that foresight raises the problem of the end of action, which must dictate and inspire the means. The problem of the future, then, would be relatively simple: instead of trying to predict what future discoveries will be, we must focus on the needs to be satisfied. In other words, human problems will take precedence over technical ones, and the ends will guide the means developed. In the end, it's all very Cartesian: we set the ends, and the means will necessarily follow. Yet, at a time when technical and scientific discoveries are constantly opening up almost infinite possibilities never before imagined, such a vision is surprising. This is not how the world has evolved. It is not the way of the entrepreneur, who, on the contrary, starts from the means available to imagine new possibilities. Such an approach would never have led to the creation of Google or the iPhone. When a group of experts imagines the needs to be met, it always ends badly.

Despite its interest and the richness of its work, foresight suffers from the same limitation as all futurology: if the future cannot be predicted, it must be built. If it is to be built, the "science of the future" so longed for by Berger must be a science of action. However learned, however versed in alternative approaches, however informed about reality, the futurist is only an observer.

So it's those who build the future-entrepreneurs and innovators-who must be addressed, and to whom we must provide the tools for decision-making and imagination. In the end, foresight has little to offer. Once the interesting prolegomena on the limits of prediction and the construction of the future have been set out, it boils down to bringing together people from different backgrounds (in fact, mostly technocrats, specialists, in short, experts again and again) to think about the future. Gaston Berger recognized the limits of prediction and the need to build the future, not guess at it, but he failed to offer a satisfactory alternative approach. We can pay tribute to Gaston Berger, but we can't do much with him. When he writes that foresight liberates man from fatality, he may be right, but among the things that liberate man from fatality, foresight is not the most important. People have long since freed themselves without it, and they have done so through innovation and entrepreneurship.

Sixth Approach: Modeling

Modeling consists of constructing a simplified representation of the system whose evolution we wish to study, based on a certain number of variables and the relationships between these variables, in other words empirical laws. This is what INSEE, French national institute for statistics, typically does with Mesange, its 500-equation model of the French economy. This model is then used to make predictions. Models are widely used in economics and finance and often reach a high degree of sophistication, especially now that the computing power available is almost infinite. The problem is that no matter how sophisticated a model is, and no matter how powerful the computer that runs it, it is necessarily a simplification of reality. It cannot include all the variables and their relationships in the system under consideration. This is especially true for the complex systems that are the subject of this book. As we have seen, such systems are open-ended, meaning that the number of variables that govern them is potentially infinite. At some point, therefore, it will be necessary to stop including certain rules and variables. This is the famous distinction between the map and the territory it is supposed to represent. The map shows paths, slopes, and watercourses, but not trees and flowers, which are considered useless to those seeking their route. The purpose of the model is therefore to privilege certain variables and exclude others. This simplification is the sine qua non for its implementation. In a complicated system, such exclusion is not very difficult, since we are able to determine which variables are important and which are not. The more you include, the better you represent the behavior of the system, and after a while the progress becomes marginal, because the inclusion of an additional rule or variable only marginally improves the representativeness of the system: there is a linear progression towards the optimum. This makes sense for a flight simulator because the airplane is a complicated object. But in the case of a complex system, the situation is quite different. It's very difficult to identify the variables that matter, and especially the causal relationships that connect them. As we've seen in the case of Tunisia, if you had to model the evolution of the country, it's unlikely that you would include an unknown street vendor named Mohamed Bouazizi in your "country risk" model. You would thus miss the key variable, and your model would collapse. In contrast to the model-building approach, it's precisely the outliers that you should be looking for.

Claude Shannon, one of the fathers of information theory, also believed that new and surprising information is more valuable than that which continues an existing sequence. This is a profound observation, since it directly contradicts the practice of modeling, which consists precisely in eliminating outliers that are considered anomalous. The non-linear nature of the systems we're dealing with means that an approximation misses the important detail, the one that counts, as we saw above with our Tunisian example. This is what Taleb captured with the notion of *extremistan*: a detail (or at least what is seen as such by the model designer) can topple the system, which is then very difficult to model. As Gaston Berger notes: "It is rather useless to foresee the consequences of a few artificially isolated factors, when in fact they must come into play in the midst of a large number of others which the abstract study has precisely failed to take into account."[44] As the Wikipedia article on the Mesange model modestly and no doubt humorously notes in its Limitations section, and which is worth quoting in extenso: "The behavior of the economy depends more and more on globalized financial speculation, the behavior of banks (cf. economic crisis of 2008-2010), and consumer behavior itself involves a great deal of uncertainty and remains difficult to model (For example, in the event of a prolonged crisis, precautionary savings, lower household investment), consumer fatigue, war, a major global pandemic, a serious event (e.g. the 'Chernobyl effect' in Ukraine or Belarus) or, on the contrary, an unexpected innovation (the Internet and mobile telephony were not foreseen by previous forecasts and models). New phenomena may emerge, such as the depletion of natural resources, the rise in sea levels,

[44] Berger, Massé, and Bourbon-Busset, De la prospective, op. cit.

or simply the aging of the population (the delayed effect of the baby boom, known as the 'papy-boom'), which is expected to peak in France around 2030 and then begin to decline." In essence, the vast majority of what will determine the behavior of the system, i.e., the final outcome, is totally unpredictable and cannot be modeled; the exercise is hopeless, forecasts are revised ad infinitum, but that doesn't stop our forecasters in the least. Shackle concludes soberly: "To admit that there is novelty, in the sense of things that are fundamentally irreducible, waiting to be encountered for the first time, is to admit that we cannot construct a model that will reveal the historical course of a society over even a limited period of time."[45] Let's bet that, thanks to advances in technology, Mesange's next model will have 5,000 equations instead of 500, and that it will still be just as useless.

The Difficulty of Defining the System to be Modeled: A Casino Story

Defining the system to be modeled is also difficult, as Nassim Taleb illustrates with the misadventure that befell a casino.[46] *In theory, risk management for a casino is relatively simple: it's a matter of monitoring the tables to prevent cheating. The probabilities of each game are known exactly, which is obviously a crucial advantage for this industry. Any player whose statistical series deviates from the theoretical one can be immediately suspected and monitored. The risk model is therefore easy to define. After all, we're rolling dice! And yet, one of the major Las Vegas casinos lost a fortune after a series of events. Four of them were completely outside their risk models. First, the casino lost more than $100 million when the tiger trainer of its flagship show was attacked by his animal after years without incident, forcing the casino to cancel the show and causing a sharp drop in hotel bookings and thus casino attendance. The casino discovered that it was actually a show connected to a hotel and casino, not the other way around. Second, a contractor was injured during construction and, angry at not being properly compensated, tried to blow up the casino! Fortunately, he was stopped in time. Third, the casino discovered that one of its employees had neglected to fill out a tax form for years, for no apparent reason. The casino had to pay a very large fine. Fourth, the owner's daughter was briefly kidnapped, forcing him to dip into the casino's reserves to pay*

[45] George L. S. Shackle, *Epistemics and Economics: A Critique of Economic Doctrines* (Transaction Publishers, 1991), p. 26.
[46] Taleb, *The Black Swan*, p. 181.

the ransom. Taleb then observes that the total value of these black swans, completely outside the model, crushes the modeled risks (the gambling) by a factor of 1000. The casino spent hundreds of millions of dollars on game theory and high-tech surveillance, while most of its risks, by value, came from outside its risk model. In other words, it didn't understand the perimeter of its business and had no awareness of what its business model really was (a hotel, plus a show, plus a casino, in that order). In a world of rapid change, the business model can actually evolve without the company being aware of it, which can lead to surprises.

Seventh Approach: Weak Signals and Trends

The idea behind weak signals is that an event is always preceded by information that allows us to anticipate it. If we can detect these signals and interpret them correctly, we can anticipate events. Hence, the police monitor fertilizer purchases because they contain nitrate, which is used to make bombs. Cosmetics brands send product managers to trendy places to spot future fashion trends. This is a useful exercise, but it has its limitations. First, weak signals can be used to mislead the enemy. Bin Laden spread numerous rumors of attacks to exhaust Western services. Second, their usefulness quickly diminishes. If the terrorists know that the police are monitoring fertilizer purchases, which is bound to happen at some point, they will find other ways to carry out their attacks (with simple Kalashnikovs, for example). The result is a cat-and-mouse game in which the terrorists always have the initiative, and yesterday's interesting signals are at best useless, at worst misleading (a lack of fertilizer purchases may indicate a reduced risk of attacks). But the main limitation of weak signals lies in their interpretation.

Two months before the 9/11 attacks, an FBI agent in Arizona alerted his headquarters that several Middle Easterners were training at a flight school and recommended a national investigation. In fact, they weren't interested in learning how to take off or land, which is odd, let's face it! A classic example of a weak signal. And yet no one was concerned, and after the attack there was considerable controversy about the alleged incompetence of the police and intelligence services. And yet the inaction can be explained. On the one hand, the owner of the flight school later explained that he had many wealthy clients who just wanted to have fun by taking over the controls of their private jet for a few minutes during the flight, without making the effort to learn how to land or take off. On the other hand, an FBI agent's job is to witness strange things all day long, so he must choose which ones to pursue and which ones to drop because he can't handle them all. One strange thing leads to another. The officer filled out his report and gave it to his superior, who probably felt that there were more urgent and important things to deal with (drug trafficking, bank robberies, violence) than student pilots who didn't want to learn how to take off or land.

Of course, it's easy to criticize this decision after the fact, but before, in the fog of action, when faced with dozens of potential cases of murder, trafficking, violence, etc., we can understand the officer's obligation to decide. The question is, on what basis are these decisions made? American researcher Roberta Wohlstetter sheds some interesting light on this question. In her pioneering work on the Japanese surprise attack on Pearl Harbor on December 7, 1941, she showed that the failure of the Americans to anticipate the attack could not be attributed to a lack of attention to weak signals. In fact, the American Navy had broken the codes of the Japanese Navy. It therefore had massive signals in the form of conversations with Japanese admirals. But they found the hypothesis of an attack on Pearl Harbor so absurd that they refused to consider it. An exercise on the subject in the spring of 1941 was even rejected. Although this has fueled conspiracy theories ever since, a look at a map shows just how crazy the Japanese undertaking was: Pearl Harbor is over 3,000 miles (6,300 km) from Japan and launching an armada that far from its bases would push the technology available to the Japanese at the time to the limits of what was feasible. Objectively speaking, it was madness. The U.S. Navy therefore based its refusal to consider such an attack on two strong assumptions that seemed perfectly reasonable at the time: first, the technical impossibility, and second, the fact that it seemed suicidal for a small country like Japan to feel capable of attacking a country as powerful as the United States.

Weak signals are therefore sorted and interpreted based on hypotheses developed about the system under study. The Americans project their rationality onto the Japanese, while the latter are completely unaware that they are awakening a giant. The surprise is therefore not a problem of weak signals, but of assumptions. It's because their assumptions are wrong that the Americans are surprised. The same applies to the flight school on September 11. If the FBI had told its agents that it suspected an attack on airliners, thereby changing its working hypothesis, the officer who reported strange behavior at a flight school would surely have been listened to. But without a hypothesis, it's impossible to extract the relevant small signals from the mass of information this officer is drowning in every day. And with big data spewing out mountains of data, it doesn't get any better over time. So we interpret the world based on assumptions (but also on beliefs and values, i.e. mental models), and it's these that guide our work of understanding the world. Knowledge expert Haridimos Tsoukas writes: "Understanding presupposes the existence of an Archimedean point, a standpoint from which the world can be viewed, considered, and interpreted."[47] Hypotheses provide just such an Archimedean point. Peter Drucker, one of management's greatest writers, wrote: "Executives who make effective decisions know that you don't start with facts. You start with assumptions... It is impossible to start with facts. There are no facts unless you have a criterion of relevance."[48]

Of course, a hypothesis can be wrong, with dramatic consequences. This is illustrated by the case of the Germanwings plane crash in March 2015. After 9/11, it was decided to equip the cockpits of commercial aircrafts with an armored door that could only be opened from the inside. This would prevent a terrorist from taking control of the aircraft. But this decision was based on the not-so-explicit assumption that the danger was necessarily in the cabin, not in the cockpit. This assumption proved fragile when the cockpit was occupied by Andreas Lubitz, a depressed co-pilot who waited for the pilot to go to the bathroom before locking the door and committing suicide by flying the plane into the mountain. During the crash, the pilot desperately tried to open the door, but it was designed not to open! The design of our systems is always based on assumptions, but these assumptions can turn out to be wrong, producing unintended effects with sometimes dramatic consequences. We must therefore make these assumptions explicit, discuss them regularly, and define an institutional means of challenging them.

Only with hypotheses can we distinguish useful signals from noise. Without hypotheses to sort them out, all we have is a huge pile of data that we don't know what to do with, or worse, that we can do with as we please. In the end, despite the theoretical interest of the notion of a weak signal, its practical scope remains limited and its use risky given the sheer amount of pre-event information available today.

---

[47] Haridimos Tsoukas, *Complex Knowledge: Studies in Organizational Epistemology* (Oxford University Press, 2005), p. 23.
[48] Peter F. Drucker, *Management: Tasks, Responsibilities, Practices* (HarperBusiness, 1973).

What About Trends?

I'm often told that in such an uncertain world there are certain trends, such as the depletion of natural resources or demographic change! Well, no! Let's look at the question of natural resources from the point of view of two of them: oil and aluminum. In 2008, the price of a barrel of oil peaked at $132. What happened? Consumers quickly adjusted their behavior. The press reported that people were moving to be closer to work. Car-sharing took off. But high prices also meant that some wells that were costly to operate suddenly became profitable. All these responses had the effect of increasing supply and decreasing consumption fairly quickly, driving prices down. But more importantly, in the longer term, if the price stays high, it will encourage investment in alternative energy, which will reduce demand.

In addition to the price effect, there's also a technology effect. Let's take the historical example of aluminum to see how that works. Aluminum has been known since ancient times, but no one knew how to extract it. In 1854, Sainte-Claire Deville developed a chemical process based on the reduction of aluminum chloride with sodium. The new metal caused a sensation, rivaling gold and silver: jewelry and prestige objects were made of aluminum. But because the process was slow and inefficient, aluminum was expensive to produce and therefore scarce. In 1890, a new electrolytic process was developed that allowed mass production: aluminum could now be produced in abundance. As we can see, the scarcity of a resource depends largely on the technology developed by humans. The certainty of geological laws is therefore relative. The availability of a resource, far from obeying an immutable geological law, depends on two factors: price and technological knowledge. When a resource becomes scarce, its price rises, slowing consumption and encouraging substitution. There is no such thing as a definite trend, due to the dynamic nature of the environment and the intrinsic novelty generated by the flow of time.

Eighth Approach: Theory

Theory is used when the available data do not allow us to "construct" an empirical law. This is especially true for rare or unprecedented events, such as global warming or the impact of solar flares on communication networks, because we cannot learn from their occurrence. In the absence of empirical evidence, theory is the only way to predict. In the field of strategy, Philippe Baumard observes that "what the writers of military treatises are fighting against is *idiotês* in the Greek sense, that is, a reality that is self-sufficient, singular, with no possible repetition. [...] The treatise on strategy plays an essential role here: to fight against the expansion of the realm of the absurd, to show that there is an art, models, reproducible knowledge."[49] In short, please give us a theory! This is often based on a strong concept, a paradigm or a mental model that helps make sense of the world and proposes an explanatory law. The domino theory is a good example of such a theory. It was developed by the Eisenhower administration in the 1950s in the context of the Cold War. It predicted that if one country fell into communism, its neighbors would inevitably follow through a contagion effect. It served as the basis for the United States' decision to intervene in Vietnam, which was seen as the first of the dominoes in Southeast Asia.

Similarly, the theory of "democratic transition" emerged after the fall of communism in the 1990s. It predicted that every dictatorship will eventually evolve into some form of liberal democracy. It became the basis of thought for a whole generation of analysts and politicians. Unfortunately, the recent return of countries such as Hungary, Turkey, and Russia to illiberal democratic regimes, or even autocracies with democratic trappings, has completely invalidated it. Once again, this was no more than an empirical "law", and empirical laws end abruptly. Another example of a theory is that of the disappearance of the State. In the 1990s, it was common among engineers, especially in the hacker movement, to think that the Internet would allow individuals to free themselves from its tutelage. Typical of this thinking is *The Sovereign Individual*[50], a landmark work in the techno-libertarian world. Many of its categorical predictions, however, have been contradicted by the facts, the most important of which is the strong takeover of the Internet by states, both democratic and less democratic. The authors simply forgot that the Internet operates on a fixed, immobile, and fragile infrastructure (servers and cables) that is easy for states to control. For the same reason, the Internet giants, which often grew up in a libertarian culture, have become multinationals that cannot resist the demands of the states on whose territory they operate. The terrorist attacks of 2001, followed by the financial crisis of 2008 and the Covid-19 crisis of 2020, have all contributed to a significant resurgence of the power of the State, thus overturning all the predictions of the 1990s of an inevitable decline in its

---

[49] Philippe Baumard, *Le Vide stratégique* (CNRS, 2012), p. 28.

[50] James Dale Davidson and William Rees-Mogg, *The Sovereign Individual: Mastering the Transition to the Information Age* (Touchstone, 2008).

economic and political importance. Social systems are therefore areas in which it is very difficult to establish laws, and those that seem to work one day end up being disproved.

The development of the Enlightenment in the 18th century was seen as making war less likely. Thanks to the Enlightenment, it was thought, people would become better because they would be better educated, and war would disappear. In 1784, French philosopher Condorcet wrote: "[...] the great probability that in the future we may expect fewer great changes, fewer great revolutions than in the past: the progress of enlightenment of all kinds and in all parts of Europe, the spirit of moderation and peace which prevails there, the kind of contempt into which Machiavellianism is beginning to fall, seem to assure us that wars and revolutions will be less frequent in the future."[51] This was written five years before the French Revolution and the Terror that cost him his life. Before World War I, it was widely believed that the development of trade and relations between countries would make war impossible, as it would be too destructive. This was the argument of Norman Angell's The Great Illusion,[52] published in 1913, which had a considerable influence on the European intelligentsia. It's easy to see how we can fall prey to theories that are seductive, seemingly full of common sense, but profoundly false.

In 2005, Thomas Friedman's book, *The World is Flat*[53], was a huge success (7 million copies sold). His thesis was that globalization was inevitable and that borders would soon become meaningless. In it he wrote: "The beginning of the 21st century will be remembered not for military conflicts or political events, but for a whole new century of globalization - a 'flattening' of the world". We know what happened instead. Let's beware of gurus, their "laws" and "inevitable" trends. The great theories that explain the world often end abruptly, at the expense not of those who promulgated them, but of those who believed in them.

Disruptions are an important case where theory can partially help anticipate the course of events. This is the contribution of researcher Clayton Christensen, one of the pioneers in this field.[54] As we mentioned

---

[51] Quoted in: Bertrand de Jouvenel, *The Art of Conjecture*, (Routledge, 2017), p. 83.

[52] Norman Angell, *The Great Illusion* (Forgotten Books, 2016)

[53] Thomas Friedman, *The World is Flat: A Brief History of the Twenty-first Century* (Farrar Straus & Giroux, 2005)

[54] Christensen's work is presented and discussed in my book: *A Manager's*

at the beginning of this book, disruption is a profound change in a company's competitive environment. It involves a change in the criteria that define a market. For example, the property-sharing website Airbnb represents a disruption for hotels: whereas hotel chains have based their performance on the consistency of the user experience regardless of the hotel chosen, Airbnb does exactly the opposite. It is basing its success on extreme variation from one location to the next. A company that has spent thirty years fine-tuning its organization to ensure a consistent experience, and training and evaluating its people to do so, can't turn everything upside down overnight to take the opposite approach. This makes it very difficult for Hilton to create Airbnb without immediately compromising its current business. But despite its success, Airbnb's model is not at all attractive to Hilton. The two have radically different, incompatible business models. We can therefore expect that Hilton will find the market exploited by Airbnb unattractive from its point of view and will find it difficult to respond to its development. Christensen's theory therefore predicts that in a disruptive situation, the incumbent leader will tend to stay on the sidelines, not finding the opportunity offered by the disruption attractive and leaving the initiative to a new entrant. Intel CEO Andy Grove said that after reading Christensen's book in 1997, he realized that the theory could apply to his company. Intel was in danger of getting trapped at the high end of the market, leaving the low end to new competitors. He set out to create an entry-level processor, and thus was born the Celeron, a great success that has ensured Intel's solid presence in this segment. The Celeron case is a very good example of anticipation: "Predict what's going to happen and adapt your behavior accordingly". Thanks to Christensen's theory, Grove was able to anticipate his company's exit from an important segment. He adjusted his behavior accordingly by creating the entry-level unit, thus avoiding the expected failure. This does not mean, however, that Christensen's theory is an absolute predictor of an organization's response to a disruption in its environment. This response still depends on many factors, and the theory does not predict the time scale over which a disruption will have its effects.

Ninth Approach: Analogy

Another important way to predict the evolution of a system is to refer to an analogous situation. Let's say that an intelligence agency is trying to

---

Guide to Disruptive Innovation: Why Great Companies Fail in the Face of Disruption and How to Make Sure Your Company Doesn't (Diateino, 2018).

anticipate a terrorist attack in the late 1990s. The idea seems to be to use suicide planes against buildings. This would be an unprecedented event. Understandably, it would be foolish for the agency to contact insurers and ask for their statistical tables on suicide aircraft in order to calculate the probability of such an event occurring. So how can they proceed? One way is to identify similar situations.

-- During World War II, Japan used the technique of dropping planes on military targets to cause widespread destruction (the famous *kamikaze*).

-- In 1945, a B-25 bomber crashed into the Empire State Building in New York on a foggy day, killing fourteen people.

-- In 1993, several bombs exploded in the basement of the World Trade Center, indicating that the building was a prime target for terrorists.

-- In 1994, an Air France airliner was hijacked by Algerian terrorists. They were neutralized by police at the Marseille airport during a stopover, but it was later discovered that they had intended to crash the plane into the Eiffel Tower.

-- In Tom Clancy's novel *Debt of Honor*, published the same year, a Japanese pilot crashes his plane into the Capitol during a meeting, killing most of the U.S. government.

-- In January 1995, Philippine police uncovered the Bojinka terrorist plot, which consisted of hijacking eleven planes and ramming one of them into the CIA headquarters.

What can we learn from this? 1) The use of suicide planes was not new. 2) This use was known and operationally integrated by some terrorists. 3) Terrorists were actively interested in major symbolic targets in the US. The idea of hijacking a civilian aircraft and flying it into a symbolic American target was therefore entirely plausible. It should be noted at this point that no more can be said. Adding or subtracting an analogous event would in no way change the "probability" of such an event occurring. What we do know is that it was within the realm of possibility (intellectually, technically, and operationally), and that it was being considered by terrorists. This is what Shackle calls an "epistemic possibility," a non-impossibility from which we can begin to work.

For any analogous event, it's important to note the differences with the event under consideration, to avoid bad analogies leading to false anticipations, such as the one that led to Covid-19 being said to be less serious than the flu. For example, during the invasion of Iraq in 2003, the U.S. government predicted that once the Iraqi army was defeated and

Saddam Hussein's power was removed, the Iraqi people would quickly build a strong democracy that would give the United States a solid ally in that part of the world. The historical model for this was Germany in 1945. Nothing worked out as planned because there are significant differences between Germany and Iraq, including geographic, cultural, demographic, religious, and historical.

MANAGEMENT TOOLS IN THE FACE OF UNCERTAINTY

As we said at the beginning of this book, while our world is mainly characterized by uncertainty and nonlinearity, the management tools we use are mostly designed for a world of risk, under the assumption of continuous evolution.

NPV (Net Present Value), a widely used investment tool, is a case in point. NPV is used to assess the advisability of investing in a project. Essentially, and in simplified terms, it consists of comparing the expected flow of expenses with the expected flow of income over a given period (say, five years). If the latter is greater than the former, the project is worth investing in. It is important to note that these are discounted cash flows because they consider the presence of time. Time means that a dollar received today is worth more than a dollar received a year from now. The model's assumptions are numerous and very important for understanding its limitations. First, as we have seen, it assumes a known and, above all, constant rate of inflation, which is not always the case in some countries, and sometimes unexpectedly so. However, the result of the calculation is very sensitive to a small variation in the discount rate. In a world that changes little, or whose change is linear, this is acceptable. In a non-linear world, it's reckless.

Second, for the formula to work, we need to calculate what's called a "terminal" value, i.e., we assume that after the last year (the 5th in our example), the flows will continue at a growth rate we define to infinity. Here's the problem: in our world, nothing is infinite, and the choice of the growth rate, which has a huge impact on the result, is completely arbitrary.

Third, the tool bases the decision on a comparison between expected income and expenses. As we saw with Richard Cantillon, while expenditures are relatively easy to predict, at least in the short run, the same cannot be said for revenues. In a context of uncertainty, it's almost impossible to correctly estimate the revenue of a new product. The calculation very quickly becomes a guessing game, where you can put just about anything into the revenue figure, with a forecasting approach based on foundations that are, to say the least, fragile.

Finally, the model is based on the very important, but implicit, assumption that "the rest" of the company's business will continue unchanged. An investment decision is always a choice between two options: to invest or not to invest. In this case, not to invest is only conceivable if the current business continues, as the proposed investment is merely an optional extra. In times of disruption, however, the current business may well collapse! NPV is completely inappropriate for reasoning in times of discontinuity and uncertainty.

PREDICTION: A TRULY LOST CAUSE?

Advantage to Foxes?

The principle that the more you know about a subject, the better your decision will be is widely accepted. However, researcher Philip Tetlock has conducted some intriguing experiments that show, on the contrary, that experts tend to be more wrong than non-experts when it comes to prediction.[55] In particular, he conducted a major research project in which he asked a group of experts to make predictions on various indicators (GDP, inflation, etc.) over several years. All in all, a massive project with 150,000 predictions made by 743 experts on 199 world events. At the same time, he asked a group of chimpanzees to throw arrows at the possible answers. The result? The chimps outperformed the experts! Even relatively simple algorithms performed better.

Why do experts make more mistakes than non-experts when faced with discontinuity? First, because their expertise is a store of knowledge, and knowledge can only refer to the past, to what has worked before. Gaston Berger observes: "The technician is often the man of the past, and a proven method is often a method that is outdated or about to become outdated."[56] By definition, a discontinuity calls into question what has been working, and thus de facto the expert's knowledge. Discontinuity is precisely the moment when experts' knowledge is no longer valid. They are the last person who should be consulted!

Second, because discontinuity, by definition, occurs outside the framework of expertise. The expert therefore doesn't see it, at least

---

[55] Philip E. Tetlock, *Expert Political Judgment: How Good Is It? How Can We Know?* (Princeton University Press, 2006)

[56] Berger, Massé and Bourbon-Busset, *De la prospective*, op. cit.

initially, and when he does, he may tend not to take it seriously. In 1876, for example, a telegraph expert would have viewed the incipient development of the telephone, which was initially of very poor quality and did not allow communication beyond a few hundred meters, with a healthy dose of skepticism. We mentioned above the reaction of the president of Western Union, the American telegraph leader, who called the telegraph a useless electrical toy. And indeed, it was true at the time: the telephone was no match for the telegraph, a technological marvel that provided secure, near-instantaneous communication with the rest of the world. The error of foresight lay not only in the inability (or refusal) to imagine that this new technology would evolve and compensate for its initial weaknesses (simplification, improved quality, increased communication range), but above all in the failure to appreciate the importance of voice, which distinguished the telephone from the telegraph, and what it would change in communication. At that time, the telegraph was used by governments and large corporations for administrative exchanges (sending instructions and reports). It was a culture of administrative and business writing that made it possible to leave traces. Compared to this, the telephone seemed to the expert to be useless, but above all dangerous: no trace remained of the words exchanged. Compared to the applications of the time, it was of no interest, which explains the expert's reaction. The success of the telephone came from the development of new uses, such as chat, exchange of practical information, etc., with new users, not from the conversion of telegraph users to the telephone.

Third, experts make more mistakes because they are competent in a necessarily narrow field. This is the condition of his competence. The more expert, the narrower the field, and the more exposed to discontinuity, which comes from outside the field. Understanding discontinuity, on the other hand, requires not only openness, i.e., thinking beyond the current framework, but also a more general competence that enables the linking of a priori separate domains.

To illustrate this, Philip Tetlock contrasts hedgehogs and foxes, using a distinction made by the writer Isaiah Berlin. A hedgehog knows only one big thing, while a fox knows many little things. According to Tetlock, intellectually aggressive hedgehogs know one big thing and, under the banner of parsimony, try to extend the explanatory power of that big thing and "cover up" new cases; they are more often wrong. Foxes, on the other hand, are more eclectic. They know a lot of little things and improvise ad hoc solutions to keep up with a rapidly changing world. As a result, Tetlock believes they are more successful at making predictions. His research is therefore an incentive to develop horizontal generalist knowledge, which is better able to connect unexpected domains, rather than vertical expertise, which is quickly locked in and forced into domains where it is irrelevant. A fourth reason why experts make mistakes when faced with discontinuity is that they are more confident than non-experts. They will find it harder to imagine a profound change in their environment, the one they have known for a long time and, above all, the one on which they have built their expertise, and thus their legitimacy and identity. After all, experts have much to lose from a discontinuity that renders their knowledge obsolete, since it is the basis of their power. In other words, turkeys rarely vote for Christmas.[57]

Predicting Successfully Anyway?

Despite his somewhat depressing results on experts, Tetlock persists in believing that one can improve one's ability to predict. One unexpected result of his research on experts has been to highlight a category he calls *superforecasters*, who seem to stand out from normal experts by achieving very good results in their forecasts. According to him, they have the following characteristics: they are intelligent (but no more so than average) and always develop a knowledge of the field under study. They practice forecasting regularly to learn from their mistakes. They work as part of a team. They are more open-minded (foxes) and have a good grasp of probabilities, enabling them to avoid the usual biases.[58] They work slowly and don't hesitate to revise past forecasts.[59]

Tetlock's work may therefore give us hope that we can improve our forecasting performance. In this vision, forecasting is a subject like any other: with the right tools and good practice, everyone can improve. Behind this is always the assumption that the better you know the field,

---

[57] This is not so much about the expertise itself as it is about the attitude of the expert. Very often the expert is overconfident and has a poor sense of the limits of his expertise. Expertise is more essential than ever in a complex world, but it must be thought through dynamically and implemented with epistemic humility. To quote Isaac Asimov, if knowledge is sometimes a problem, we cannot solve it by ignorance.

[58] Philip Tetlock and Dan Gardner, *Superforecasting: The Art and Science of Prediction* (Random House Books, 2016).

[59] Walter Frick, "What Research Tells Us About Making Accurate Predictions", Harvard Business Review, February 2, 2015.

the more likely you are to make a good forecast. Thomas Fingar makes this point in field of intelligence.[60] As head of the CIA's clandestine service in the early 2000s, he was tasked with reforming the agency's operations in the wake of the Iraq WMD fiasco. The CIA's prediction that Iraq had an arsenal of weapons of mass destruction was one of the key arguments for the U.S. invasion in 2003. After the invasion, this prediction proved false, and no weapons were ever found, despite intensive searches. Fingar's approach was to improve analysis processes: to summarize his approach, if we do a better job and use our information better, we'll be less wrong.

But it's not at all clear that more information leads to better predictions. In fact, Taleb argues the opposite. He cites the example of a legendary Wall Street broker from the 1980s. He specialized in the Swiss franc, of which he was a recognized expert. He correctly predicted the dollar's sharp decline against the Swiss currency in the 1980s. However, Taleb recounts that a brief conversation with him revealed that he was unable to locate Switzerland correctly on a map. He had never been there and knew absolutely nothing about the country. One might have thought that his expertise was based on a detailed knowledge of each canton and an ability to anticipate, for example, the impact of a vote on this or that issue on the exchange rate of the Swiss franc, but this was not the case.[61] There is therefore no cause-and-effect relationship between the accumulation of technical knowledge about a subject and the ability to predict correctly. This may come as a surprise, but if we simply acknowledge that prediction is impossible, it's easy to see that knowledge makes no difference. Indeed, Tetlock's great limitation is his unspoken assumption of environmental continuity. None of the superforecasters, however talented, succeeds in the face of discontinuity. Where were they during the 2016 American election? Where were they Before 9/11? Before the 2008 crisis? Before the brutal appreciation of the Swiss franc in 2015? Before the Arab Spring? Before Covid-19? Before the invasion of Ukraine? Nowhere. If the environment does not change fundamentally, they can indeed improve their forecasts. A hair's breadth here, a hair's breadth there. But in the face of discontinuity, they fail like everyone else, because like everyone else, they are faced with a challenge to the rules of thumb that have governed the past.

---

[60] Thomas Fingar, *Reducing Uncertainty - Intelligence Analysis and National Security* (Stanford University Press, 2011).
[61] Nassim Nicholas Taleb, *Antifragile: Things That Gain from Disorder* (Random House Publishing Group, 2014).

Finally, the belief in the existence of superforecasters is even counterproductive, because it creates the illusion that we can escape black swans. This is not the case, though it's a hard truth to admit - we want so much to believe that our intelligence, the massive amounts of data at our disposal, and our conceptual and technological arsenal will finally enable us to counter the nature of our environment. Perpetuating this belief may be in the interest of those who have something to sell, but they're not the ones who pay the price when the accident happens. Again, with all due respect to Tetlock, a complex world is subject to the unpredictable, and the unpredictable… is not predictable, no matter how hard you try. Tetlock-style prediction works well between catastrophes. Don't be the superforecaster's turkey.

Nate Silver, Superforecaster Extraordinaire?

Nate Silver is a good example of a professional superforecaster. Silver is an American statistician who specializes in sports and elections. He is best known for predicting the results of the 2008 presidential and senatorial elections with great accuracy. He immediately achieved guru status. He is an apostle of the use of megadata (big data). He has written a fascinating, rich, yet easy-to-read book about his forecasting work: The Signal and the Noise. In it, he examines several examples from the world of sports, politics, and business, and explains his approach. Despite his guru status, the author is relatively modest about his work. He admits that as a statistician, especially after the 2008 crisis, he knows far less about the world than he thought. He acknowledges that many predictions have failed and tries to understand why. In doing so, he joins Tetlock in remaining firmly within a forecasting paradigm that he seeks to improve. In essence, he says: "We've screwed up a lot of predictions, I'm sorry, but we're going to improve our technique, so hang in there". Or, to paraphrase Orwell's Animal Farm, "We will work harder". The faith in technique remains strongest, the hammer continues to fall relentlessly on the screw. Finally, after 420 gripping pages, it's the cry of the heart. After being invited to a conference on terrorism in 2008, he writes: "Frankly, the methods I presented at the conference were probably not very useful for national security analysis. Baseball and politics are data-rich fields that provide satisfying answers. Thousands of baseball games are played each year. Elections occur less frequently - and require a little more caution to predict - but hundreds of polls are released during each presidential campaign. All of this data is publicly available, for free or for a small fee. Terrorism, it seems, is nothing like that."[62]

This quote is interesting for two reasons. First, he recognizes that outside of a relatively linear and open field, his technique no longer applies. Once there's uncertainty, he doesn't have much to offer, so his approach only works when there's no possibility of a black swan event. That's fine for baseball games, but when it comes to terrorism or the economy, don't bother. Silver's admission, to his credit, is of course essential to the purpose of our book: a famous statistician admits that prediction is impossible in situations of uncertainty. Whole areas of human activity - in this case, those that matter most to us - suddenly disappear from his field of expertise. Sic transit! On the other hand, he writes without hesitation that, for him, politics falls within the realm of predictable phenomena. This is astonishing. It was already so in 2008, but when you consider what happened in 2016, when he completely missed the Trump phenomenon with his fine technique, it's really appalling. This is exactly the case of an expert who is unable to define correctly the scope of his expertise. It's not enough to recognize that prediction doesn't work under uncertainty; we also need to recognize that uncertainty applies to a much broader field of human action than we'd like to believe, and that politics is very much a part of that field. Mastering the ontology of one's field and the epistemology of one's profession is essential to avoiding catastrophe.

Is Forecasting a More Attainable Goal?

An interesting approach is to introduce a distinction between "to predict" and "to foresee" or "forecast". Whereas to predict means "to announce in advance what is certain to happen", to foresee means "to think, on the basis of certain data, that a future event is highly probable". To foresee is to imagine something in one's mind and make provisions for its eventuality. Prediction assumes a deterministic world, whereas forecasting can exist in a changing world because its very purpose is to trigger action.

In an article about forecasting[63], Futurist Paul Saffo returns to this distinction. Forecasting examines how hidden currents in the present can signal changes in direction for companies, societies, or the world. Thus,

---

[62] Silver, *The Signal and the Noise*, op. cit., p. 420.

[63] Paul Saffo, "Six rules for effective forecasting", Harvard Business Review, July 2007, pp. 1-11.

the primary goal of forecasting is to identify the full range of possibilities, not a limited set of illusory certainties. Unlike a prediction, a forecast must be based on logic, which distinguishes it from prophecy and the divinatory arts. But, according to Saffo, forecasting must also simplify decision making. He proposes the notion of the "cone of uncertainty", which delimits the possibilities that can arise from a given moment or event. The forecaster's job is to define the cone to help the decision maker. A cone defined too broadly will be of little use, but will leave room for opportunity. A cone defined too narrowly is blind and allows for surprises. This is an interesting notion because it underscores the fact that uncertainty is never universal; there are always areas of decision making that are less uncertain than others. According to Saffo, the art of defining the cone lies in carefully distinguishing between the highly unlikely and the completely impossible. Outliers (which he calls wildcards) define the cone's boundary. A good bound consists of elements on the edge of plausibility. These are outcomes that could happen, but that we find difficult to imagine.

Like Tetlock, Saffo believes that you can improve your ability to predict with a few principles and good practices. According to him, if you must predict, predict often - and be the first to be proven wrong. The way to do this is to make a prediction as quickly as possible and then discredit it with new data. The approach he advocates is to formulate a series of predictions that turn out to be wrong as quickly as possible, thus refining the cone to the point where you can base an answer on the prediction contained within its boundaries, and have strong opinions to draw conclusions quickly, while readily accepting to abandon them when you encounter contradictory evidence. Sure, but in practice, how do you define the right cone width? How do you know for sure that an area is not uncertain? You don't. In fact, Saffo's thinking is linear. Like others before him, his method collapses in the face of an unprecedented event: indeed, he himself acknowledges this almost from the start with his wildcards at the edge of the cone, i.e., unprecedented events. Like so many others before him, Saffo's approach is to treat these events as aberrations exogenous to the system. The very use of the term wildcard is telling. It preserves the purity of the model, but certainly not the durability of its user!

Quantification: The Quest for the Holy Grail

With the Internet, search engines, artificial intelligence, and big data, the problem of gathering information seems finally solved. We'll have all the information we need, and all we'll have to do is process it. That's what Chris Anderson, editor-in-chief of the avant-garde tech magazine Wired, argued in 2008. In his view, the sheer volume of data is rendering theory and even the scientific method useless.[64]

This belief in the omnipotence of data is not new. As early as 1986, Admiral Turner, director of the CIA at the time of the Iran fiasco, marveled at the progress of technology, particularly satellites: "We should soon be able to track most activity on the earth's surface, day and night, in good weather or bad."[65] Building on the incredible developments in new technologies, in the 2000s the United States developed the concept of TIA, for *Total Information Awareness*. The goal of TIA was to collect detailed information about individuals on a massive scale to anticipate and prevent crimes before they were even committed. The term has fallen into disuse, but this is now the approach of the NSA (National Security Agency), which is putting its enormous technical and human resources into the program, developing preventive surveillance of all communications in whatever form.

This belief in the almighty power of numbers obtained through technology to understand the present and predict the future is a manifestation of the scientism that permeates our society. This translates into a desire to apply the principles and methods of science to intellectual and moral life. It is a misleading extension of the ideas and methods of science to social issues. Most regrettably, the science that is singled out in this way is that of Newton, which modern science itself has long since abandoned. Scientism is a legacy of 1950s positivism, the belief that human systems are amenable to Newtonian solutions, and that complex geopolitical situations and social movements can be understood by counting physical devices or analyzing Internet flows.

At a time when surprises are multiplying, whether in the political, economic, financial, social, scientific, or religious spheres, such a belief

[64] Chris Anderson, "The End of Theory: The Data Deluge Makes the Scientific Method Obsolete", Wired, 2008.

[65] Milo Jones and Philippe Silberzahn, *Constructing Cassandra: Reframing Intelligence Failure at the CIA, 1947-2001* (Stanford University Press, 2013).

is problematic. To think that what allows us to understand and anticipate the evolution of a country like Yemen or Chad is to be found in a search engine is incredibly naive: it would already be wrong in a technologically advanced country like the United States (which, let's not forget, was incapable of anticipating Trump's victory two days before), but it makes no sense in countries where the Internet barely exists. What's in the head of a Peshawar street vendor sensitive to Taliban rhetoric is unlikely to be found thanks to Google. Shackle was writing about economics, but his point can be extended to all social sciences: "By tacitly assuming that the right approach can always be discovered through ordered thought, and that this is how human practice is formed, economics has forbidden itself to understand the vast domain of human action where disorder is the essence of the situation."[66] How could Turner's "all activities" be translated into computerized data? How could this tool be used to understand the thoughts of a Korean teenager? A Black Lives Matter activist? A Russian hacker? Predict the hostility of Sunnis when their enthusiastic support was expected during the 2003 invasion of Iraq? How can we think that being able to track these activities will give us enough clues to anticipate an attack? And what about the secrets? Could tracking "most of the activities" of the Russians have helped the U.S. anticipate the collapse of the Soviet system? Far from it! Especially since they ignored the wealth of information they already had. To "track the activities" of targets without their knowledge is certainly a fine technical feat, but to understand the enemy or a competitor is quite another matter.

As historian John Gaddis points out, one of the basic techniques of science, calculation, has taken precedence over one of its goals, which is to anticipate what will happen. As early as 1932, the ever-modern Charles de Gaulle wrote: "To believe that one possesses a means of avoiding the surprises of circumstances is only to give the mind the illusion of being able to neglect the mystery of the unknown."[67] A century later, nothing has changed. Writing today, military historian Martin Van Creveld offers a grim diagnosis: "For all their high-tech arsenal, today's armed forces seem no more capable of handling information than they were a century or a millennium ago. Although modern means undoubtedly allow more information to be gathered and analyzed faster than ever before, regardless of distance, movement, or weather conditions, the ability to approach certainty has not improved

---

[66] Shackle, *Epistemics and Economics*, p. 23.

[67] Charles de Gaulle, *Le Fil de l'épée*, (Perrin, 2015), p. 195.

one iota."[68] We can extend this observation without reservation to companies that succumb to the pleasures of scientism and spend fortunes on smart, "digital", "big data", artificial intelligence, or other information systems without improving their ability to understand their environment, and whose managers haven't seen a real customer in ages. This is because, as researcher Haridimos Tsoukas observes, "the human domain is fundamentally the domain of doxa (opinion), not episteme (science)."[69] Again, we see the importance of hypotheses (mental models), and naive rationality quickly reaches its limits. The workings of complex human systems cannot be reduced to a series of numbers and causal relationships.

As the historian François Hartog nicely puts it, counting bubbles is not the way to understand the movement of the sea. The ideas developed for a particular rigorous science cannot be applied to moral, ethical, and political problems, because science cannot answer questions of meaning or value. That is simply not its purpose. And imitating its methods, as many subjects such as economics try to do, will not solve the problem. As Aristotle already pointed out, a scientistic approach leads to moral monstrosity, because "the law is always something general, and there are cases in which it is not possible to formulate a general statement that applies to them with rectitude." Principles are formulated with a paradigmatic situation in mind, but life presents complexities and contingencies never imagined. In these situations, moral judgment is required, and judgment isn't a matter of rules. Rather, it is acquired through sensitive observation of numerous cases and constant reflection on one's mistakes. Not only does the accumulation of numbers fail to understand human problems, but it also fails to anticipate behavior. Let's take a closer look at some of the limitations of the quantitative approach to human systems.

What's Important Isn't Necessarily Quantifiable

In 1969, a CIA officer conducted a simple but highly instructive experiment: she went to live in Moscow for a week as a normal Moscow resident. She quickly realized that the simplest of daily activities - shopping - was very time-consuming and complicated. One day, for example, it took her more than six hours to buy cabbage, a basic ingredient in everyday Russian cooking. The lesson she learned from

---

[68] Martin Van Creveld, Technology and War: From 2000 B.C. to the Present, Touchstone, 1991, p. 266.

[69] Tsoukas, *Complex Knowledge*, op. cit. p. 219.

this experience is that by estimating Soviet GDP (a jealously guarded secret that the CIA tried its best to estimate) based on production alone, the West was making a big mistake by not taking into account the very low productivity of the system. If it took ten minutes to buy one kilogram of cabbage in the U.S., but six hours in the USSR, then one couldn't compare the GDPs of each country simply by establishing a purchasing power parity. Soviet GDP was significantly overestimated because the calculation did not consider unquantifiable dimensions.[70] We now know that much of the wheat harvest, which would have been enough to feed the USSR, rotted on the ground, and that another significant portion was lost in transit due to logistics failures from producer to consumer. The mismanagement was systemic and completely unimaginable to an American analyst living in an efficient society. Highlighting this mismanagement, given its magnitude, might even have seemed suspicious, since it could have been interpreted as a deviation from the imperative of objectivity (we are not here to criticize the Soviet system, but to measure its GDP scientifically). By ignoring what could not be quantified, i.e. by decontextualizing the phenomenon under study, Western analysts produced erroneous results that, until the end, gave an impression of the solidity of the system that did not correspond to reality. We can generalize this typical example to all modern management and analysis systems, which are based entirely on the measurement of quantifiable elements, which leads them to miss the point.

An opposite approach is that of the financier George Soros.[71] His team, though made up of top-notch financiers, is known for its limited taste for quantitative models and for considering human factors derived directly from contact with the field. In 1991, fearing a devaluation of the markka, the Finnish currency, following the collapse of the USSR, its main trading partner, Soros's currency expert decided to spend a few days in a Helsinki hotel to get a feel for the atmosphere. There he spent several boozy evenings with the cream of Finnish business and finance, as well as with industrialists and trade unionists. "These people were preparing for devaluation", he recalls, "and I could hear it in their voices". He came back convinced that a devaluation was imminent, which could not be deduced from any figures or models, liquidated his positions and even

---

[70] This overestimation was confirmed after the fall of the USSR. See: Jones and Silberzahn, *Constructing Cassandra*.

[71] Source: Christian Madsbjerg, *Sensemaking: The Power of the Humanities in the Age of the Algorithm*, (Hachette Books, 2017), p. 63.

turned them into positions against the markka. A few days later, the markka devalued by 18%. The point here is not to say that Soros has found an infallible method for anticipating currency trends - and alcohol abuse remains dangerous - but to show that the important things to consider are rarely deduced from models and are more easily found on the ground. None of this could be modeled or quantified, none of it could be found in the impressive models developed by the other financial institutions located a few blocks from Soros's offices, which lost billions in the process. It's easier to fiddle with a spreadsheet in a comfortable office in the City of London than to spend a week at the end of the world drinking with strangers.

What's Quantifiable Isn't Necessarily Important

A drunk is looking for his car keys under a lamppost. A passerby offers to help. After a few unsuccessful moments, the passerby asks, "Did you really lose them under the lamppost?" The drunk replies, "No, but at least there's light". It's a hackneyed joke, but it illustrates the reality of many quantitative analyses that have more to do with our drunkard's approach than with a genuine approach to understanding complex problems.[72] We accumulate data because it's easy, or at least we accumulate data that's easy to collect, and because it allows us to indulge in a technological debauchery with results that are always impressive to civilians: "Look how good I am with my high-resolution satellite, I know where Boris buys his potatoes and what cigarettes he smokes!" This led an exasperated former staff director of the House Intelligence Committee to tell a CIA Deputy Director bluntly: "We don't give you brownie points for collecting intelligence by the hardest means available."[73]

During the Vietnam War, the Pentagon regularly published figures on the number of Viet Minh soldiers killed. This was known as the body count. The very high number of enemy deaths was used as an indicator of the success of the American strategy, whose losses in men were much lower. The assumption was that these very high casualties would lead to a progressive weakening of the enemy troops, an undermining of their morale, and thus to their defeat. Promotions within the ranks of the American Army were mainly based on this count, which led to

---

[72] Indeed, the saying is that the drunkard approaches the lamppost more for support than illumination. Any resemblance to data scientists is purely coincidental.

[73] Milo Jones and Philippe Silberzahn, *Constructing Cassandra.*

competition between units and massive falsification of the numbers, as we know today. We also know that civilians were included. But perhaps worst of all, these figures failed to capture the real meaning of what they purported to quantify. Yet Ho Chi Minh, the North Vietnamese leader, had understood as early as 1946 that this logic would not lead to victory, presciently declaring to the French: "You can kill ten of our men for every one of yours we kill, but even with this ratio you will lose, and we will win". Indeed, this was a war of national liberation coupled with a war of ideology, and the fundamental asymmetry of motivation between the two sides somehow redressed the balance. Napoleon had captured this essential element well: "Three-fourths of war is moral."[74] In other words, what makes the difference - the morale of the troops - is completely unquantifiable. One Vietnamese soldier indoctrinated and mobilized for his country's independence could therefore be the equivalent of ten American soldiers who didn't know why they were there and just wanted to go home. The United States had blinded itself to the underlying problem with a mountain of numbers.[75] The current vogue for big data is developmental blindness squared. As economist Simon Johnson and MIT artificial intelligence specialist Jonathan Ruane point out, today's algorithms are very good at pattern recognition when fed very large amounts of data - such as identifying an object in a YouTube video or detecting credit card fraud - but they're much less good at situations that don't fit the usual patterns, or simply when the data is insufficient or of poor quality.[76] Once again, our systems are designed for continuity and, above all, regularity, but not for the unprecedented; for stable causalities, not for social systems. Writing in the context of revolutions, Zachary Shore points out that quantitative analysis cannot help, because such episodes are not iterative (they don't repeat identically), and so no data set is available to build a model to reveal their timing, scale, or nature.[77] Welcome to a world of novelty!

---

[74] Letter from Napoleon I to Joseph Napoleon, Saint-Cloud, August 21, 1808.
[75] Kenneth Cukier and Viktor Mayer-Schönberger, "The Dictatorship of Data", MIT Technology Review, May 31, 2013. Halberstam, in *The Best and the Brightest*, also describes very well the blindness created by numbers in the case of the Vietnam War.
[76] Simon Johnson and Jonathan Ruane, "Jobs in the Age of Artificial Intelligence", Project Syndicate, May 30, 2017.
[77] Zachary Shore, *A Sense of the Enemy: The High Stakes History of Reading Your Enemy's Mind*, Oxford University Press, 2014, p. 180.

Quantification Can be Misleading

One way for the CIA to assess the strength of the Soviet regime was to measure its military arsenal and count its missiles. The assumption was that the number of missiles was a good indicator of Soviet wealth, since the more resources a country had, the more missiles it could finance. However, counting Russian missiles to assess the strength of the Soviet system assumes that, as in Western countries, the military comes last in the budgetary process. Thus, the number of missiles does indeed reflect economic health. In the USSR, however, the opposite was true: the military came first. The USSR was, in fact, a war economy, an essential fact that has completely escaped Western analysts. The more missiles the Soviets had, the poorer they became. An American senator, more lucid than the CIA analysts, once declared: "The USSR is an Upper Volta with missiles."[78] It was a very accurate characterization of the USSR, albeit derogatory to the Upper Volta. The missile count, based on a false mental model, thus contributed to a totally erroneous assessment of the health of the Soviet system. As we can see, even a purely quantitative approach to a problem is not necessarily objective: you can't eliminate the subjective dimension, you can't separate the "facts" from the identity of the person who selects and analyzes them.

When Quantification is Misleading: The Yom Kippur War

The Yom Kippur War of October 1973, when Israel was attacked by several Arab countries, is a good example of how numbers can be misleading. On paper, Israel didn't stand a chance. The Egyptians deployed 650,000 troops. Syria, Iraq, and other Arab countries added about 250,000. Faced with these 900,000 combat-ready men, Israel had only 375,000 soldiers, including 240,000 reservists. But the war was really a war of tanks, and Israel's chances looked even slimmer: 2,100 tanks against the coalition's 4,500. And yet, despite a total surprise and a very difficult first few days, Israel ended up winning the war. One reason was that the Egyptians were unable to maintain their tanks properly because they had not invested in training crews to repair them. When a tank broke down or was hit, repair crews had to be called in, which is dangerous in a combat situation. Israeli crews, on the other hand, were trained to cope and to continue fighting by any means necessary. In the end, the right parameter to look at to predict the outcome was not the raw number of tanks, but the average life of a tank.

---

[78] Milo Jones and Philippe Silberzahn, *Constructing Cassandra.*

With this new variable, the balance was almost restored, at least on paper.[79]

Quantitative obsession sometimes takes on grotesque proportions. In the summer of 2003, the NSA drew up a list of 160 possible targets (sites and events) for terrorist attacks. By the end of 2003, this list had grown to 1,849 targets. By 2005, it had grown to 77,769 sites. By 2015, the figure had risen to over 300,000 targets, including world-class events such as the Indiana Pork and Apple Festival and the annual Mule Day Parade in Columbia, Tennessee.[80] But as statistician Nate Silver notes, numbers have no ability to speak for themselves, and their passive accumulation serves no purpose.[81] We do it because it's easy, not because it's useful, and because doing what would be useful would be much more complicated and less rewarding.

Beyond the excesses that technology allows, we can't help but think that this ridiculous obsession with data accumulation is actually a formidable distraction that not only does nothing to prevent the next terrorist attack but may actually make it easier. Indeed, the danger of this accumulation is to multiply what statisticians call false positives, or false alarms. This is what happened in the June 2017 London attack. The terrorists were all known to the police, but they were not arrested before they acted. The reason? Britain's security services were drowning in the immense amount of data, police reports, public denunciations, and intelligence leads. They maintain a database of some 25,000 "persons of interest", making it impossible to monitor them all effectively - assuming, of course, that the next terrorists are on that list, which experience suggests is unlikely. What's more, the study of modus operandi shows that the personalities, trajectories, behaviors, and personal histories of terrorists do not form a stable pattern but, on the contrary, a broad spectrum, which makes quantitative analysis impossible. As we have emphasized, the condition for the relevance of a quantitative approach is the stability of the phenomenon under study over time, which is clearly not the case here. In fact, it's in the terrorists' interest that this is not the case - it's

[79] Shore, *A Sense of the Enemy*, p. 172.

[80] Milo Jones and Philippe Silberzahn, "Snowden and the challenge of intelligence: the practical case against the NSA's big data", Forbes, July 11, 2013.

[81] Silver, *The Signal and the Noise: Why So Many Predictions Fail - but Some Don't* (Penguin Press, 2012).

the condition for their success. So why build such a useless arsenal? In practice, too much data blinds us, as Tsoukas concludes: "The more information we have about the world, the more we tend to distance ourselves from what's going on in the world, and the less able we are to understand its complexity."[82]

Today's Data can't Predict Tomorrow

At the end of the eighteenth century, New York, like all the world's great cities, stank. One hundred and fifty thousand horses carried people and goods through the streets of Manhattan, producing 45,000 tons (!) of manure per month, which, in addition to the odor, posed obvious sanitary and logistical problems for disposal. In 1898, planners from around the world met to discuss solutions to this crisis. The meeting was a failure, with participants unable to imagine transportation without horses. Less than fifteen years later, cars outnumbered horses in New York, and the dystopian visions of manure were forgotten.[83] If city planners had access to big data, machine learning, and modern management, these tools would not have helped them at all. They would have simply confirmed their existing concerns. It is an illusion to be able to describe and understand a system based on quantitative data. It is even more illusory to think that we can predict its evolution. This limitation is also evident in the case of elections. The American elections are the subject of one of the most massive exercises in data collection, based on polls, measurements, studies, and so on.

However, Donald Trump's victory in 2016 defied virtually all predictions, calling into question the idea that the analysis of large amounts of data can correctly predict events.[84] A few months later, the same thing happened again in France with the presidential elections, which confounded the best predictions several times in a row with completely unexpected events: The defeat of the incumbent François Hollande, unprecedented in the Fifth Republic; the defeat of Nicolas Sarkozy, a former president, in the primaries of his own party, also an unprecedented phenomenon; and the surprise victory of François Fillon, who then succumbed to scandal when everything seemed to assure him

---

[82] Haridimos Tsoukas, *Complex Knowledge: Studies in Organizational Epistemology* (Oxford: Oxford University Press, 2005), p. 23.

[83] Eliot Peper, "Why Business Leaders Need to Read More Science Fiction", Harvard Business Review, July 2017.

[84] Steve Lohr and Natasha Singer, "How Data Failed Us in Calling an Election", The New York Times, November 10, 2016.

of victory in the presidential election; the unexpected emergence of Emmanuel Macron, little known to the public a few months earlier, his first-round victory, and then his election. The prediction error was then repeated in the British election in June 2017. Such errors occur in technologically advanced societies, with massive data of all kinds, where dozens of polling organizations conduct study after study, ad nauseam, and yet always end in forecasting disaster. If such disasters occur in hyper-connected and so-called hyper-informed societies, what can we say about less "advanced" countries?

A Mass of Data Allows You to Show What you Want

The logician Willard Quine showed that there are always logically consistent theories and families of interpretations that can correspond to a given set of facts. In other words, given enough data, anything can be shown! The more data we have, the easier it is to find correlations that allow us to prove whatever we want.[85] Of course, big data is always about correlation, never causation, but this subtlety is often overlooked by the average person. As Nate Silver confirms: "Finding relationships is easy in any data-rich environment; it's what mediocre players do. The key is to determine whether those relationships represent noise or signal."[86] Which is why, in the age of big data, and contrary to what we hear everywhere, our predictions should be even more fragile. In other words, big data, big surprises!

The Limits of the Normal Distribution Hypothesis

In *The Black Swan*, Nassim Taleb develops at length the idea that the main cause of the modeling errors that led to the financial disaster of 2008 was the assumption of a normal distribution of events. The argument may seem technical, but it's fundamental and worth explaining in detail.

Imagine that we draw lots to measure the height of individuals in a given population, say the inhabitants of a small town. The first individual is 1.85 m tall. The average of our sample (reduced for the moment to a single individual) is therefore 1.85 m. We choose a second individual who is 1.65 m. The average becomes 1.75 m. The addition of the second individual has shifted the average by 10 cm. Let's choose a third

---

[85] Dan Brown's *Da Vinci Code* is a great example of how, if you look hard enough, you can find signs everywhere and come up with a great story based on them.

[86] Silver, *The Signal and the Noise*, p. 240.

individual who is 1.70m. The average is now 1.73m. Then we choose a fourth individual who is 1.60m. The average is now 1.70. A fifth individual who is 1.65, and the average is now 1.69m. What we observe is that the effect of each new individual on the average decreases as the number of individuals increases. Even an individual whose height is significantly below the average (1.60 m) only shifts the average by 3 cm. In other words, as the sample size increases, it "converges" towards an average that varies less and less and which should be 1.75 m, the average height of the people in the village. Once the sample has grown to about twenty individuals, even a giant or a dwarf will no longer move this average. The system is inherently stable. Nassim Taleb calls this type of system *mediocristan.*

Most people will be 1.75 m tall. Many will be either a little below (say 1.70m) or a little above (say1.80m). A slightly smaller number will be 1.65 m or 1.85 m. The further you move away from the average, the fewer individuals there will be. Since the maximum measured height of a human being is 2.72 m (which is extremely rare), we know that there will be no one taller than 2.72 m in our sample. The variation between an individual's height and the sample mean is called the standard deviation. A low standard deviation means that most individuals are close to 1.75 m tall. A high standard deviation, on the other hand, means that individuals are very different from the mean.

The distribution is bell-shaped. If this distribution follows a normal distribution, we will find 50% of individuals whose height is below average and 50% whose height is above average. This is called the median. The characteristic of the normal distribution is that the mean and the median correspond to the same values. This reflects the fact that the different values are homogeneously distributed, and the larger the sample, the greater the homogeneity. Again, we have an inherently stable system.

Now let's look at how knowing the distribution can be useful for anticipation. Let's choose a new inhabitant. What is the probability that she will be less than 1.65 m tall? The available statistical tools give us a value of 15.9%. Knowing that our sample has a normal distribution allows us to predict that an individual will be a certain height. There are several types of distributions and knowing that the system under study follows a particular distribution allows us to mobilize the appropriate tools to calculate the probability of occurrence of a particular event. The normal distribution is widespread, and many professions follow it. For example, the income of a doctor or a shopkeeper is generally characterized by a normal distribution, in the sense that there is no reason for it to vary greatly from one year to the next.

But many phenomena that cannot be represented by a normal distribution. Let's return to our previous exercise in the small town, but this time let's look at the wealth of the residents. The first resident we meet has assets of $50,000. This is our initial average. The second resident has assets of $2,000. The average drops sharply by 48% to $26,000. The third resident has assets of $1,000,000. The average is now $350,667, a jump of 1,249%. The fourth has $20,000 in assets and the average drops by 24%. The fifth has assets of $10,000,000, again pushing the average up by 726%. As you can see, this is an inherently unstable system. When an individual is added, the average can change significantly, either positively or negatively. Unlike height, the average wealth of the sample does not converge to a stable mean as the sample size increases but continues to evolve with large variations. If billionaire Bill Gates happens to visit the town that day, his inclusion alone can literally explode the sample and crush all other observations, with the average even changing scale.

Such a system is what Nassim Taleb calls *extremistan*, in the sense that it is subject to the tyranny of single, extreme values. In extremistan, the impact of an extreme has nothing to do with sample size. One observation (one event) can ruin years of previous observations; the system can be out of balance at any moment, regardless of the history of the previous series; it is inherently unstable and can topple over with each new event, as we saw above with the turkey. Taleb notes that the difficulty arises from the fact that most models, especially in finance, are wrongly built on the assumption of a normal distribution of events. However, as we saw in the first chapter, the systems we're interested in evolve in sudden jumps; they're characterized by extremes, they're actually extremist. By applying the wrong model to a given reality, we inevitably expose ourselves to a prediction error. This is what happened in 2008, and so many times before, so many times since, and certainly so many times in the future.

THE DOG THAT DOESN'T BARK OR THE ABSENCE OF A PROBLEM

In 2001, Enron, the darling of Wall Street, declared bankruptcy. The affair revealed that its apparent success was based on fraudulent financial arrangements. The bankruptcy was a huge scandal, all the more so since the company had for years been regarded as a model of the "new economy", indeed of capitalism.[87] Just two months earlier, Goldman Sachs had called it the best of the best. At the ensuing trial, the judge ruled that former CEO Jeffrey Skilling had repeatedly lied to investors, including his own employees, about various aspects of Enron.[88] The case was made: the company had built its success on misconduct that it had cleverly concealed.

Journalist Malcolm Gladwell's analysis of the scandal shows that this is not the case. Enron is obviously a gigantic fraud. But he shows that this fraud was born and flourished in broad daylight, in plain sight, and that Enron never hid anything about its activities. Crooks, certainly; liars, not at all. How do we know? Well, simply by looking at how the affair happened. It didn't happen because a whistleblower came forward with confidential information, but simply because a journalist got a call from a financier suggesting that he take a closer look at Enron's books than the analysts of the day were doing. He thought they were bizarre. The journalist went to work, pulled the accounts off the Internet, put them through the wringer, and unraveled the whole thing. All the data he used was public, easily accessible within minutes. Admittedly, the complexity of the financial arrangements required a great deal of work and, above all, the shuffling of large quantities of documents, but everything was there, nothing was hidden, there were no lies. All that was needed was to analyze the data, but for years no one did, and Enron was able to thrive (so to speak).

Enron's problem was threefold: first, the overabundance of data could discourage suspicious minds; second, there was no reason to question the data or suspect fraud because the company was not only well known but, more importantly, held up as a model of success by all financial experts. For a long time, Enron was a non-problem; third, this universal celebration by all the experts made it difficult for any of them to

---

[87] This author still remembers, while studying management in a business school in London in 1997, a presentation on Enron by his fellow students in a finance course. The presentation was dithyrambic, Enron was presented as a pioneer, a model company, and the presentation ended with a heartfelt cry from one of the presenters: "Gosh, I love these guys." Once again, the experts had been fooled. More importantly, they had intimidated and silenced the non-experts, including this author, with the logic of their arguments.

[88] "The evidence established that the defendant repeatedly lied to investors, including Enron's own employees, about various aspects of Enron's business", quoted by Malcolm Gladwell in *Open secrets: Enron, intelligence, and the perils of too much information*, The New Yorker, January 1, 2007.

question Enron publicly. This undoubtedly explains why the financier behind the story chose to contact a journalist rather than blow the whistle himself.

It is often assumed that the analytical process begins with an identified problem that needs to be solved. For example, the first stage of the analytical process, as defined by Sherman Kent, the founding father of the CIA's Analytical Intelligence School, is "1 - The emergence of a problem that requires the attention of the intelligence team."[89] The problem appears, usually in the form of an order from the decision maker, and the work can begin. But this is not always the case. Very often there is no identified problem, and the first task is to identify it, even before trying to solve it. In other words, "the dog doesn't bark", to paraphrase Arthur Conan Doyle, and you have to decide that a situation is (perhaps) a problem worth analyzing. The American writer David Foster Wallace once said that what is important in life is not so much the ability to think as the ability to choose what to think about. So there is a "dark matter" of problems or issues unknown to us, in which lurk a myriad of potential black swans. That's why it's not a good idea to ask the question of decision in terms of problem solving.

---

[89] Sherman Kent, *Strategic Intelligence for American World Policy* (Princeton University Press, 1949).

Sociology: Collective Decision-Making in Uncertainty

"It's not on the comet, where we draw up our plans, that we take action; our thinking becomes clearer as we perceive the concrete situation, which in turn becomes clearer not only through operative action, but also through co-acting thinking."

Karl Mannheim

In this chapter, we look at the different actors involved in decision making in uncertainty. Who plans? Who will act? Who defines the issues to be addressed within the organization? It's a matter of looking at the interplay of the actors that make up the system in which the decision-making process takes place. This is the sociological dimension, sociology being the study of human social facts. The system referred to is not limited to the organization to which the actor belongs but goes far beyond it. For example, an analyst is part of a department, which is itself part of the management of an organization, which is itself developed within the intelligence community, which is itself part of the government. These entities do not have the same interests or the same vision of a particular issue: an innovative entity may want to launch a product in response to a disruption it anticipates, but this launch is strongly resisted by a business unit that fears that its flagship product will be cannibalized.

THE INDIVIDUAL IN THE WORLD

In the previous chapter, we explored the epistemological dimension of uncertainty by considering the world as exogenous. This was a simplification. When a scientist manipulates chemicals in an experiment, he is not part of the system he is studying. Nor does that system of chemicals have the capacity to observe the scientist and wonder what he or she is going to do. The system is not reflexive, it doesn't watch itself evolve, and it can't learn from one experiment to the next. It is also repetitive: you can do the same experiment a thousand times under the same conditions and get the same result a thousand times. The same cannot be said of social systems, as we saw earlier. Actors and decision-makers no longer face an environment that they observe from the outside; they are part of it and act within it; they are both actor and object. This shift in perspective is by no means obvious to us. The sociologist Michel Crozier once remarked that research on the relationship between the organization and its environment is still trapped in a Cartesian conception of the environment as a set of impersonal factors whose objective characteristics are somehow automatically imposed on organizations. The result is a one-sided conception of environmental influences that - by neglecting or ignoring the possibilities for organizations to play with or even manipulate the demands and constraints of the environment - more or less explicitly favors the adaptation processes of organizations.[90] And yet, as the philosopher Thierry Ménissier observes: "Since the political actor is also a historical agent, no viewpoint outside history is available to him."[91] It is therefore necessary to study the interaction of the actors that make up the system in which the anticipation exercise takes place. What questions are asked and ignored? How does anticipation fit into the organizational process in which it takes place? How does the personality of the actor and the group to which he belongs influence anticipation?

THE NEW AND THE CHALLENGE OF IDENTITY

Assumptions and Identity

We have repeatedly stressed the importance of hypotheses in the exercise of anticipation. Assumptions led the great minds of the 19th century to believe that cities were destined to drown in horse manure. The 2008 crisis showed that financial models assumed a normal distribution of events, which contributed to a massive underestimation of the possibility of defaults on toxic loans. In Fukushima, the protective

---

[90] Michel Crozier and Erhard Friedberg, *Actors and Systems: The Politics of Collective Action* (Univ of Chicago Press, 1980), p. 153.

[91] Thierry Ménissier, *Machiavel ou la politique du centaure* (Hermann, 2010), p. 166.

walls of the nuclear power plant were built to a height of 5.20 m, on the assumption that a tidal wave could not be higher than 5 m. The CIA assessed the economic strength of the Soviet regime based on the number of missiles produced, on the assumption that this number was a good indicator. We make sense of the world based on assumptions that reflect our mental models. Decision makers' mental models of how the world works strongly influence their selection and interpretation of signals.

These models are notoriously difficult to challenge, and for a very good reason: they're useful. They provide us with cognitive shortcuts for making sense of the world. They make us more efficient and productive. Without them, life would be hell, and we'd have to spend our time constructing a representation of the world. The problem is that they are mostly unconscious and taken for granted. We fail to update them when they change, and they end up resisting our way of dealing with them. The question is, where do our mental models come from?

To answer this question, let's take a brief historical detour and consider a famous photograph, that of Osama Bin Laden sitting with two of his associates in front of a cave hidden somewhere in Afghanistan. All three are dressed in grimy military fatigues. In front of them are Kalashnikovs, the poor man's machine gun. It's the late 1990s. Bin Laden had declared war on the United States. He did so in a 1998 letter to William Perry, Bill Clinton's secretary of defense. Interestingly, the letter was written in verse, a poem.

Now imagine William Perry's reaction. He leads the most powerful army in the world, unrivaled since the collapse of the USSR a few years earlier, which has just crushed Iraq in a matter of days. He reads the declaration of war and sees this photo. Does he run for cover? Probably not. A poem declaring war isn't serious. Besides, a bearded, poorly dressed man standing in front of a cave looks more like a caveman than a dangerous enemy. Not surprisingly, the threat is quickly forgotten.

Now let's put ourselves in the shoes of a Peshawar resident who also sees this photo. As a Muslim, he will not fail to remember that the cave has a special significance in Islam: it was in a cave that the Prophet Mohammed took refuge when he fled Mecca in 622 to escape assassination. It was also a cave (Hira) where Muhammad retreated to meditate, and it was there that he received his first revelations from God through the archangel Jabril (Gabriel) during the month of Ramadan. A Muslim also knows that everything important in Islam is written in verses. Hence, Bin Laden's photo is anything but innocent. He is clearly trying to follow in the footsteps of the Prophet in order to legitimize his actions among Muslims. For non-Muslims, however, it works in the opposite direction: he is underestimated and seen as a caveman. By motivating his friends and deceiving his enemies, Bin Laden uses one of the oldest military tactics. But above all, the case reveals that the hypotheses formulated on the basis of the observation of the photo are entirely based on the identity of the observer. The hypotheses by which we make sense of the world around us are therefore a reflection of our identity, both individual and collective, i.e., of our mental models.[92]

Knowledge is not Enough: The Organization Trapped by its Identity

Until the 1970s, the Swiss watch industry dominated the world with approximately 70% of the global watch market. By the end of the 1980s, that share had fallen to 5%. The reason? The invention of quartz, which made it possible to produce precise watches at low cost. The Japanese took advantage of this technology and developed a mass market at the expense of the Swiss. But it was the Swiss who invented it! In his work on innovation mentioned above, researcher Clayton Christensen shows that most organizations that failed in the face of disruption knew all about it. Often, they were at the origin of the disruption. Kodak knew in 1981 that digital would replace film in photography by 1995-2000 but failed to meet the challenge. Not for lack of trying: Kodak was a pioneer in digital photography, investing heavily to develop innovative products and lead the market. But the company's efforts were always hampered by its concern to preserve its film business, which had been a cash cow for so many years. Knowing that the future is digital is one thing, accepting it and making the hard choices is quite another. For Kodak, betting on digital meant writing off an extraordinary history, throwing away what had made up its identity: a century of innovation in film, its factories, its development labs, its R&D centers with their cutting-edge chemists, its dealer network; it meant voluntarily amputating itself. Similarly, quartz made it possible to produce precise watches at low cost, a market that the Swiss watch industry, proud of its tradition of mechanical excellence, looked upon with contempt. Going low-cost would damage the image of the entire industry.

It's not that organizations can't anticipate disruption; they usually do, but they are unable to respond because of a very strong conflict with their identity, which anchors them in their current activity and prevents

---

92 Source: Milo Jones and Philippe Silberzahn, *Constructing Cassandra.*

them from banking on future activity. A decision can therefore never be separated from the person who makes it, and this importance of identity in decision making in uncertain situations is valid at both the individual and the institutional level.

The Need for Forecasting is a Social Construct

We have shown that the capacity for perfect forecasting is consubstantial with the rational actor model that underlies our decision-making tools. Without it, the model breaks down. But the need to forecast is not simply the result of the need to stay within this model. It has much deeper roots. The historian Mircea Eliade reminds us that "archaic humanity defended itself as best it could against everything new and irreversible in history"[93], because novelty is a factor of uncertainty, and uncertainty creates fear. The ancestral fear of the future and its dangers did not disappear with agricultural civilization and the advent of industrial society. Even today, the indeterminacy of the future is almost universally perceived as a major problem by philosophers, politicians, and businessmen alike. Indeed, as sociologist François Dupuy observes: "Whatever the uncertainty of the world, a leader is always asked to have a 'clear strategy', not because it is right, but because it reassures all those who fear the unpredictability of the future."[94] The business leader is thus supposed to be a "reducer" of uncertainty in the eyes of the organization's stakeholders, mainly investors and employees. Our paradigms, such as the French Constitution, which now includes a clause imposing the precautionary principle, are designed to protect what already exists in the face of future risks. The desire to control nature and reduce the element of chance has permeated Western thought for at least two millennia. It is reflected in Descartes' development of his famous method to, as he put it, "make ourselves masters and possessors of nature."[95] Reflecting this belief in the power of knowledge to protect us from the vagaries of nature, Saint-Simon, a philosopher, advocated a form of government controlled by a council of scientists, artists, craftsmen, and entrepreneurs and dominated by the primary sector, which needed to be planned to create wealth and improve living

---

[93] Quoted in: Stephen Jay Gould, *Time's Arrow, Time's Cycle: Myth and Metaphor in the Discovery of Geological Time* (Harvard University Press, 1987), p. 29.

[94] Francois Dupuy, *Are we all lost in management? On Management Thinking Derailers* (Diateino, 2018).

[95] René Descartes, *Discourse on Method* (Hackett Publishing Company, 1999).

standards. In modern times, the scientific and industrial revolution has introduced even more uncertainty and upheaval, while the capitalist system, with its dynamic of creative destruction, is also a generator of uncertainty.

We live in a state of permanent disruption. Uberization, a term coined after the emergence of the company Uber, which attacks the taxi monopoly, affects all industries. Many observers are more sensitive to what is lost than what is created, to what we see than what we don't see[96], are worried about this destabilizing evolution, and are turning to the State, which they see as the only guarantor of protection against the vagaries of the future. Whereas the market is seen as disruptive and short-termist, the State alone can anticipate major issues and taking long-term action. The idea that social phenomena can be understood in the same way as physical phenomena, promoted by Cartesian rationalism, was famously described as scientistic hubris by the economist Friedrich von Hayek, who blamed the École Polytechnique for being one of its most ardent promoters.[97] Pierre Massé, one of the leading figures of State planning in France, wrote: "Everyone seems to agree on this first point - the need for a country like ours to define and practice a voluntary regional policy, instead of leaving the location of activities to the natural mechanisms of the economy."[98] Massé's book on the subject bears a telling title: *The Plan, or anti-chance*. For people like him, it is intolerable to leave the world at the mercy of chance and, by extension, the market. This belief in the need to steer the world's great evolutions, and in the incapacity of the market to do so, unlike the State, which has the knowledge and patience to do so, remains highly topical. We have already mentioned the errors in predicting the inevitable rise of Japan. In 1991, Philippe Delmas, a high-level French civil servant, wrote a book entitled *The Master of Clocks*, in which he used Japan's success to point out what he saw as the limits of free market to defend the role of the State as the only entity capable of long-term management. The State is the master of the clocks and the only one who can set the pace of development.[99] As we can see, the need to predict is not only a consequence of our hope for rationality, nor is it self-evident; it is also

---

96 To use the famous expression of the economist Frédéric Bastiat.

97 Friedrich von Hayek, *The Counter-Revolution of Science* (Liberty Fund, 1952).

98 Pierre Massé, *Le Plan ou l'anti-hasard* (Gallimard, 1965).

99 We didn't hear the same Philippe Delmas criticize the role of the State in Japan's decline, which began just as he was extolling its strength.

the result of very deep ideologies that reflect very strong cultures and identities.

Individual Bias in Prediction

The importance of identity is also reflected in the way decision makers approach forecasting, with the notion of bias. A bias is an error that is unintentionally introduced into reasoning. Like any analytical exercise, forecasting is not free of bias. There is an abundance of literature on the subject[100], and it is beyond the scope of this book to list all these biases. Most of them concern the individual. Let's look at a few that relate to the individual in relation to the institution to which he belongs.

Identity bias

Identity doesn't just play a role in the propensity to predict. It also influences the predictions that are made. Forecasting exercises are often presented as objective work, carried out by experts who have no stake in what they are forecasting, a kind of weather service. Again, the model is positivistic, that of scientists dealing with numbers and facts without any personal involvement. But this is far from the case. Because they are made by humans, all forecasts are subject to identity bias. This is illustrated by the Théry report.

Entitled *The information superhighway*, this report was written in 1994 by Gérard Théry, Alain Bonnafé and Michel Guieysse and addressed to the then French Prime Minister. Reading it more than thirty years later is very instructive. It shows how three of France's most competent technocrats saw the future of the information superhighway and the role the Internet would play in it. The importance of the latter was recognized, but not taken seriously. We read: "Its cooperative mode of operation is not designed to provide commercial services. Its wide openness to all types of users and services reveals its limitations, in particular its inability to provide high quality real-time voice or image services." This was written at the very moment when the Internet revolution was about to explode in the United States, when Marc Andreessen created Netscape, which would introduce the first Internet browser, and when a certain Jeff Bezos created Amazon, today one of the world's largest commerce sites.

---

[100] Daniel Kahneman's *Thinking fast and slow*, packed with examples and easy to read, is an excellent exposition of the main biases by one of the leading experts in the field.

Why do smart people make such mistakes? Charitable souls are quick to point out that in 1994, many of the tools needed to turn the Internet into a truly robust commercial network were still lacking. The network was still in its infancy and accessible only through a very slow connection. It was hard to imagine its evolution. Granted, thousands of entrepreneurs were doing just that at the time. But it's not the lack of foresight that's interesting here. In fact, this is not the first time that experts have completely failed to predict an evolution in their environment, as we discussed at length above. Beyond what I call the epistemic arrogance of those who know and are wrong, we need to dig a little deeper and ask ourselves who Gérard Théry is. He's the inventor of the Minitel, a cheap terminal launched in France in the 1980s. Minitel was great French technocratic success and was in a way the precursor of the Internet. Minitel was a closed version of the information highway. A model in which the telecom operator, a State monopoly at the time, designed the system and fully controlled the technical and commercial aspects of the services offered. The Internet, on the other hand, is the open, somewhat anarchic system that emerged from a military research project and was taken over by academics. The Minitel is Descartes; the Internet is Montaigne. These are two opposing cultural models. In this report, the authors judge the Internet according to what they know and what models their thinking, i.e., Minitel. Thus, the absence of a directory on the Internet, which is due to its open and decentralized nature, seems to them to be redhibitory. As an open network, the Internet doesn't seem as credible or secure as Minitel, and so on. This is a very classic phenomenon in strategy: the vision we develop of our environment is shaped by our social and professional identity. Minitel was the failed forerunner of the Internet. It came before, it was a pioneer, but in 1994 it was clearly no match for the newcomer. For Théry and his colleagues, such a situation must be unbearable. How could a network with so many flaws, built by hippies, replace our technological jewel? So it's not surprising that the report is skeptical about the Internet's prospects. Identity bias turns the author, perhaps unwittingly, into a defender of his cause. Théry's case is not unique. The economist Tim Harford cites an experiment carried out at the Experimental Science Center of the University of Oxford. Participants were divided into two groups: farmers, who would earn more if wheat prices were high, and bakers, who would earn more if they were low. They were then shown a graph purporting to show the price of wheat and asked to predict the future price, with a reward for accurate predictions. Despite being paid for their accuracy, the farmer-participants consistently predicted higher wheat prices than the bakers. Harford concludes: "Everyone predicted what they hoped would happen."[101]

The conclusion is not that we should try to make forecasting more objective. This is largely a Cartesian illusion that may even prove counterproductive. It's probably much better to recognize that forecasts are always largely shaped by the identity and interests of those who make them, and to use them as such.

Pessimism

Pessimism can have a profound effect on forecasting. Surprisingly, during the Cold War and into the 1980s, the West was pessimistic about the outcome of its confrontation with the Eastern Bloc. For example, with the launch of the Sputnik satellite in 1957, the United States believed that the USSR was winning the technological race. Its invasion of Afghanistan in 1978 was seen as a daring operation and a major strategic advance by a growing empire. Indeed, the back cover of *Le Grand Frère* (Big brother), a book devoted to the development of the Soviet empire by Hélène Carrère d'Encausse, a leading expert on Eastern Europe at the time, read: "Despite these spectacular cracks, the system continues to grow stronger." The book was published in 1983, just six years before the fall of the Berlin Wall. Policy was therefore built around this pessimism. Yet we now know that the invasion of Afghanistan was in fact a disastrous initiative by a group of senile, misguided leaders that hastened the fall of an economically and socially strained empire by bleeding it dry.

Pessimism can lead to unfortunate decisions based on false predictions: the writer Stefan Zweig committed suicide with his wife in 1942, in despair over the triumphs of Nazism, from which he had fled. His magnificent testament, *The World of Yesterday: Memories of a European*, evoked the "golden age" of Europe (especially the cosmopolitan, creative prewar Vienna where he had grown up) and concluded that civilization had failed. Yet his suicide came just as the war was turning in the Allies' favor and civilization was about to triumph over barbarism. Less known is Chris Gueffroy, the last person killed by East German border guards as he tried to cross the Berlin Wall in February 1989, just nine months before it fell.

---

[101] "Why forecasters failed to predict Trump's victory", timharford.com, November 30, 2016.

Persistence of Belief Even in the Face of Contradictory Evidence

The scene takes place in 2018 during an intervention with a client, a very large French company. I'm lucky enough to be speaking just before the CEO. My speech is over, I give way to him. The topic is uncertainty. It's rare to hear a CEO speak on this topic, and the speech is quite interesting and quite sophisticated. But in the middle of the talk, no doubt to underscore how difficult it can be to manage the disruptions that are occurring in most industries, creating situations that seem to make no sense at all, the CEO declares, "Amazon has never made money. The implication is that this is an aberration, and the party will soon be over". It's a truism. I hear it all the time. Back in 1997, a respected financial analyst sounded the alarm that Amazon was going to the wall. The CEO of Amazon could walk on water and multiply loaves of bread, and there would still be some grumpy people who would say: "Sure, but he's not making any money." Amazon has been disrupting retail for almost thirty years now, but the fact that it doesn't make money would be enough to allow us to minimize its impact. This is a grave mistake. Amazon is a steamroller that is revolutionizing mass retail from top to bottom. You'd have to be deaf and blind (or work in retail) not to see this. What's more, Amazon is making money! This case is a good illustration of our ultimately human capacity to perpetuate a false belief, if only to keep our heads in the sand and our illusions alive for as long as possible. And no amount of additional data will change that.

Our appetite for accumulating data is partly explained by the belief that the more data we have on an issue, the better our understanding of it, and therefore the better the quality of our decision. But this is wrong for two reasons. The first is that additional information does not generally cause us to change our minds. On the contrary, once we've formed an opinion, it's very difficult to change it. An experiment conducted in 1975 by a group of researchers at Stanford University illustrates this.[102] First, they gave students suicide notes. The students were asked to distinguish between fake and real letters. The researchers then trick half the group into believing that they have gotten excellent results, and the other half into believing that they have gotten very poor results. They then reveal the deception by telling the participants that none of them did better than the others. The researchers then asked the students to estimate how many letters they had correctly identified. An interesting thing happened: those

[102] Elisabeth Kolbert, "Why Facts Don't Change Our Minds", The New Yorker, February 27, 2017.

who had been led to believe that they had scored well felt that they had done quite well in the exercise and greatly overestimated their performance. Conversely, those who had been led to believe that they had done poorly felt that they had done rather poorly in the exercise and greatly underestimated their performance - even after they had been told the truth, that their performance was simply average! One of the researchers concluded that our beliefs, once formed, are remarkably long-lasting, even when they are completely disproved.

Hundreds of experiments later confirmed these findings, and historical examples abound: British intelligence had heard about German-Soviet negotiations in 1939, but they couldn't accept the idea of a pact between the two enemy brothers, so they ignored the information. Similarly, the development of the iPhone was an open secret in the mobile industry in 2006, but its announcement took everyone by surprise. Why doesn't conflicting information cause us, who consider ourselves rational, to change our opinions? The economists Roland Bénabou and Jean Tirole have studied this question. They observe that a belief is an economic good like any other: people invest time and resources in developing it and derive value from it. This investment is part of their identity and deserves to be preserved and defended. Because these beliefs are no longer simply tools for making decisions, but are valued as such, information that challenges them is not welcomed. People then engage in what Bénabou and Tirole call "motivated reasoning" to deal with this challenge. Motivated reasoning takes three forms: strategic ignorance, when we simply avoid the information in question; denial, when we invent a reason to ignore the information; and self-signaling, when we invent our own tools to interpret the information in a way that favors our beliefs. Motivated reasoning is a cognitive bias to which educated people are particularly susceptible because they are intellectually better equipped for self-signaling. Hence, no doubt, George Orwell's famous observation that there are ideas so absurd that only an educated mind can believe them, because education enables us to construct an explanation for just about anything.

Group Reinforcement of Individual Beliefs

Beliefs are naturally reinforced by group membership. We tend to join groups that share our beliefs (a right-wing reader is unlikely to subscribe to a left-wing newspaper to hear the arguments of the opposing party), which reinforces them. For groups that we don't choose (e.g., our coworkers), the dynamic is different: an individual will tend not to assert his disagreement if he bears the cost of the group's error; the gain would be negligible (symbolic victory of "I was right") and the cost high (collective cost and hostility of the group in which he must remain anyway). The social incentive to engage in motivated reasoning is therefore very strong.[103] Reason, then, has evolved not to enable us to solve abstract logical problems, nor even to help us draw conclusions from unknown data, but to solve the problems of group life. The need to conform to group decisions, a condition of our survival, thus takes precedence over the search for truth. Kahneman soberly concludes: "Facts that challenge basic beliefs - and thus threaten people's lives and self-esteem - are simply not absorbed". He adds, "We know that people can maintain unshakable faith in any idea, no matter how absurd, if it's supported by a community of like-minded believers."[104]

We are far from being "analytical machines". On the contrary, our ability to reason is profoundly influenced by our identity and guided by our survival goals, which often include the need to remain a member of a social group. In short, it's better for survival to be wrong with your group than right outside it. Herein lies an explanation for the puzzle we mentioned in the introduction to this book: regardless of the evidence of its harmfulness, regardless of the number of examples of costly failure, it is extremely difficult, if not impossible, to remove the predictive paradigm from management practice. The latter is entirely based on it. Why do intelligent people continue to use an approach that is so obviously dangerous and contrary to their own interests? Because their investment in the predictive paradigm is so important, so longstanding, that to challenge it would be very costly and would challenge their very identity. And as if that weren't enough, it would also put them at odds with their group, which is also potentially extremely costly. This is what I'm most often told: "My boss will never accept that I stop making my annual forecasts. And even if the boss would agree, his own boss would not". As we can see, the difficulty is both individual and systemic. A vice practiced by all is no longer a vice, but a practice. But there are assumptions behind it: If you don't predict, what are you afraid of? Not knowing where I'm going. Is it a problem if you don't know where you're going? Yes, because I don't know what to decide. The predictive paradigm is firmly rooted in an institutionalized set of beliefs. It's easy to see why it's not enough to "know" that prediction is a risky business to abandon it, especially since the cost of wrong predictions is usually borne by society - or, in the case of banks, by taxpayers. A manager

---

[103] Source for this section: "How to be wrong", The Economist, June 10, 2017.
[104] Kahneman, *Thinking fast and slow*, p. 217.

therefore has little to lose if his predictions are wrong; it's seen as the price he must pay to build his business. On the other hand, he can lose a lot by deviating from group practices. If the cost of a harmful practice is socialized, it can be perpetuated. However, if its adherents are "brought back into the equation" - what Taleb calls "skin in the game"[105] - and pay for the consequences, it may disappear.

Reinforcement of Initial Opinion

A second reason why an excess of information does not improve the quality of our decisions is that it increases our confidence in our initial opinion. This was shown in an experiment conducted by researcher Stuart Oskamp with clinical psychologists and subsequently confirmed. This is important because overconfidence in medicine has long been associated with higher rates of diagnostic error: the more confident doctors are in their diagnosis, the more likely they are to be wrong.[106] Daniel Kahneman gives another example. He began his career with military service in the Israeli army. After graduating with a degree in psychology, he was assigned to a team responsible for assessing the potential of cadets upon their arrival at military school. Confronted with the actual performance of the cadets a few years after graduation, he had to face the facts: his ability to predict performance was poor. But most interestingly, while the irrefutable evidence of his failures should have undermined his confidence in his ability to judge candidates, it didn't: "We generally knew that our predictions were little better than a random guess, but we continued to think and act as if they were valid". He adds: "The most striking part of this story is that our knowledge of a general rule - which we couldn't predict - had no effect on our confidence in specific cases."[107] Note that we are dealing with a highly intelligent, highly educated person - a future Nobel Prize winner. We can easily extend this result to other professions. Hence, we have the infernal chain of obsession with data: the increase in available data reinforces the initial opinion and increases confidence in one's diagnosis, which increases the risk of error.

---

[105] Nassim Nicholas Taleb, *Skin in the Game: Hidden Asymmetries in Daily Life* (Random House, 2020).

[106] E S Berner and M L Graber, "Overconfidence as a cause of diagnostic error in medicine", American journal of Medicine, no 121, May 2008.

[107] Kahneman, *Thinking fast and slow*, p. 212.

Wisdom Versus Intelligence

The fact that intelligent people do not change their minds in the face of contradictory information suggests that intelligence is sometimes an obstacle to wisdom. Nassim Taleb explores this question in *The Black Swan*. He imagines a dialogue between two fictional characters, Fat Tony and Dr. John. Born in Brooklyn, a working-class neighborhood in New York, Fat Tony is a street kid. He left school as soon as he could and made his own way in life. He made a modest fortune in real estate and finance, buying up properties mortgaged to banks at low prices. His life is a big mess; he eats whatever he can get his hands on, doesn't have a desk or even a diary, doesn't exercise, and relies on his intuitive understanding of human psychology rather than learned theories. Dr. John is the opposite of Fat Tony. He's an engineer who works as an actuary for an insurance company. He has a Ph.D. in physics and lives in New Jersey, a middle-class state next to New York. His life is meticulously organized; he's efficient, and he pays strict attention to his diet. Taleb brings them together in a bar and asks them the following question:

Taleb. - Suppose a coin is not rigged, that is, it has an equal chance of coming up heads or tails every time it is flipped. I flip it 99 times and get heads every time. What is the probability of getting tails on the next flip?

Dr. John. - Trivial question. 50%, of course, since you specify equal probability for each side and independence between tosses.

Fat Tony. - No more than 1%, of course.

Taleb. - Why do you ask? I told you that the coin is not rigged, which means that there is a 50% probability for each side.

Fat Tony (in his characteristic way). - Either you're full of shit or you're a perfect sucker for this 50% story. The game is obviously rigged. It can't be an honest game.

Taleb. - But Dr. John said 50%.

Fat Tony. - I know these nerdy guys from my banking days. They think too slow. You can rip them off.

Taleb then mischievously asks the reader: "Which of Fat Tony or Dr. John would you like to see elected mayor of New York?"

Dr. John thinks entirely within the framework he's been given. He never questions it. Beyond the frame is forbidden territory, and what's more, it's invisible to him. Fat Tony, on the other hand, systematically rejects any framework. No matter how many people tell him or even guarantee him that the game is not rigged, he does not believe such assurances, even from someone he should trust. Dr. John is fragile. As long as the outside of the frame doesn't affect the inside, as long as the rules he's been given are correct, his approach is superior in terms of performance. Fat Tony, on the other hand, is robust. He can't really tell you the probability that the coin will come up tails, but he knows without hesitation that it's far from 50% and that the coin is rigged, despite the assurances of an honorable person. He doesn't even need to know whether Taleb is lying or mistaken.

The very nature of black swans is that they come from outside the frame, so if you limit your thinking to the frame, sooner or later you will be exposed to one. Taleb observes that good pupils often fall victim in their careers to this inability to question the frame, let alone see it or even realize there *is* a frame. He adds: "There is a sterile, obscurantist quality often associated with academic knowledge that gets in the way of understanding what happens in real life."[108] And yet Aristotle placed the capacity for astonishment at the origin of all philosophy. To face the unprecedented, it's essential to be able to question an obvious rule and, above all, to understand that the "framework" is in flux. Question to the reader: How many Fat Tonys do you have in your company? If your team consists entirely of Dr. Johns, you're fragile, meaning your sensitivity to black swans is at its highest; it's only a matter of time before one falls on your head. As Madsbjerg observes: "I see the lack of culture at the highest levels of the largest organizations. Too many leaders are isolated in their worldview. They have lost touch with the humanity of their customers and stakeholders and, as a result, confuse quantitative model representations with real life."[109] He adds: "Their fixation on numerical data often masks staggering deficiencies, and many of them will shatter on the glass ceiling of the business world. (…) They simply don't have the intellectual sophistication to reach the heights of leadership in their organizations."

The Best of Us

There are many examples of disastrous results produced by intelligent people precisely because they were more intelligent than wise, but none is as striking as that of the Vietnam War. This was masterfully described by David Halberstam.[110] Upon taking office, Kennedy surrounded

[108] Taleb, *The Black Swan*, p. 174.

[109] Christian Madsbjerg, *Sensemaking: The Power of the Humanities in the Age of the Algorithm* (New York, NY: Hachette Books, 2017), p. xiv.

himself with the most brilliant experts in the United States, supplied by the establishment. Halberstam observes that if there was one thing that united these men, their followers, and their subordinates, it was the belief that intelligence and rationality could solve everything. In this, they mirrored their leader: Kennedy was aloof, hyper-cerebral, and always embarrassed by emotional outbursts; indeed, he thought only of rationality and brains, nothing else. And yet this brilliant team would be responsible for one of the greatest self-inflicted disasters the United States has ever known: the Vietnam War. The limitations of these experts had been recognized early by the old-timers: at the beginning of the administration, Lyndon Johnson, the vice president of relatively modest origins, shared his amazement at the brilliance of his advisors with his friend Sam Rayburn, a longtime member of the Senate. Rayburn, concerned about their lack of contact with reality, replied: "Well, Lyndon, you may be right, and they're probably as smart as you say, but I'd feel a lot better if just one of them ever ran for sheriff."[111]

Halberstam describes the errors of judgment, the inability to truly understand the nature of the problem and the stakes of the various players, the trap into which the U.S. government would gradually fall of its own accord by turning a struggle for the independence of a minor country into an issue of strategic importance to the United States. The growing importance of the Vietnam question was only the result of its neglect, never of the actors sitting around a table to decide that the question was important. In the end, the experts were trapped like children by the complexity and sophistication of the geopolitical process, which was completely beyond them, but which they pretended to control with their bombers and their statistics. Nothing ever happened as they expected, but they never abandoned their approach. Just calculate more, spend more, bomb more, and it'll all work out in the end. One must "keep one's options open", they repeated, the classic antiphon of the prudent Cartesian, which means never choosing any of them to make it work and thus becoming a prisoner of events. An example cited in the book is the use of aviation. The obsession of the experts was not to get involved and to resolve the war as quickly as possible without putting men on the ground. So, they decided to use aviation. Aviation is the preferred tool of the Cartesian in khaki: you come from afar, drop the

---

[110] David Halberstam, *The Best and the Brightest* (Ballantine Books, 1993). This remarkable book should be required reading for any student, or practitioner, of management.

[111] Halberstam, *The Best and the Brightest*, op. cit., p. 41.

bombs, and you're back home for dinner. No commitment, nothing personal. So, the decision to bomb was made. The military carried it out. But planes mean airports. So, an airport had to be built in Vietnam. Pilots had to be housed, and ground personnel were needed to ensure operations. So, a regiment was needed to protect the airport. To ensure that this regiment was not an easy target, it had to be large enough. This required significant resources, logistics, and support personnel that also needed to be protected. So, without seeming to do so, what began as a decision to avoid committing human resources on the ground becomes, through slippage and chain of events, a very heavy human commitment. In the end, we find ourselves with thousands of men on the ground. The Cartesian disregard of operations as mere implementation of strategy has the perverse effect of leading to the very thing it was intended to avoid: the presence of troops on the ground.

The striking thing about the Vietnam War is that the shortcomings of the decision-makers it exposed were not new. They were the same ones that led to the defeat of Athens in the Peloponnesian War over two thousand years ago. As General Vincent Desportes explains: "Pericles, the Athenian strategist, built his argument on false assumptions: he based his strategy on his own vision of Lacedemonian rationality, believing that Sparta would soon understand the futility of its efforts against the defensive posture adopted by Athens [...]. [...] He was wrong. Year after year, Sparta continued to ravage Athenian lands, gradually destroying the ancient city's wealth and driving it into the strategic errors that would lead to its downfall."[112] Sam Rayburn was right: In the face of uncertainty and in the fog of action, what is needed is not so much brains as wisdom, and wisdom can only be acquired in the field from a posture of humility that is sadly rare among superior minds.

Anticipation and the Question of "the Other"

A fundamental source of uncertainty in decision making is the behavior of other actors, especially adversaries or competitors. In 1962, when the CIA was surprised by strong Russian troop movements into Cuba and a sharp increase in naval traffic, the hypothesis of secret missile installations was considered but quickly dismissed. The reason? The Russians would never take such a risk. The CIA saw them as cold calculators. This was far from reality. The First Secretary, Nikita Khrushchev, was psychologically fragile. He had been humiliated by the

[112] Desportes, *Décider dans l'incertitude*, op. cit. p. 17.

size of Kennedy's plane when they met in Vienna in 1961 and despised the American president as a spineless rich kid. He was also outraged that the U.S. had installed nuclear missiles in Turkey. In other words, the Cuban missile crisis had a more crucial personal dimension than the strictly rational, impersonal, and calculative approach could comprehend. In essence, the CIA's scientism failed utterly, with the consequence of bringing the world to the brink of nuclear annihilation. A better understanding of Khrushchev's personality, and especially of the importance of the personal dimension in the affair, would have made it possible to expand the range of possibilities and to consider as plausible developments that were otherwise considered impossible. When we work on social systems, the decision necessarily has a human dimension, which raises the question of "the other": his or her way of thinking, motivation, etc. We must make a considerable effort to understand the "other" and his or her role in the process. It's called *placing people*.[113] It's not an easy exercise, especially if you dislike your opponent. But not doing it is potentially very costly: you can't properly anticipate the actions of an opponent you don't understand. This exercise in understanding must be profound, and it should raise no ethical problems. Lack of understanding can be very costly and lead to strategic surprises. But trying to put yourself in the shoes of your adversary is difficult and not without risk.

Zachary Shore shows that the main danger of this approach is that we project our own rationality onto the reasoning we attribute to our adversary.[114] Shore cites the example of Stalin, who, despite being warned by numerous reliable sources of Germany's preparations for invading the USSR, refused to believe it until the very end because he thought it was Hitler's strategic mistake and that Hitler was necessarily aware of it. What Stalin couldn't admit was that Hitler was first and foremost an ideologue, and that he placed above all else what he saw as his mission: to create a "living space" in eastern Germany free of "inferior populations". The hyper-rational Stalin thus failed to understand his opponent's true motivation and sense of priorities. Worse, he projected his own rationality onto his opponent. Another problem is ignoring the decision maker's entourage. For example, Pericles' strategy relied heavily on his reading of the Spartan king

---

[113] The leading work on the subject is Richard E. Neustadt and Ernest R. May, *Thinking in Time: The Uses of History for Decision-Makers* (Free Press, 1988).
[114] Zachary Shore, *A Sense of the Enemy. The High Stakes History of Reading Your Enemy's Mind* (Oxford: OUP USA, 2014).

Archidamus. He believed that Archidamus preferred to appease Athens rather than fight. This was true, but he was not the only decision maker. He was influenced by the Spartan war party, which eventually overtook him and forced the conflict. In his analysis, Shore warns against what he calls the *continuity heuristic*, which we called above the immortality argument: it consists of anticipating the opponent's decisions by studying his past decisions. This approach was the basis of the Center for the Analysis of Personality and Political Behavior, created by the CIA in 1965. Its founder and director, Jerrold Post, explained: "One of the reasons for evaluating the individual in the context of his history is that, other things being equal, his reactions under similar circumstances are the best basis for predicting his future behavior."[115] Unfortunately, it's false. Shore observes that studying an individual's past doesn't reveal what we really need to know: his or her deepest motivations. What's more, he adds, "in international politics, the most important decisions an adversary can be expected to make are usually made in a very different context from the one he may have experienced before. Here, as elsewhere, tomorrow is not like today, and the assumption of continuity in unprecedented situations leads to disaster". Shore therefore recommends taking an interest in past situations where the adversary has changed its approach, what he calls pattern breaking. For example, he points to Adolf Hitler's decision in 1934 to sacrifice SA leader Ernst Röhm, his friend and early political supporter, during the infamous "Night of the Long Knives". After the Nazi victory in 1933, the SA became a major paramilitary force in Germany. It formed the ideological core of the Nazi movement and kept street violence alive. This violence was useful for Hitler's rise to power, but it worried conservative circles and the Army, especially as Röhm sought to take control of the latter.

The SA, made up of indoctrinated but poorly trained thugs, was far from having the legitimacy and capacity to do so. Conservative circles, as well as the still very weak Reichswehr Army, demanded that it be brought to heel. Instead of ideological purity and revolution, Hitler finally sided with the traditional Army, which was quite a departure for an ideologue. In retrospect, this choice can be seen as a clear indication that he needed a strong army, and that war was part of his plans from 1934 onward.

Instead of putting oneself in the shoes of one's adversary, Shore recommends an approach he calls *strategic empathy*, which is the ability

---

[115] Shore, *A Sense of the Enemy*, p. 165.

to identify with others and feel what they feel. It requires developing a deep understanding of one's adversary while trying to disregard one's own cultural and ideological filters. Shore gives a historical example of a little-known but crucial player in the Vietnam War. This was Lê Duan, leader of the Communist Party of Vietnam (North), the country's ruling party. From the beginning of the conflict, Lê Duan made a conscious effort to understand American dynamics. He realized early on, for example, that the American people would find it difficult to endure a protracted war in a distant land, so he opted for a war of attrition. Shore devotes long pages to describing Lê Duan's understanding of the United States, a relatively rare viewpoint in the literature on Vietnam, of which there are dozens, but almost all written by Americans and from an American point of view. This deliberate effort on the part of the Vietnamese leader certainly contrasts with the attitudes of many other leaders. On the eve of escalation in Vietnam in 1965, the North Vietnamese leader correctly understood the three most important constraints on the United States: its vulnerability to high casualties, its difficulty in maintaining popular support for the war over time, and the diversity of its other commitments in the world that would prevent concentration of the political apparatus over time.

Anticipating the behavior of others, however, remains a highly complex task. Edward Luttwak emphasizes the paradoxical nature of strategy[116], observing that it may be in the opponent's interest to behave in an abnormal way to surprise us. For example, if he must choose between two roads, one open and wide and the other steep, narrow, and longer, it may be in his interest to choose the second one because he thinks we won't expect it. Anticipating your action also means considering this paradoxical dimension of your opponent's decision. It should be noted, however, that this type of reasoning can quickly get into a recursive loop, leading to what intelligence specialists call the "wilderness of mirrors".[117]Our opponent will take the most difficult route to surprise us. But we know he's cunning, so we expect him to take that route. But he also knows that we're smart, and we know that he's smart, so we expect him to go that way. So it's actually in his interest to take the easier way. And so on. As we can see, this exercise in rational anticipation leads to a

[116] Edward N. Luttwak, *Strategy – The Logic of War & Peace* (Harvard University Press 2002).

[117] The expression "wilderness of mirrors" was used by the legendary American counter-espionage chief James J. Angleton to describe his work; its origin lies in the poem Gerontion by T. S. Eliot.

dead end, because in the end we don't know which choice would be the most rational for our opponent, not to mention the fact that we are then ascribing to him a rationality, and even a knowledge, that he may not have: does he even know that this second way exists? Anticipation raises the question of the other, but the answer is highly complex.

MAKING SENSE OF THE UNCERTAIN: IDENTITY IN THE FACE OF THE UNPRECEDENTED

In his book *Le Passé d'une illusion* (The Past of an Illusion)[118], the historian François Furet describes the inability of intellectuals in the 1930s to grasp the unprecedented nature of the Stalinist dictatorship. The Russian Revolution was seen as a continuation of the French Revolution, and as such enjoyed a benevolence that continues to this day. The French Revolution was liberal in inspiration, and the Terror was merely a by-product that lasted only a few weeks. Terror, on the other hand, was consubstantial with the Soviet regime and lasted at least thirty years. The two regimes were completely different in nature. Hannah Arendt explains this misconception as follows: "Totalitarian rule [is] an instituted fact which, since it is unprecedented, cannot be understood by the usual categories of political thought."[119] Faced with an unprecedented and evolving situation, it is essential to answer the following questions: What does this evolution mean? How can we understand it? How is it specific? What are its implications? This is what researcher Karl Weick calls sensemaking.

In the face of the unprecedented, there is no hypothesis. There may not even be an identified problem. Such was the case with Enron: the company's reputation for innovation and financial excellence was such that no one could even think of questioning it. The revelation of the fraud, and especially its scale, was a major shock to the business world. To question something is to take a stand on it. Simply deciding that something is a question is a political act. This is anathema to scientists like Sherman Kent, who are helpless in such situations. The problem with the unprecedented is that what we're facing bears no resemblance, either in nature or in degree, to what we've known before. The concepts we've been using (our mental models) to make sense of what we're experiencing are becoming obsolete. We must create a new framework

---

118 François Furet, *Le Passé d'une illusion: Essai sur l'idée communiste au XXe siècle*, Robert Laffont, 1995.

119 Hannah Arendt, *Between Past and Future* (Penguin Publishing Group, 2006).

for thinking about the new event. Weick uses the term "cosmological episode" to describe an event that comes as such a surprise that it leads to a loss of meaning for what is happening.

The extermination of the Jews of Europe by the Nazis in the 1940s is such a cosmological episode. Persecution of Jews had always existed, at least since the Middle Ages. Spain expelled Jews or forced them to convert as early as 1492. In Eastern Europe in particular, pogroms (attacks on Jews by mobs) had been common since the mid-19th century, with the tacit complicity, or at least passivity, of the state, which found easy scapegoats. Until then, however, genocide had never been systematically and industrially organized by a State with the clear intention of completely exterminating a given population. In fact, the Nazi operation was called the "Final Solution". It was therefore an entirely new phenomenon in its scope and ambition. The biography of Simone Veil, née Jacob, a former minister who recently died, sheds an interesting and frightening light on the difficulty of making sense of the unprecedented. After France's defeat in June 1940, the Jacob family took refuge in Nice. In 1941, the father, André, an architect, had to register his family with the prefecture. In a way, there was nothing more banal and harmless than a census. The family had nothing to reproach itself for. The Jacobs were a French family like any other, bourgeois, apolitical and law-abiding. Despite the German occupation, it was the French police who had to take the census. This was reassuring, or so it seemed. André Jacob decided to register. He immediately lost the right to practice his profession, and material difficulties began. The whole family was finally arrested and deported in 1944, and only Simone and his sister Denise returned from the camps alive.

What signs could have alerted André Jacob to the danger he was in? First, there had already been a genocide: the genocide of the Armenians by the Turkish state was a precedent, albeit on a smaller scale, but indicative of the capacity of an authoritarian state to exterminate a racial or religious minority. Second, the events in Germany since 1933, with the loss of rights and persecutions, in particular the Kristallnacht of 1937, a gigantic pogrom organized by the Nazis, showed that they took Hitler's plans in his book *Mein Kampf* seriously. The many Jews who had fled Germany could also testify to the reality of this persecution. Third, the Dreyfus Affair had revealed a deep-seated anti-Semitism in many sectors of the French population, which animated the political movements that had just gained influence with the advent of the Vichy regime. Besides, a census had to serve a purpose... but what? For a Jew at that time, the dilemma was terrible. On the one hand, the signs of danger were mounting: Vichy's racial laws of September 1940, compulsory censuses, disenfranchisement, harassment, the presence of the Germans, who had been pursuing an active anti-Semitic policy for several years, virulent anti-Semitic attacks in French newspapers, etc. On the other hand, how to imagine the worst? How to imagine that a state would invest immense resources in the extermination of its fellow citizens? That industrial techniques would be applied to mass death? That the wonderful German bureaucracy would be mobilized for this project? How to imagine that the dead would number in the millions? That the French State would be an active accomplice? That French policemen would put children in cattle cars before quietly going home for an aperitif? France had been the first country to grant full citizenship to Jews in 1791. Persecuted in many European countries, Jews had always sought refuge in France. Despite the tensions, despite the mistakes of the Dreyfus Affair, the French state had always protected them. All this weighed heavily when a family had to decide whether to participate in the census. The danger was clearly perceived, but not taking part in the census meant becoming an outlaw. For an integrated, bourgeois family, this was unthinkable. It's extremely difficult, both intellectually and emotionally, to accept that one has left continuity behind and is on the slippery slope of the unprecedented. This can take a long time while the event unfolds at our expense.

The Difficulty of Making Sense of the Unprecedented: The Example of September 11, 2001

An example of the considerable time it takes to make sense of an unprecedented situation is the terrorist attacks of September 11, 2001. Let's look at the NBC 4 New York video[120], which begins its coverage ten minutes after the first impact on one of the World Trade Center towers. For the first twelve minutes of the broadcast, the two commentators describe what they see. They know a plane hit the tower, but not once do they consider it an attack. Then something amazing happens. At the twelve-minute mark, a plane appears in the upper right corner of the screen and hits the second tower. A huge explosion follows at 12'30. The journalists comment on the explosion, but don't seem to have seen the plane, which is obscured by the first tower. They keep talking and again don't think for a moment that the second explosion, in

[120] https://www.youtube.com/watch?v=58TpAXMk2bI

a separate tower, a few minutes apart, was probably also caused by a plane, so it couldn't have been an accident. But they keep talking about an explosion. The slowness of consciousness is staggering. At 15'22, one of the journalists plays the video, but only the few seconds before the explosion, so we don't see the plane coming (it is covered by the first tower, which has already been hit). For the first time, he considers the possibility of a second plane, but does not continue. Then, at the 17-minute mark, a witness calls in and points out to the two journalists that their own footage does indeed show a second plane. The network then replays the footage further up, and this time the plane is clearly visible. At 18'32, one of the journalists mentions the possibility of a deliberate attack. However, at 26 minutes, the other journalist, summarizing what she knows, immediately clarifies: "I wouldn't call it an attack." When the first journalist learns that the FBI has just announced an investigation into the hijacking of two planes, he hesitates before repeating "terrorist attack," but his colleague stops him, pointing out that "we don't know enough and that it's not certain that the two facts are connected". So, two planes hit a tower 20 minutes apart, two witnesses confirm that the planes flew very low and went straight into the towers, but the idea of an attack still seems inconceivable to the two journalists. At the 29-minute mark, the journalist again quotes the FBI as saying it was a deliberate attack, but again with great caution. At the 38-minute mark, the journalists interview a commercial pilot on air who witnessed the first attack. The pilot explains that the plane flew straight into the tower and showed no signs of technical problems or distress. He is then interrupted by a statement from President Bush, who clearly refers to this as a terrorist attack. The newscaster, however, summarizes it as a "suspected" terrorist attack. The interview with the pilot continues. He points out that there is no way a commercial airliner could have been in that area and at that altitude. He adds that a pilot in trouble could have easily avoided the towers. He concludes: "Whoever was at the controls deliberately flew into the tower". Yet the two journalists are still talking about a "probable" terrorist attack, more than 40 minutes into the report, 50 minutes after the first impact. And then, at 52 minutes, the announcement of the attack on the Pentagon comes in and ends the debate. It took the two journalists almost an hour to admit without reservation that this was a terrorist attack, even though the facts were clear from the second impact.

This is not to impugn the two journalists, but to underline once again how difficult it is for us to admit that we are faced with a totally unprecedented situation.

FLAWS IN THE ORGANIZATIONAL PROCESS

Anticipation and the Organizational Process: The Intelligence Cycle

In the foregoing, we have proposed a shift from an objective to a subjective position, placing the individual and his or her identity at the center of the approach to uncertainty. Let's now extend this development by addressing the identity of the organization within which the individual operates in uncertainty. The work of anticipation takes place not in vitro, like an organic chemistry experiment, but in vivo, between people, in an institutional context, and is integrated into the processes of the organization within which it takes place. In intelligence, this organizational process is captured and diagrammed by what we call the *intelligence cycle*. This allows us to link the anticipation exercise to the organizational process, and it is valid for any type of organization. The different stages of this cycle are as follows:

1. Expressing the need: the decision maker defines what needs to be researched; this is the question posed.

2. Information Gathering: The information needed to answer the question is gathered through various means.

3. Analysis: The analysis of the collected information consists in transforming it into usable information. Explanations are eliminated, others are favored, estimates are made, different sources are cross-referenced, and so on.

4. Production: Production consists of creating communication documents containing the necessary and relevant information, tailored to the target audience (the chairman, the CEO, a minister, a commission of inquiry). This stage may require coordination between different departments.

5. Dissemination: Dissemination of the analysis produced is the exercise of communicating the content of the intelligence to the decision maker. This can take the form of a report, an oral presentation, etc. This is a cycle in which the results found and the exchange with the decision-maker can lead to a new expression of need.

The model has been rightly criticized: it obviously reflects a positivist (reality exists and I observe it without being part of it) and Cartesian (I gather information, I use this information to inform my thinking, then I make my decision; everything is well sequenced) attitude, but it is nevertheless useful to schematize the process. In any case, it allows us to point out the major pitfalls in the anticipation process. Above all, it allows us to see that anticipation errors do not originate at the level of analysis alone, but at each of the five stages of the cycle.[121] Let's take a closer look at each one.

Expressing the Need: The Risk of the Wrong Puzzle

In the ideal intelligence model, a decision maker poses a question to the analysts. This is the starting point of the cycle conceived by Sherman Kent. This is the customer-supplier model, which is also the commercial language used by the CIA: customer, supplier, product. In other words, in this model, there is no issue that is not initially a question for the decision maker. This is problematic because there are many important issues where this is not the case. Or if we wait for the decision maker to ask it, it will be too late. For example, when the CIA asked the new President Clinton at the beginning of his term in 1992 what his priorities were, terrorism ranked only third. As a result, the CIA focused on other issues, with the consequences we know. The needs assessment phase, in which the problem to be addressed is defined, is obviously crucial, because it also determines which problems will be ignored, whether intentionally or not. This is where the term "solving the wrong puzzle" comes into play.

Refusal to Understand

Because management is generally thought of in terms of "problem solving", we focus on a visible problem and ignore an invisible or more diffuse problem, as we mentioned in the case of Enron. Let's look at this phenomenon using terrorism as an example. Blindness to a development can be the direct result of a desire not to understand one's environment. This is explained in a very interesting article by Gilles Kepel and Bernard Rougier, published in the daily *Libération*.[122] The article shows how French universities have refused to try to understand the rise of

---

[121] This issue is covered extensively in Milo Jones and Philippe Silberzahn, *Constructing Cassandra*.

[122] Gilles Kepel, "'Radicalization' and 'Islamophobia': the king is naked", Libération, March 14, 2016.

Islamic terrorism. This is underscored by Sciences Po's closure of its specialized program on these issues in December 2010, the same month as the Arab Spring. According to Kepel and Rougier, this closure "wiped out entire fields of knowledge and, in particular, the ability of young researchers to read Salafist and jihadist propaganda literature in the original Arabic." The refusal to understand an adversary and, more generally, a phenomenon that concerns us, or should concern us, is unfortunately nothing new. This explains the Cuban Missile Crisis in particular[123]. Even today, the CIA, which was completely blindsided by the Soviet attempt in October 1962 to secretly place missiles in Cuba to threaten the United States, considers this an aberration, a mistake for which the CIA cannot be held accountable and which it could not have been expected to anticipate. In particular, the CIA failed to understand the deep-seated motivations and unstable personality of Soviet leader Nikita Khrushchev. The result? The world came very close to nuclear war.

In *Constructing Cassandra*, Milo Jones and I link this inability to understand to the agency's scientistic identity and cultural construction, which precludes the consideration of human elements in decision-making. To a large extent, the adversary is not understood because we refuse to try to understand him, simply because we don't think it's necessary. What's more, we often find our opponents repulsive; we feel too far removed from them. Why go to the field when a good satellite can take wonderful pictures for us? The refusal to understand our adversary develops what strategy specialist Edward Luttwak calls *strategic autism*, in which the decision maker isolates himself in his own world. I have faced this refusal to understand myself. In a seminar on strategic surprise for military officers, I mentioned the Charlie Hebdo and Bataclan terrorist attacks and the need to better understand the attackers if we were to anticipate the next ones. The response of one of the participants? We don't need to worry about that. Just bomb Daech and the problem will be solved. Granted, this was all in jest, but there was an underlying sincerity: an almost desperate desire to believe that there could be a simple solution to a complex problem. That our technology would suffice. That we didn't need to bother to understand; that all we needed was to launch our planes. Trying to understand would even be an admission of weakness, "a girl thing", as a participant in another seminar told me. The refusal to understand, fueled by arrogance, dogmatism, and intellectual laziness, is everywhere. Nothing expresses

---

123 Milo Jones and Philippe Silberzahn, *Constructing Cassandra.*

this alleged narrow-mindedness better than the incredible statement of the then Prime Minister Manuel Valls: "To understand is already to excuse". Refusing to understand is, on the contrary, applying an old model to a new reality, the best recipe for disaster. This intellectual laziness is commonplace, and it exists in the corporate world as well. Modern management places so much emphasis on the imperative of action that it becomes the focus of everyone's attention. In my seminars, I always have a hard time convincing people that they can't act too quickly; that they need to sit down and understand, and only then can they act, or sometimes decide *not* to act.

Intellectual climate that prohibits certain questions

Kepel and Rougier also mention in their article the fear of being accused of Islamophobia. They are right. Libels laws haven't reduced racism at all, but they have reduced our ability to think about the world to understand it, by forbidding us to generate hypotheses, to pursue certain avenues, and even to collect certain data. Together with the current intellectual climate leading to a culture of cancellation, i.e., attempts to prohibit certain people from expressing themselves, they are part of this infernal mechanism we develop to blind ourselves. They make anticipation more difficult by creating de facto blinders, making the next disaster more likely and its cost higher.

Counterproductive Performance Measurement

Analysts or researchers do not operate in an institutional vacuum. Like any employees, they are regularly evaluated on the basis of their professional activities. The way they are evaluated will naturally influence the way they work. In academic research, this evaluation is increasingly based on published articles. This is an individual evaluation, not an evaluation of teamwork. This evolution in the criteria used to evaluate researchers discourages time-consuming, in-depth research in favor of articles written quickly to keep up with the times. The system for measuring research performance also contributes to our blindness. When researchers are evaluated every year based on the articles they publish, they stop taking the time to understand a phenomenon in depth, an approach that would take several years to produce a result. This is problematic in a discontinuous environment. We must look to ourselves for the causes of our blindness in the face of unprecedented phenomena that we do not understand and therefore cannot anticipate.

Information Gathering: Technology and the Human Factor

The collection phase can be disturbed in several ways: easy information can be collected (laziness) or, on the contrary, difficult information can be collected (technical exploitation) instead of relevant information. This is very common today with the ease of information technology. We can also use technology naively, without realizing that every technology exists in a cultural and social context. The basic goal of scientists is to remove the human dimension from the decision-making process and to limit themselves to the purely objective parameters. This explains their interest in technology. But the human factor never disappears, and there is no technology that operates in a social vacuum. A good example is the role of the U-2 spy plane in the Cuban Missile Crisis.[124]

On October 14, 1962, the U-2 flew over Cuba and revealed that long-range nuclear missile launch sites were under construction. This was the beginning of the Cuban Missile Crisis. It was a triumph for the CIA. The U-2 is a marvel of engineering. With a wingspan of 30 m, it flies at an altitude of 20,000 m, twice as high as a commercial airliner, and has a range of 5,300 km. Best of all, its high-resolution cameras can take 12 km of film! Launched in 1957, it is still in service at the time of writing. On October 15, 1962, about 900 photos were extracted from this 12 km of film (it took a whole day to develop and analyze them, this was pre-digital!), providing irrefutable proof of the existence of Soviet missile sites in Cuba. The official story was as follows: the USSR was preparing a surprise attack against the USA. Thanks to its advanced technology, the CIA was able to discover the plot in time to warn the president. Armed with this information, he was able to resolve the crisis in favor of the United States, as the Russians agreed to dismantle their facilities.

However, if we examine the conditions of the U-2 flight, a very different story emerges. First, as mentioned above, the CIA, which had noted strange phenomena around Cuba (troop movements, greatly increased shipping traffic, construction sites in the middle of nowhere, etc.), nevertheless refused to consider the possibility of nuclear missiles. In its Special Report SNIE 85-3-62 to the President, dated September 19, 1962, the CIA wrote categorically: "We believe that the military buildup which began in July does not reflect a radically new Soviet policy toward Cuba, either in terms of military commitments or the role of Cuba in overall Soviet strategy." This is despite the fact that the Russian

---

[124] The source for this section is Milo Jones and Philippe Silberzahn, *Constructing Cassandra.*

operation began in May and the first nuclear missiles arrived on the island a week before. Second, the last U-2 flight was on August 29. Between August 29 and October 14, the plane did not fly. In other words, during this crucial period, when the CIA knew that something was going on in Cuba, it did not use its technological lifeline and was therefore blind.

So why didn't the U-2 fly? Why didn't the CIA use its technology to get to the bottom of it? To understand this, we must put ourselves in the context of the time. The world had just gone through the Berlin Crisis of 1961, with the building of the Wall greatly increasing international tensions. It was the height of the Cold War. The U-2 was also known as the "spy plane". Its ability to fly so high over any region that it was not necessary to ask permission from the countries it flew over was frowned upon by the latter, who saw it as proof of American arrogance, which could get away with anything thanks to its technological prowess. Soviet propaganda had skillfully presented the U-2 as a symbol of imperialism, and each flight brought its share of articles denouncing its use. The overflight of Cuba was even more sensitive because the island was seen by many as a symbol of revolution, celebrated by Western intellectuals for whom it was a bath of youth. Again, the United States' efforts to overthrow the Castro regime did not sit well with some international opinion. In essence, each U-2 flight was seen as a provocation, even within the U.S. government.

At a crucial meeting on the issue, Secretary of State Dean Rusk pressured the CIA not to fly the plane during the Berlin negotiations. At that meeting, however, CIA Director John McCone was absent; he was represented by his number two, who therefore had less political clout in the face of pressure from Rusk, who was close to the president. Why was McCone absent from this crucial meeting? Simply because he was... on his honeymoon! Married late, he was in Nice, far from the action. So the CIA hesitated, but since it didn't think anything important was going on in Cuba, it finally agreed not to fly the U-2. McCone, for his part, was convinced that the matter was serious, but he was not followed by the organization of which he was the head. Why wasn't he? Because he was new at the helm of the CIA, having been appointed after the Bay of Pigs and the forced departure of all the agency's "old hands". He was frowned upon internally. What's more, he was not from the intelligence world; he was a businessman; he was also a Catholic in a Protestant organization, and he was a Republican in a Democratic administration. A Republican CIA director appointed by a Democratic president? Yes, because after the Bay of Pigs, Kennedy wanted someone who would be untouchable by his opponents.

That's how the various elements of a tragedy that almost ended in disaster were set in motion. Despite the power of its technology, the CIA was blind because the conditions under which it could use this technology were dictated by its human and institutional environment, with which it had to negotiate. It's not enough to have the ultimate big data tool, 1962 edition, to know and anticipate everything; it's also necessary to be able to use it in a way that makes sense and is useful, and above all to understand its limitations. No technology is omnipotent, and even less so in human systems. We're a long way from scientism.

The question remains: why did the U-2 finally fly on October 14, 1962? Well, because he couldn't stand it any longer, knowing that his subordinates weren't following him, McCone cut short his honeymoon, returned to CIA headquarters, and ordered the flights to resume immediately. The CIA discovered the missiles, and the United States realized suddenly that it was on the brink of a major strategic disaster. Here we're much closer to Shakespeare than to the positivist model of strategy based on diagrams, the study of positions, and the rational calculation of interests. We have the facets of personality, marriage, propaganda, Kennedy's impatience with the CIA's failures, cultural and religious differences, divergent interests between the CIA and the State Department, and so on. In short, technology is nothing without the context in which it operates. Understanding this context is fundamental to the decision maker. This is all the more difficult in a Cartesian world that separates thought from action, where those who appreciate the context despise the technology or, on the contrary, worship it without understanding it, and those who master it ignore the context or deny its importance.

Analysis: The Importance of Context

Context also plays a part in the analysis phase when data and hypotheses are examined. This is not simply an intellectual exercise; it is also, and above all, an organizational and even bureaucratic process. Generally speaking, a report or presentation must be validated by at least one hierarchical level before being sent to its addressee. Anyone who has worked in a large company and had to make a presentation to senior management knows that this is a complicated process requiring several meetings, fine-tuning and even negotiations on what to say and what not to say, and how to say it. The main victim of such a process is necessarily the truth, or spontaneity, which is inexorably filtered by the preparatory stages and meetings.

This author experienced it firsthand. The scene takes place in 2015, in a training program I'm conducting for the executives of an automobile manufacturer. After discussing Nokia, we turn to Tesla, the electric car pioneer. Some in the room get it: "It seems to me that if you replace Nokia with us, and Apple with Tesla, we're in exactly the same situation as Nokia was in 2007". But not everyone agrees. One attendee points out that Tesla's production is tiny, and that he believes it will never be able to produce in large quantities (at the time, Tesla was only producing about 80,000 cars a year, which is very small). Another adds, "It's much more complicated to make a car than a phone!" The similarity to Nokia's attitude is striking. First, there's the contempt for the opponent: he's small and will never make it. The fact that a complete amateur from nowhere can produce a car in a relatively large series in just a few months, when it should be impossible, raises no questions. Then there's the turkey syndrome: the one that judges that tomorrow will always be like today. Tesla is small, so it will always be small. It has a small market share, so it will always be small. The idea that it could increase its production capacity and impose itself on the market, like Apple did to Nokia, does not enter the minds of some participants. It's hard to argue with that, especially since the example evokes strong emotions and shows that we've put our finger on an issue that directly questions the identity of the participants (who work for one of the leaders in their market).

My response was essentially this: we don't know if Tesla will succeed, of course. We know that the company has manufacturing problems, that its CEO, Elon Musk, is setting overly ambitious goals and taking huge risks. But we also know that he's a very good entrepreneur, and that he's already done things that everyone said were impossible, like sending rockets in the sky (he has successfully disrupted the space and energy markets). Tesla is a gamble, but I would take it seriously. My participants didn't like it. My seminar was poorly evaluated, and I never worked for the company again.

Since then, Tesla has ramped up production to 1.37 million in 2022, and everyone is now taking it seriously, albeit belatedly. The players who mocked Tesla were like Nokia or Microsoft dismissing Apple's iPhone. It's really an absurd gamble to say, as I heard in another industry, "Nokia's parallel to us doesn't hold up". It's just too risky. Yet, because it challenges their identity, companies may refuse to consider certain hypotheses, sometimes with disastrous consequences.

The Impossible Option: Abandon Vietnam

Historian Frank Gavin explains that in the 1960s it was perfectly possible to defend the idea that it was in the United States' interest to get out of Vietnam; that the country was, in fact, of no great strategic interest to them. But the American administration's theory at the time was the domino effect, i.e., that the fall of Vietnam would automatically lead to the fall of the other countries of Southeast Asia, which nothing suggested (and indeed neither Thailand, Burma, Malaysia, Indonesia, nor Singapore fell). In Gavin's view, there was also an advantage to not getting involved: by abandoning Vietnam, the U.S. would no longer pose an immediate threat to China, opening the possibility of a rapprochement with that country in the face of the USSR. In fact, this is what happened: after a gradual reduction of their presence, the last Americans left Vietnam in 1973, and a year earlier, Nixon had been in Beijing, creating a break between two giants within the communist world and thus causing a major strategic upheaval. But this kind of option is sometimes difficult to imagine. To understand why, we need to look back at the historical context in which the Vietnam question was approached by the American government, and in particular by Kennedy, who took the initial decisions to get involved. In 1949, after a long civil war, Mao's Communists took power in China. In the context of the Cold War, the "loss" of China was traumatic for the United States. Although they had refused to intervene directly, the Americans had strongly supported Chiang Kai-Shek's Nationalists. Democratic President Harry Truman was accused by Republicans of having lost China and of being weak in the face of growing Communism, an accusation that would stick with the Democrats for a long time (we were just emerging from the McCarthy era). In the Prague coup of 1948, the Communists seized power in Czechoslovakia, and immediately thereafter, in 1950, the Korean War began, a surprise attack by the Communist North, supported by China, against the South, which was repulsed only in extremis. The affair ended in compromise, but not in victory. From then on, after China, Czechoslovakia, and Korea, it was extremely difficult not to see the Vietnam affair as a new episode in a great Communist conspiracy that had to be resisted with all possible means.

It was against this backdrop, where accusations of democratic weakness toward the Communists remained strong, that President Kennedy took the matter in hand. The unfortunate Bay of Pigs episode, the aborted April 1961 attempt by U.S.-backed rebels to overthrow the fledgling Communist government in Cuba, added to the impression of Communist progress and American, and especially Democratic, weakness. The last thing the President wanted was to appear weak in the face of this threat. This context strongly conditioned his response and de facto reduced the number of options considered: it was simply out of the question to state coldly that Vietnam was of no strategic importance to the United States, or that the country had other priorities. We can see how the decision is very much constrained by the context, by the preferences of the actors, and by the self-imposed blockages in exploring their options or even in creating possible options. For many reasons, we are still far from the ideal decision-making situation described in textbooks, where the decision maker is free, or thinks he is free, to consider all possible options.

Social Pressure

Nor is analysis impervious to social pressures. This author was once asked to analyze the reasons for the failure of a company's innovative product. The project had been initiated by the CEO, who had been seduced by the social impact of the product, which was intended to improve health conditions in developing countries. From the beginning of the project, technical difficulties became apparent. The technology on which the product was based was far from perfected, and industrialization had not been studied. The project quickly fell behind schedule. Finally, a prototype passed a performance test. Everyone was relieved, and the project moved into the industrialization phase. However, an R&D engineer pointed out that the test had been conducted under very specific, unrealistic conditions and that the product would not pass a full battery of real-world tests. But because of the delay, management ignored these warnings and exerted strong pressure to proceed. The engineer was accused of complicating matters and not having a "winning attitude". The pressure was so great that he went on sick leave. As it turned out, the product did not meet the required level of performance. A few months later, the project was buried for good, leaving the company with a bill of 30 million euros. The engineer was right, he had correctly anticipated the technical failure, but it had cost him personally to share his concerns with his superiors. In this context,

Kahneman notes that optimism is highly valued in our personal and professional environments, and that it's not a good idea to express doubts. An objective appreciation of uncertainty should be the norm - but it's not what people and organizations want. Extreme uncertainty is paralyzing in dangerous situations. Admitting that you don't know is socially unacceptable when the stakes are high. Acting on presumed knowledge, even if it turns out to be wrong, is often the preferred solution.

Influencing Performance Criteria

Conformity is often valued more than being right. When he was studying management in 1997, this author took a course in financial analysis. He thought that the role of an analyst was to analyze a company's numbers, discuss its strategy with management, study its environment, and then, based on these analyses, make a stock price forecast. But this is not the case, as the professor pointed out. The analyst's job is not to predict the company's performance, but to predict what the market will think of the company, because that is what ultimately determines the share price. The analyst's measure of success is therefore not the quality of his work, but his ability to keep up with the market. You must avoid recommending that a stock be sold when everyone else is recommending that it be bought, and vice versa, because even if the market doesn't end up moving in the expected direction, everyone was wrong, so it doesn't matter. What we need to anticipate is not the performance of the stock, but what the market will think of the future performance of the stock. Again, we see that anticipation is based on a very strong social constraint, far from the ideal model of a purely calculating mind.

Production and Dissemination: The Relationship Between Decision-Maker and Advisor

The main danger in the production and dissemination phases is the elimination of extreme hypotheses (the statistician's outliers), as these may not be accepted by the decision-maker or other departments. In fact, there is often a need for consensus, which increases as one moves up the hierarchy. In the fall of 1978, the CIA was unable to produce a report on developments in Iran, then in the throes of revolution, because the various intelligence agencies it was supposed to coordinate, but over which it had no authority, could not agree on its conclusions, thus preventing the agency from producing a report. It remained silent while the regime of a key U.S. ally was collapsing. The situation was repeated in 1984 when the CIA's Soviet Economic Division attempted to estimate the USSR's budgetary capabilities. According to them, the USSR would not be able to balance its budget without borrowing from abroad or cutting military spending, which turned out to be true. The problem was that the rest of the intelligence community at the time, especially the Pentagon, was convinced that the USSR was getting stronger and was therefore unwilling to discuss such a possibility, so the CIA's argument did not make it into its own final report to the president. The consensus imperative suppresses extreme hypotheses, which is a problem in the face of the unprecedented.

Separating the Analyst from the Decision Maker

Complex decision-making often takes place in an institutional context in which an analyst, the producer of information, advises a decision-maker, the consumer of that information. The analyst's role is to advise the decision maker and guide him or her to the best decision. This division of roles reflects a Cartesian model that distinguishes between thinking and doing. However, the relationship between the two is highly complex, and this model has been problematic from the beginning. This problem is explored in a famous 1949 article in the CIA's internal journal, *Studies in Intelligence*, which remains highly relevant more than sixty years later.[125] The article recounts a controversy on the subject within the agency itself, between Sherman Kent and Wilmoore Kendall. Sherman Kent was the legendary founder of the CIA's Analytical Branch, which he headed until 1967 and on which he left a profound mark. Kendall, who spent some time at the CIA, was more of an academic. The controversy arose from Kendall's review of Kent's 1949 book, *Strategic Intelligence for American World Policy*, in which Kent laid out his doctrine. Kent notes that effective links between analysts and decision-makers, while clearly essential to the smooth functioning of both groups and their constructive relationship, are difficult to establish. The solution he recommends is to ensure the objectivity of researchers and provide analysts with institutional independence. To ensure their relevance, he urges them to seek clear "directives" from the decision-maker. In this model, the analyst's role is to answer the decision maker's questions without trying to influence the decision or even the definition of the problem under study. The "problem" is defined by the decision maker, and the analyst's role is to provide him with the information he needs to solve it. We're in a Cartesian distinction between thinker and

---

[125] Jack Davis, "The Kent-Kendall Debate of 1949", Studies in Intelligence 36, no. 5, 1992, pp. 91-103.

doer, in a positivist paradigm of objective information, and in a "customer-supplier" approach that assumes that the customer knows exactly what he wants, is perfectly capable of defining his needs, and that the supplier's only role is to satisfy them.

For Kent, the key is to avoid a situation in which the analyst becomes an advocate, trying to influence both the definition of the problem and the possible solutions. The analyst must never bring himself into the equation. Kendall rejects what he calls Kent's "ideal". Instead, he sees the role of intelligence as helping political leaders achieve their foreign policy objectives, largely by identifying those elements of an issue that are sensitive to their influence. Moreover, Kendall observes that if the mission of intelligence is to inform decision making with the best that specialized knowledge can provide, then Kent's aversion to considering policy and social science theory is counterproductive. Defining the problem may be difficult, but it's certainly the most important part, and for Kendall, only strong analyst involvement can enable him to contribute; he must bring himself into the equation. Nevertheless, Kent's position prevailed, and the famous intelligence-policy divide, or the separation between intelligence and policy (decision-makers), became an article of faith in the American intelligence community and anathema to advocacy. In his book on the future of war[126], researcher and military strategy specialist Thomas Barnett revisits this issue and highlights two limitations of this separation.

First, this approach weakens the analysis by forcing analysts to describe what every other country in the world will do in response to a set of events, while leaving the U.S. essentially static. Indeed, to imagine possible U.S. responses would be to invade domestic politics and approach advocacy. Thus, if one imagines hostile action by China against Taiwan, the analyst cannot make any assumptions about the American response, because to do so would be to go beyond analysis and into the political realm. Only when analysts are allowed to imagine possible U.S. moves - and this can only be done with policymakers - can a dynamic approach to analysis truly be achieved. Of course, in the process we may come close to advocacy, Kent's greatest heresy, but it's worth the effort. A strictly Cartesian "client-supplier" vision like Kent's ignores the creativity that can come from a strategic conversation

[126] Thomas P. M. Barnett, *The Pentagon's New Map: War and Peace in the Twenty-First Century*, Reprint Edition, Berkley, 2005.

between analyst and decision-maker, in which options not initially imagined can emerge.

It was this conversation that Kennedy facilitated during the 1962 missile crisis. At the first meeting of the Executive Committee, when the missiles had just been discovered, the option recommended to him was a preemptive nuclear bombing of Cuba.[127] Kennedy was not enthusiastic about the proposal. How did he argue? He thought out loud and said, "If we bomb Cuba preemptively, how will future generations judge us?" He shifted his perspective: in the face of radical uncertainty, he looked at the present from the future, not the other way around. Above all, he questioned the values that would underpin the decision. From this perspective, the bombing seemed much less defensible. He then asked the participants to think about other options, leaving the room several times so as not to influence the discussion too much. The result was a creative response, the blockade, which resolved the crisis and was seen as a triumph for the president.[128]

Second, according to Barnett, an illusory separation between intelligence and decision virtually forces analysts to imagine the future as a pure and simple continuation of the present, the dangers of which we have amply demonstrated, since, again, to imagine an unprecedented event without a specific command from the decision maker would be to invade the political domain. The analysis should not be limited to projecting trends but should assess the possible strategic interaction between decision-makers and their policy objectives. This requires a creative, iterative, and interactive approach. In a world of uncertainty, Kendall's vision of the decision as the result of a strategic conversation with an entrepreneurial attitude is profoundly relevant.

---

[127] Kennedy's advisors assumed that Cuba would have to be leveled very quickly before it acquired nuclear capability with the activation of the missiles under construction. Long afterward, however, it was learned that Russian *tactical* nuclear missiles were already operational. Had this option been chosen, the American strike would have been immediately followed by a Cuban counterstrike. Once again, we see the role of assumptions and their disastrous consequences when they are proven wrong.

[128] Kennedy's handling of the committee to facilitate a creative solution has become legendary. The reference book on this subject is Graham Allison and Philip Zelikow, *Essence of Decision*, (Longman, 1999).

Convincing the Decision Maker

Typically, the analyst's role is to provide the decision maker with what Paul Saffo calls an "effective forecast". This is important because decision-making under uncertainty cannot be reduced to calculation; it always involves a significant degree of judgment. Effective forecasting expands understanding by revealing overlooked possibilities and uncovering unexamined assumptions about expected outcomes. Often, however, it is the analysts who identify the problem and must point it out to the decision maker, who may have many other things on his or her mind. This runs counter to the intelligence cycle, which assumes that the decision maker will always drive the issue. From then on, the difficulty is to convince the decision maker of the importance of the question. The analyst doesn't work for a weather service that provides apolitical data. Quite the contrary. As a British intelligence veteran once remarked, "Salesmanship is part of the game".

The tricky part is that it's difficult for an analyst to consider possibilities that are too "out there" without losing his audience. Very often, his conclusions about an anticipated event are not to the "client's" liking, either because they run counter to his beliefs or because they come at the wrong time, and he is therefore not prepared to accept them. For example, in the 1990s, Bill Clinton believed that terrorism had ended with the collapse of the USSR, and so he placed the issue very low on his list of priorities. As noted above, the belief at the time - marked by the PLO (Palestine Liberation Organization) renunciation of terrorism that made the Oslo Israeli-Palestinian Accords possible - was that today's terrorists were tomorrow's statesmen and should therefore be called "militants" rather than "terrorists". In this context, it was difficult to convince Clinton of the danger posed by a rich man's son "playing the financial terrorist" (i.e., Bin Laden). Attacks on the United States, such as the bombings of the American embassies in Nairobi, Kenya, and Dar es Salaam, Tanzania, which killed more than 200 people, were thus seen as aberrations, not as harbingers of trouble to come. As Philippe Baumard observes: "It is an eternal truth of intelligence that it is useful to decision-makers only insofar as it conforms to their own views, or if they can use it to sell their own political arguments."[129] Again, we come to the limits of the prohibition against advocacy. If the analyst is truly convinced of the reality of an anticipated event and fails to convince the decision maker, should he or she continue and insist until the case is

---

[129] Baumard, *Le Vide stratégique*, p. 172.

won? Insisting would be tantamount to advocacy... It's not easy, because your career may be on the line. Michael Scheuer, head of the CIA's Bin Laden unit before the 9/11 attacks, was so frustrated that the agency wasn't taking the Saudi terrorist seriously that he decided one day to write directly to the director and urge him to get things moving, jumping several hierarchical levels in the process. The response was swift: he was fired a few weeks before the attacks! Selling is part of the job, and if the "customer" doesn't want to buy the "problem", then in a sense the problem doesn't exist, at least from an organizational point of view, until it imposes itself on the organization, sometimes brutally when it's too late.

Criteria for Success

If this is the case, what are the success criteria for the analyst or consultant? Failure to anticipate leads to surprise, which can be costly. Because anticipation is flawed, behavior is not adapted to the event that occurs. In *Constructing Cassandra*, we define surprise as "the sudden realization that one has been operating on the basis of an erroneous estimate, rendering one incapable of anticipating an event with a significant impact on one's vital interests". As we can see, the key is an erroneous assessment of one's environment. Therefore, it is essential to understand it. This may seem obvious, but in his work with analysts, this author is always surprised to find that they often know little about their environment. Conversely, how can anticipation be considered successful? The question is not as simple as it seems. One might consider it successful when the event of interest is perfectly predictable (date, time, place, modalities). But this is often not possible or even necessary. What matters is that the prediction is sufficient to allow action to be taken, to prevent the event, to manage it properly, or to take advantage of it, depending on its nature. More generally, it's about giving the decision maker enough degrees of freedom to act with respect to the event so as not to be subject to it. For example, knowing that an individual is actively preparing an attack is enough to apprehend him and thus prevent the anticipated event, without needing to know the details of the project. In the words of researcher Paul Saffo, the criterion for success may therefore be: "Being able to provide the decision maker with *enough information* to take *meaningful action* in the face of a given development."[130] Prediction, i.e., knowing exactly what will happen in the future, is therefore not necessary to achieve this goal. The key word

[130] Saffo, "Six rules for effective forecasting", op. cit.

here is *enough*. It's about getting enough information to act, not to predict, which lowers the bar of difficulty considerably.

THE PUBLIC DECISION MAKER FACED WITH UNCERTAINTY

We mentioned earlier that, contrary to what we might have thought a few decades ago, the development of science and technology has brought more uncertainty, not less. This is a particular challenge for public decision-makers. There was a time, especially in France, when the decision-maker was king. The embodiment of Auguste Comte's positivism, exercised by the experts who graduated from our top schools, the State was a long-term player, deciding alone whether to launch a nuclear program or the high-speed train. Two developments are undermining the power of the public expert. The first is the increasing complexity of decisions. The development of science and technology makes it increasingly difficult to master problems. What's more, many areas are genuinely uncertain, and scientists disagree of many important topics. Decisions must be made on projects whose consequences will be felt for decades to come, and no one can predict them. Many of the proposals on these issues are simply undecidable. No amount of additional information will solve the problem. With these complex issues, we again reach the limits of the Cartesian logic of decision making, which assumes perfect information and possible rational anticipation; we must decide when we have very little information about the consequences of our decisions, and therefore our expertise is largely inadequate.

The sociologists Michel Callon, Pierre Lascoumes, and Yannick Barthe note three difficulties in studying this question: first, the list of options is not unambiguous. Some are easy to identify, but others are more or less deliberately ignored. Specific work is needed to identify those that could be improved. This is a creative approach, closer to entrepreneurship than to expertise in a closed, well-identified world. The attitude is different. Second, the conditions under which each option will work, and in particular the system components that will make it work, are not identifiable. Finally, the interactions between these components are also unidentifiable.

The second development that undermines the power of the public expert is the fact that individuals, better informed than previous generations, now have their own expertise, or counter-expertise, and are no longer willing to accept the expert's verdict without challenge. This change obviously undermines the power of the expert, who derives from his knowledge and the ignorance of others. He now must deal with them. A good example is the determined action of parents of children with muscular dystrophy, who have forced research to take an interest in this hitherto neglected disease and have become key players. Of course, this evolution can lead to aberrations if the information is false (fake news), as we saw with the reluctance to vaccinate against Covid. Science and technology can no longer be managed by the political institutions we have, insofar as they have historically derived their authority from their expertise. We must accept that expert knowledge is not the only kind of knowledge possible, and especially that these big questions are not just technical or computational. They always have political, social, and ethical dimensions. To ignore these developments is to expose oneself to hostile reactions, which can be very strong. This is what happened to the Monsanto group, which conceived the introduction of its GMO products in purely technical terms and completely failed to anticipate the strong opposition, justified or not, that its products aroused.[131]

We are thus witnessing the failure of what Callon, Lascoumes, and Barthe call the "Alexander model" of decision making, where the expert draws his sword and cuts the Gordian knot of the complex problem. The self-confidence of the male warrior must now be replaced, not by inaction, but by measured action, the only kind possible in situations of extreme uncertainty. Above all, this action can no longer be taken without the participation of those involved in the decision. Indeed, when decisions in the face of uncertainty can no longer be made on the basis of objective criteria of knowledge and predictive calculation, because the questions are undecidable, they can only be made subjectively, that is, by agreement with others, on the basis of values at least as much as facts. This is what Callon, Lascoumes, and Barthe call "technical democracy", which consists in involving stakeholders in decision-making: patients for medical decisions, residents and farmers for nuclear waste treatment, and so on. Stakeholders are thus involved in decision-making, in a process of co-determination of the future. For the experts, this is a revolution, and like all revolutions, it's a difficult step. No one

[131] The loss of power of the expert naturally exposes him to abuses, if the expertise of some carries as much weight as the ignorance of others. However, today's citizens have wide access to the means of information that enable them to become experts. This is not to say that ignorance has the same rights as expertise, but rather that expertise can now be found everywhere. As for separating the wheat from the chaff, that's the whole point, as the controversy surrounding hydroxychloroquine during the Covid-19 crisis showed.

willingly accepts a reduction in power. Technical democracy need not fear controversy. On the contrary, it is an appropriate response to the growing uncertainties created by technoscience, a response based on the organization of collective experimentation and learning. If we can't know a priori, we have to do it. In this way, the idea of technical democracy embodies two key concepts that we'll explore in more detail below in relation to entrepreneurship: the involvement of stakeholders in the project of co-creating the future, and creative action rather than a priori calculation.

PART 2: SURVIVING AND THRIVING IN UNCERTAINTY

Montaigne is Back

"I usually reply to those who ask me why I travel: that I know what I'm fleeing from, not what I'm looking for."

Montaigne

The dominance of Cartesianism is the result of a formidable assault that took place in the seventeenth century, when it brutally replaced Renaissance philosophers such as Montaigne. Today, however, this model is being challenged by modern philosophical, economic, and scientific thought. This questioning allows us to think about action in a radically different way. In an uncertain world, after a hiatus of four hundred years, Montaigne is more relevant than ever.

HOW WE GOT HERE: THE TRIUMPH OF DESCARTES

The world was not always Cartesian, or even Platonic. In fact, there was a time between Plato and Descartes when thinking was very different. Renaissance humanism in the 15th and 16th centuries welcomed the complexity, uncertainty, diversity, and chaos of the world with interest, even delight. But all that changed in the seventeenth century, when rationalism took its place. But why? The answer to this question is provided by philosopher Stephen Toulmin in his book *The Hidden Agenda of Modernity*.[132] Toulmin notes that before 1600, theoretical inquiry was counterbalanced by concrete discussions, practical questions such as the specific conditions under which it was morally acceptable for a sovereign to wage war or for a subject to kill a tyrant. From Erasmus to

[132] Stephen Toulmin, *Cosmopolis: The Hidden Agenda of Modernity* (University of Chicago Press, 1992).

Shakespeare and Montaigne, the writings of the Renaissance humanists displayed an openness and skeptical tolerance that were innovative features of this new secular culture. What was not entirely new, however, was that the scholars and educators of the time were indeed indebted to a crucial feature of Aristotle's ethics, politics, and rhetoric: a sensitivity to the "circumstantial" character of a practical question. A theologian of European renown, Erasmus was torn between Catholicism and Protestantism. Asked by both the Pope and Luther to choose - his support was crucial - he refused. Why choose between black and white, true and false, when truth is inevitably gray and uncertain? Shakespeare explored page after page the depths of the human soul and the circumstances that are the reality of great tragedies and great battles. There are no models or axioms with him! His plays, more than four hundred years after they were written, still explain far better than many calculations and learned models how human tragedies happen.

But above all, Montaigne. Montaigne is a very unconventional philosopher. He writes in the first person and speaks about himself. He is immediately and always in the equation: "Thus, reader, I myself am the subject of my book", he writes. Not to present himself, but to observe himself in action and to learn from it. He doesn't create grand theories, he doesn't seek the truth, he only denounces the lies and hypocrisies of his fellow men, howls against injustice, but doesn't try to prevent it by creating yet another philosophical system. He knows what to hate: injustice, great men, fanaticism, but he offers nothing in exchange. There will be time to make proposals when we've explored the world. In a modest approach typical of his thought, Montaigne, like Erasmus, argued that it was better to suspend judgment on questions of general theory and concentrate on accumulating a rich perspective. Montaigne thus embraced uncertainty with joy, with pleasure, with the eagerness of a child who doesn't know where he's going but knows he's going to have fun. Like the naturalists of his time, he rejoiced in the richness, complexity, and variety of the world that was being discovered, especially through travel - it was the age of great discoveries - and the study of nature. Montaigne does not hide his weaknesses, not to correct himself, but to *know* himself. He admits laziness, gluttony, and cowardice. Mayor of Bordeaux almost against his will, he flees from the plague, abandoning the inhabitants for whom he is responsible, in an episode of little glory, and just as well: he distrusts glory like the plague. Montaigne is a peaceful revolutionary. With him, there's no need to prefer one thing to another, or to despise whole swaths of human existence. Montaigne is also a skeptic who doesn't like skepticism. For him, the first duty is to be oneself. Philosophy begins with oneself, has oneself as its object and oneself as its end, nothing more - no system! - and nothing less. By refusing, unlike so many philosophers before and after him, to divide man into strengths and weaknesses, he finally makes it possible to describe him truthfully, so that knowledge of the facts prevents us from jumping to value judgments. Montaigne doesn't fit easily into any intellectual system, and this is undoubtedly one of the reasons for the relative obscurity into which he quickly fell. Above all, he quickly fell out of step with the times.

From 1600 on, most philosophers devoted themselves to questions of abstract and universal theory, to the exclusion of concrete questions. Where Montaigne rejoiced in the richness and ambiguity of the world, the new philosophers of the time saw only chaos and confusion. Modern philosophy thus set aside all questions of argumentation - among particular people in particular situations, dealing with concrete cases where various things are at stake - in favor of proofs that could be written down and judged in writing. It moved into a higher stratosphere where nature and ethics conform to abstract, timeless, and universal theories.

According to Toulmin, it thus made four fundamental changes in humanism, in a veritable counter-revolution:

-- rhetoric, the art of language and discussion, which was the way of doing philosophy, gave way to formal logic;

-- the discussion of special cases gave way to general principles;

-- concrete variety gave way to abstract axioms;

-- the transitory gave way to the timeless.

What explains this change? As always, if we want to understand a difficult question, we must start from the historical context. Since the beginning of the 16th century, the Reformation had been gaining momentum, and conflicts within the Christian religion threatened to escalate. In this context, French King Henry IV, a Protestant who had converted to Catholicism to be crowned, pursued a cautious policy of reconciliation between the two parties, which naturally brought him attacks from both. He believed that it was possible to be an honest Catholic or Protestant and still be a loyal subject of the kingdom. At a time when each party was demanding to choose sides, he defended a compromise solution that separated national loyalties from religious affiliations. Henri IV's pragmatic approach to politics is reminiscent of Montaigne's in the intellectual sphere, and it's no coincidence: the two were very close. Henri no more allowed doctrinal dogmatism to overtake political pragmatism than Montaigne allowed philosophical dogmatism to overtake the testimony of familiar experience. Both men placed the modest claims of experience above the fanatical demands of doctrinal loyalty and were thus skeptics (in the true sense of the word) and, above all, moderns. But on May 14, 1610, Henry IV was assassinated. The event sent shock waves throughout Europe. What people saw was that a policy of religious tolerance had been tried and failed. After Henri, it no longer stood a chance. The intellectual debate between the Protestant Reformers and their Counter-Reformation opponents came to an end, and there was no alternative to the sword and the torch. Both sides hardened their positions, and in 1618 the conflict finally broke out. The quest for certainty would become the Thirty Years' War, and it devastated Europe, leaving a field of ruins in its wake.

Trying to "prove" with the sword that one's side is right on a matter of faith would quickly seem rather futile, but both sides were caught in a vicious circle and the situation spiraled out of control. The more brutal the war became, with massacre following massacre, the more the adherents of each religious system sought a way to prove their doctrine right. Montaigne's epistemological caution and modesty had become unacceptable, unthinkable, obsolete: the time had come for clarity, for universal truth, for certainty. If humanist uncertainty, ambiguity, and the acceptance of pluralism had in practice only led to an intensification of religious wars, so the thinking went, then it was time to find a rational means of demonstrating the essential accuracy or inaccuracy of philosophical and theological doctrines. What war couldn't decide, "science" had to. The times called for men of spirit to propose a means of access to the truth, a truth that could not be denied and based on which society could rebuild itself after the massacre. To do this, this truth had to be independent of human contingencies and passions. And it was Descartes who responded to this call.

Descartes persuaded his age to abandon fields of study rich in content and context, such as ethnography, history, or poetry, and to focus exclusively on abstract, decontextualized fields, such as geometry, dynamics, and epistemology. His hope, and that of his successors, was to eventually bring all subjects under the umbrella of an unquestioned formal theory. With Descartes and his "new philosophy" we move from a style of philosophy that gives equal weight to questions of local, temporal practice and universal, timeless theory to a style in which only the latter has the right to exist. Descartes was therefore less the murderer of humanism, which died in 1618, than its gravedigger. Contrary to his image as a philosopher detached from material contingencies, he responded to a pressing social need, the search for certainty, that arose in troubled times. But his impact was major. It marked the transition from an era in which uncertainty was seen as a source of richness and pleasure to one in which it was the source of all evil. It did even change the very conception of the world and society, the whole being seen as a system, with God ruling over the world, the king over men (the "Sun King"), the husband over his wife, the noble over the peasant, and so on. From then on, the way was open for a way of thinking that would constantly produce tools designed to deny uncertainty, either by reducing everything to a series of equations or by attempting to plan, and by clearly separating the realm of thought from that of human passions, which were considered inferior.

CHALLENGING THE DESCARTES MODEL

Thus, since Descartes, uncertainty - the indeterminacy of the future - has been anathema to most philosophers, businesspeople, and politicians, who wish to eliminate it in order, in the words of the philosopher, to "make themselves masters and possessors of nature". This fear of uncertainty has, of course, given rise to systems of thought and theories of decision whose primary goal is to reduce it. This explains the triumph of Descartes, who precisely offered this to a Europe exhausted by religious wars. Classical economics and moral theories assume that we hesitate to make decisions because we don't know well enough the consequences of our choices or the fundamental moral principles on which our actions are based. For these theories, hesitation is due to a lack of information (about consequences, about foundations). To make the right decision, all you need is the right information (to know the consequences of your choices, the moral rules, etc.), to know what to do and how to do it right. The dominant view of thinking is therefore the idea that orientation is found first through knowledge of the world, and only later through action. According to this view, action is initiated only after meaningful goals have been defined in the world of thought and then, in a separate act of will, the decision to pursue those goals has been made. As sociologist Hans Joas notes, this view seems to assume that lethargy is the natural human state.[133]

This Cartesian view of action as the implementation of thought is dominant in Western thought. It completely shapes our teaching and our

[133] Joas, *The Creativity of Action* (Polity, 1996).

view of the world. In particular, it is reflected in the notion of the plan, in which a stage of conception is followed by a stage of implementation. The plan is a universal tool, equally at home in economics, industry, and entrepreneurship (business plan). This concept is also found in the separation between analyst and decision maker in intelligence and business intelligence. But it is being challenged.

Challenging the thinking and assumptions of Descartes is nothing new. Modern biology has long since shown that his separation of mind and body, and his view of emotion as an obstacle to rationality, is unfounded. On the contrary, neurologist Antonio Damasio has shown that the ability to express and feel emotions is indispensable for the implementation of rational behavior. This ability, along with the hidden physiological mechanisms that underlie it, helps us accomplish the daunting task of thinking about an uncertain future and programming our actions accordingly. Damasio adds: "The most primordial functions of the organism are therefore involved in the implementation of the reasoning faculty at its highest level."[134] Mind and body are intimately connected, and rationality is not possible without emotion. This is a lesson that should be pondered by many managers who think they should suppress their emotions to make better decisions.

The Cartesian model has also been challenged by authors from very different and sometimes unexpected schools of thought, all of whom were interested in human action and its conditions. The first is Machiavelli, who shows that, in the face of uncertainty, only action can reveal possibilities that no calculation or reflection could discover a priori. The economist George Shackle, writing on the epistemology of economics, shows that imagination, the source and domain of original thought, and not a priori calculation, is the indispensable resource for decision making in a non-deterministic world. The philosophical current of pragmatism challenges the strict Platonic and Cartesian separation between thought and action, and especially the subordination of the latter to the former. Instead, it theorizes creative human action.[135] Following this trend and writing in the context of entrepreneurship, researcher Saras Sarasvathy showed how entrepreneurs abandon predictive logic and use uncertainty to transform their environment by

---

[134] Antonio Damasio, *Descartes' Error: Emotion, Reason, and the Human Brain* (Penguin Books, 2005).

[135] See, for example, in the field of art: John Dewey, *Art as Experience* (TarcherPerigee, 2005).

creating new markets, new organizations, new products and services. Because they are transforming their environment, they no longer need to predict it.

In the end, what emerges from these contributions is a very different conception of acting in uncertainty, of the relationship between thinking and acting, and, above all, of our relationship to the world. According to philosopher Nelson Goodman, the world is not a given whole that we can only observe and, at best, understand. It is a construction, or rather a constant reconstruction, at the whim of culture and human history. It is made, as well as found. Philosophers, scientists, artists, and entrepreneurs are among those actively engaged in "redesigning" the world, as are all of us through our actions, large and small. It took centuries after the Cartesian eclipse for uncertainty to be recognized once again as an essential and fruitful feature of our environment, a feature that is particularly the source of capitalist profit (Frank Knight's reward for judgment in the face of uncertainty), but more generally of freedom: with uncertainty, the world is no longer deterministic, and the field of human action opens without limit. Hannah Arendt observes of this eclipse: "Our tradition of political thought began when Plato discovered that turning away from the common world of human affairs is, in sum, inherent in philosophical experience; it ended when nothing remained of that experience but the opposition of thought and action, which, by depriving thought of reality and action of meaning, renders them both meaningless."[136]

REVEALING ACTION

Machiavelli and Hidden Parties

An important challenge to the dominant model, which assumes that perfect information is necessary and a prerequisite for decision making, comes from Machiavelli, who observes that, on the contrary, only action can reveal certain possible options. Writing in the 16th century, Machiavelli revolutionized political thought and ushered in the modern era. Philosopher Thierry Ménissier explores the originality of his thought by observing that, for Machiavelli, "there is a fundamental indeterminacy of becoming, and we must speak of the permanent openness of time."[137] Since the future is uncertain and therefore

---

136 Arendt, *Between Past and Future.*

137 Thierry Ménissier, *Machiavel ou la politique du centaure.* All quotes by Thierry Ménissier in this section are taken from this book.

indeterminate, it cannot be known, and no amount of analysis will ever change this situation. In the prevailing model, as we've seen, decision making is a process that unfolds as follows: first we analyze the situation and set a goal; then we identify possible options and choose optimal one; then we take action to implement a plan to achieve that goal. This model seems so obvious that it is rarely questioned. It corresponds to what's called a *prudential* view of action: it's all about avoiding failure. The assumption is that the more information you have, the less chance you have of making a mistake. The point is not to act until you know enough. Machiavelli suggests the opposite approach: act precisely *because* you don't know. In a fundamental passage that sums up his entire thinking on the topic, he writes: "By acting, parties [options] are revealed that would have remained hidden if we had not acted". Thus, action will reveal options that could not have been known a priori without action. We act in order to know, as opposed to knowing in order to act. For example, acting will force another actor who has been ambivalent to take sides. In a business context, launching an imperfect product as quickly as possible will uncover unexpected uses that no amount of market research could have uncovered.[138]

Ménissier notes that in the Machiavellian conception, "action is constituted by the confrontation with facts (this is the meaning of the theme of 'opportunity') and above all, whatever the prudence of the rulers, these facts present themselves as an otherness that always exceeds the human power of formalization". Since precalculation is not creative, it does not allow us to imagine everything that could happen, and prudence can therefore, paradoxically, lead to risk-taking, that of missing opportunities. Action is therefore a full and equal part of the decision-making model, no longer relegated to the inferior status of mere implementation. We don't just use information to act, we act to discover important information that enables us to act more effectively. The Cartesian sequence of thought and action no longer holds. Both are closely intertwined, feeding off each other in an organic flow. Decision becomes a process, a conversation between reality and thought; it is no longer an isolated moment in time. Ménissier observes: "The Count acts in order to assess the situation, because, says Machiavelli, only the encounter between the event and his gesture will give him a precise idea

---

[138] A method implementing this type of approach in the entrepreneurial field is Lean Startup. See: Eric Ries, *The Lean Startup: How Today's Entrepreneurs Use Continuous Innovation to Create Radically Successful Businesses* (Crown, 2017).

of what he can do. The reversal with the prudential conception is radical, since here it is the gesture that directs the decision". He adds: "If we interpret this way of conceiving action in ontological terms, we can say that the possible is not determined by a calculation, nor independently of action, but by an initial assumption of responsibility for the event by the latter". He adds further: "It is necessary for the course of things to be an event for an action, before we know if and how we can act effectively - without which fate takes the initiative and imposes its sudden, unpredictable and disastrous options on men". As we can see, the actor must consider two risks: the positive risk of acting and the negative risk of missing an opportunity by not acting. The former corresponds to prudent action, the latter to creative action.[139]

Of course, there is a cost to action, and it is advisable to reduce that cost as much as possible through prior analysis, but there is also a cost to inaction in that opportunities may be lost that we are unaware of because of our inaction. Prudence also has a cost. And in the case of uncertainty, a priori analysis is particularly difficult because the "permanent openness of time" multiplies the opportunities hidden in a world that is not set in stone. Machiavellian thinking is particularly relevant in this context. And Ménissier concludes that, in this conception, "the test thus reveals and sanctions a certain relationship between nature and truth". The implications of this Machiavellian conception are profound in terms of ontology, that is, the way in which we conceive of the nature of our environment and our relationship to it. In most classical conceptions, inherited from positivism, the actor is fundamentally external to his environment. He tries to understand it and act upon it, but he is not part of it. It is symptomatic that the great strategic models, including the famous SWOT (Strengths, weaknesses, opportunities, and threats), are all based on this dichotomy between an "internal" (the organization) and an "external" (the environment). For Machiavelli, the opposite is true: "Since he is also a historical agent, the political actor is not offered a point of view external to history". The actor is fully part of his environment; he acts within it at least as much as he acts upon it. Researchers Chia and Holt believe that understanding the world as a realm of uncertainty rather than risk fundamentally changes our relationship to it. We are no longer separate, looking at our situation and deciding how to respond to the assessment of what we think has happened, is happening, and will happen in the future. Instead, we are thrown into the world, and through our actions we are constantly trying

[139] Almost all the managerial tools are devoted to managing the former.

to make sense of our condition.[140] We are fully part of the environment; we determine it as much as it determines us. "The principle of the Machiavellian theory of action is based on the fact that what happens (fate) is not external to the way we act". This inversion was later developed by the philosopher Martin Heidegger, who argued that the starting point of philosophy is not thought but being. This was in direct contradiction to Descartes, who took thought as the starting point with his famous statement: "I think, therefore I am". Seemingly subtle, the difference is in fact fundamental, for it puts the human being back at the center of the equation. Once again, the dualism of actor-environment and action-acting disappears. For Machiavelli, it's never a question of abandoning the contingent world of fate, but of staying as close as possible to the phenomena, since the aim is to tell "the truth of facts and effects."

Like a fish in water: Byzantium's Strategy for Anticipating and Deterring Attacks

A good example of the value of seeing oneself as part of the environment rather than outside of it is the strategy of the Byzantine Empire. In his book on the subject, strategy specialist Edward Luttwak analyzes how the empire was able to survive for nearly a thousand years despite being in an unfavorable geographic area and under constant attack from virtually every direction. How can such longevity be explained when the Western Empire lasted only about 600 years? According to Luttwak, it's because its leaders were able to adapt strategically to difficult circumstances and devise new ways of dealing with successive enemies. The empire relied at least as much on military force as on persuasion to recruit allies, deter threatening neighbors, and manipulate potential enemies into attacking each other instead. To achieve this strategy, the Byzantines always tried to maintain constant contact with hostile tribes and empires, even the most distant ones. This strategy had two goals: the first was to anticipate a tribe's hostile intentions by being informed as early as possible, and the second was to prevent such hostile intentions from materializing. Contact was maintained by every means possible, from espionage to trade to arranged marriages, but the basic attitude of the Empire was based on recognizing these tribes as equals with whom it was not unworthy to mix. This is a far cry from the attitude

[140] Chia and Holt, *Strategy without Design* (Cambridge University Press, 2011), p. 42.

of the Western Romans, heirs in this respect to the Greeks, who regarded foreign tribes as barbarians with whom contact was repugnant. Interestingly, Luttwak attributes the Byzantines' ease of contact to their Christian religion: since the latter regarded bathing as an invitation to sensuality, the Byzantines, being less clean, were less repulsed by the smell of barbarians than were the cleanness-obsessed Romans. This barbarian-inspired Roman revulsion is still relevant today when we look at the way terrorists are described, and the extent to which an organization like the CIA remains marked by a deep scientism that makes it view the world clinically, as something dirty and external to itself[141]*, or how marketing or financial analysts view the world through disembodied quantitative models.*

Action Determines Preferences

Action not only reveals hidden information, it also allows the actor to discover his or her preferences. Researcher Christian Walter points out that the work of psychologists Kahneman and Tversky (and many others to follow) shows that uncertainty in choice is not the result of a lack of information.[142] There is an intrinsic uncertainty, as if embedded in our neural decision-making processes, resulting from the very structure of the human brain: the possible states present in the minds of those who must decide are not separate, as economists or classical moralists imagine, but superimposed, as in Schrödinger's cat experiment in quantum physics. In essence, we can't know what we prefer until we've decided. Only the act of choosing dissolves states. It creates preferences. This underscores the importance of the concept of preference, a human dimension that points to the subjective nature of choice, which is denied by rationalism, which considers only its objective dimension. The decision-maker is inevitably "in the equation" and cannot disengage from the decision or its environment. Contrary to the maxim "there's nothing personal, it's just business", even business decisions are highly personal. By committing oneself in a direction without knowing exactly where one wants to go, the very movement of commitment brings out a preference that was unknown just before. We return to Machiavelli's idea that action reveals possible options, but here it's preferences that are revealed, or more accurately, determined. This means, according to

[141] See Milo Jones and Philippe Silberzahn, *Constructing Cassandra.*

[142] Source for this section: Christian Walter, "Les filets du diable", Philosophie magazine, February 12, 2018.

Walter, that every elementary particle behaves like someone who, by choosing, violates the axioms of Cartesian rational choice theory. What's more, the quantum superposition of states leaves open the possibility of making a different choice from the one we initially intended, at the very moment we decide to implement it: acting (choosing) has modified the initial preference! The lamentations of Medea or Saint Paul, who regretted having acted against what they wanted to do, are perfect illustrations of this. Walter concludes that forgetting this intrinsic uncertainty is at the root of the rationalist or moralist illusion that a clear vision of separate states would enable us to decide according to rational preferences or overarching values and is reflected in the advocacy of the deliberative method.[143]

CREATIVE ACTION

As we saw with Machiavelli, action reveals "hidden parties" and opens possibilities that would otherwise have been unimaginable. But action goes far beyond the simple discovery and revelation of these hidden parties. In essence, Machiavelli's paradigm remains one of discovery of an objective reality. Through action, however, the actor also creates parties and situations, not just reveals them. Much more than a revealing action, we're talking about a creative action, a notion developed by the philosophy of pragmatism. Pragmatism was born at the end of the 19th century with writers such as William James, John Dewey, and Charles Sanders Pierce. Taking as its criterion of truth the fact of working and succeeding in practice, it represents a method of thinking and grasping ideas that stands in opposition to Cartesian and rationalist conceptions. For John Dewey, the pragmatic attitude is presented as the opposite of the passive theory of knowledge. To know is not to see, as in the Cartesian tradition, but to act. Already in the Nicomachean Ethics, Aristotle wrote: "What we must learn to do, we learn by doing it."[144] For pragmatists, and again in direct contradiction to Descartes, action is not subordinate to thought; it does not consist in the pursuit of well-defined goals or the application of norms, and creativity does not consist merely in overcoming obstacles along a prescribed path. In fact, according to Dewey, man has discovered and appropriated the world through his

---

[143] On rationality and preferences, read the following article by one of the leading specialists in the field: James G March, "Bounded Rationality, Ambiguity, and the Engineering of Choice", The Bell Journal of Economics, vol. 9, no. 2, 1978, pp. 587-608.

[144] Aristotle, *Nicomachean Ethics*, Book II, 1, 1103 b.

actions; man is above all an acting being... who thinks. Thus, pragmatism is as much a theory of creativity as it is a theory of action, since it is a theory of the creativity of human action in a world open to human determination. Thus, if there are parties that can only be revealed through action, if the preferences of actors are only determined at the moment of action, and if the possible states of the environment are created by action, we can see that the distinction drawn by Plato and Descartes between thought and action, with the latter being subordinate to the former, is not only erroneous but, above all, profoundly counterproductive in an uncertain world.

Taken together, these considerations call into question the model of the two great philosophers, that of the calculating actor, detached from the context, fearful of uncertainty and human passions, who analyzes the available information before acting in a prudent manner. To do this, he needs an indisputable knowledge base that only mathematics can provide, which explains why the Cartesian vision of the world is that of a great machine with a complicated but perfectly knowable mechanism. A vision that is contradicted by the everyday experience of our environment. Montaigne, on the other hand, welcomed uncertainty and complexity. For him, uncertainty was a feast, a realm of possibilities for those who venture into it. Without realizing it, he prefigured the attitude of entrepreneurs for whom uncertainty is the raw material, which we will explore below. Uncertainty is the source of new products, new markets, new organizations, and new empires. Entrepreneurs don't protect themselves from uncertainty; they organize themselves to take advantage of it. To do so, they put action at the center of their approach. Taking their cue from the pragmatists, they see action as the source of change and novelty. A world in which uncertainty is finally recognized, in which it is no longer denied, is a world that leaves Descartes and returns to Montaigne.

FOUR POSSIBLE ATTITUDES FOR THE FUTURE

When we look at the attitudes that decision-makers can adopt when facing the future, we have distinguished two main dimensions. The first is prediction: Either I believe that I can predict the evolution of my environment, or I do not. The second dimension is control. Either I believe that I can influence the evolution of my environment, or I do not. Crossing the two dimensions gives us four possible attitudes, which are illustrated in the diagram below (Figure 9).

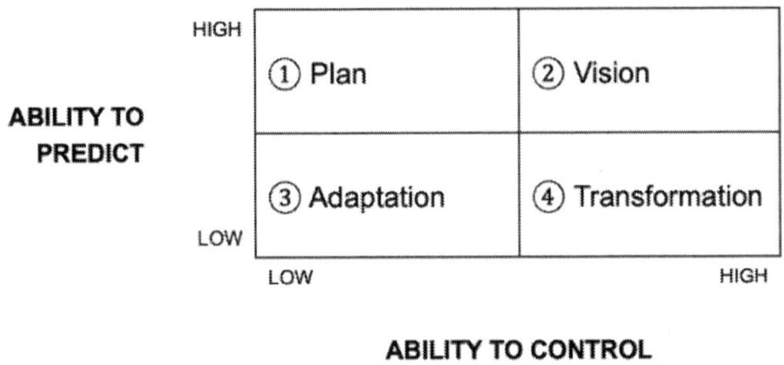

Figure 9: Four possible attitudes for the future[145]

Let's look at these four attitudes in detail.

1. High Prediction and low Control (Plan): I believe I'm capable of anticipating the evolution of the world, but not capable of influencing it. I am a "taker" of the world. I try to anticipate foreseeable changes and prepare myself to take advantage of them. This is the domain of futures studies, business plans, and scenarios. This is the approach I take when I want to open a Mexican restaurant in London, for example. The restaurant market is stable and known, and I can't influence it, so it makes sense to proceed with a relatively predictive business plan.[146]

2. High Prediction and high Control (vision): I believe I'm capable of both anticipating the evolution of my environment and influencing it to my advantage. The paradigm is that of the visionary: I make a prediction about the desired evolution of my environment and act to make it a reality. I seek to bring about the desired changes through concrete action. The entrepreneur Elon Musk, who wants to colonize Mars, is a typical example of a visionary actor.

3. Low Prediction and low Control (Adaptation): I believe I'm not capable of either anticipating or influencing the evolution of my environment. I am a "taker" of the world as events unfold. The only thing I can do is react to changes as they happen. Therefore, I organize

[145] Source: Robert Wiltbank et al, "What to do next? The case for nonpredictive strategy", Strategic Management Journal, vol. 27, 2006, p. 981-98.

[146] This is a belief, of course: it's possible that I'll start at the exact moment when a discontinuity occurs that disproves my belief (Covid-19, for example).

myself accordingly (e.g., with adaptable industrial tools). The paradigm is one of adaptation, or flexibility, agility, and responsiveness.

4. Low Prediction and high Control (transformation): I don't believe I can anticipate the evolution of the world, but I believe I can influence it. The paradigm is that of transformation, the domain of innovation and entrepreneurship. I can't have a vision of the final state of the world in the long term (for example, the electric car market in Europe in fifteen years), but I don't need one to move forward and act. It's through a series of short-term actions (small victories) that I end up transforming the world.

The transformative attitude is particularly relevant to uncertainty. It's the basis of the theory of effectuation, the logic of entrepreneurship, which we'll explore in more detail later. Since uncertainty prevents prediction, the two predictive approaches (plan and vision) are very risky in this context. The adaptation approach works well, but we've seen its limitations: we can't prepare to adapt to an infinite number of possibilities, and we'll always be one step behind the others. Adaptation works well in an environment characterized by risk (I can't predict what color my customers will want for the car they order, so I give them a choice of ten), but not for uncertainty. The two dimensions of prediction and control are complementary. An entrepreneur or innovator who creates the future he wants doesn't need to predict it. In other words, when we gain a measure of control over our environment and give ourselves the ability to change it, the need for prediction diminishes. This shift is very important: we've shown that it's dangerous to predict; of course, every time I say this, I get the response, "But what can we do about it?" Well, the idea is to make prediction unnecessary. The predictive paradigm can be summed up as: to the extent that I can predict this, I can control my projection into the future. We reverse this statement to say that to the extent that I can control the creation of the future through my actions, I no longer need to predict it. So, prediction is no longer necessary, or more pragmatically, it becomes less necessary, less central to our decision.

Military strategist and researcher Thomas Barnett advocates this approach to thinking about the future.[147] While most analysts define their profession as identifying "futures to be avoided", he prefers to focus on a "future to be created". He concludes, "What I want to do is embrace

---

[147] Barnett, *The Pentagon's New Map.*

that future and shape it from within. It's about transforming rather than predicting, using uncertainty to create".

Of the four attitudes distinguished above, two are non-predictive and correspond to the categories proposed by Barnett. These are the attitudes of adaptation and transformation. They are based on the premise that the decision maker does not base his or her reasoning on an anticipation of the environment, but rather admits that he or she cannot predict it. Adaptation responds to the need to avoid the future, while transformation responds to the need to create the future. Let's take a closer look at these two attitudes.

Futures to Avoid: Surviving Uncertainty

"I will do no harm or injustice to [my patients]."

Hippocratic Oath

As we mentioned earlier, some researchers are trying to improve our forecasting abilities. The idea is that these depend on technical tools and the skill of the forecasters. Both can be improved: the former through research, the latter through training. But this effort reflects both a naive faith in technology and, above all, a misconception of the ontology of the systems whose behavior we are trying to anticipate. Moreover, even if prediction can be marginally improved, which is highly doubtful, the fact remains that prediction will continue to make us vulnerable. Worse, the extra confidence that Tetlock's work can give us may make future black swans even more costly because we'll expect them even less. The illusion of our ability to predict increases our vulnerability. Let's look at several avenues to reduce it.

AVENUE 1: REDUCE THE USE OF PREDICTION

This is the most obvious recommendation: if a method doesn't work or is even dangerous, stop using it. This is an adaptation of the Hippocratic Oath taken by doctors: first and foremost, do no harm. If a product is toxic, we ban it. Unfortunately, as we have discussed, it is unlikely that organizations will agree to stop using prediction. The most important processes rely on prediction: budgeting, resource allocation, sales plans, business plans, product development. The predictive paradigm permeates the entire functioning of a modern organization, right down to its culture. Kenneth Arrow, the future Nobel laureate in economics, was assigned to the weather service in the Pacific during World War II. One day, he received a request from the high command for a five-day forecast. He replied that the best he could do was two days, and beyond that the forecast would be worthless. "Send it anyway," replied the requester, "we need it for planning purposes." So, we have an irreducible paradox in which a poisonous and ineffective method remains in use because its elimination would be completely disruptive to the organizations. These organizations and their managers, who pride themselves on being rational, prefer a recipe that doesn't work, or even turns out to be dangerous, to the absence of a recipe that would force them to invent a new decision-making paradigm. Recall Kahneman's observation from his own experience during his military service: "We generally knew that our predictions were little better than a random guess, but we continued to think and act as if our specific predictions were valid."[148] The problem is systemic, and therefore cultural.

AVENUE 2: WORK ON IMPACT, NOT PROBABILITIES

This is Taleb's big idea: If we admit that the uncertainty of our environment makes it impossible for us to determine the probability of an event, then we shouldn't try to improve it. That's a dead end. On the other hand, we can estimate the *impact* this event would have on us if it were to occur. I can't predict whether there will be a strike in my factory, but I can prepare for it by increasing my inventory and diversifying my production. This approach is very rich. Taleb adds: "It eliminates the need for us to understand the probabilities of a rare event (there is a fundamental limit to our knowledge of them); instead, we can focus on the impact of such an event when it occurs."[149] By eliminating, or rather more realistically reducing, the need for probabilities, we save ourselves an enormous amount of completely sterile work. This approach can be summed up as investing in preparation rather than prediction. One way to protect yourself from the impact of an event that you can't predict, and that you can't necessarily do much about, has always been to diversify your activities. That way, a shock to one business is offset by the others. Kodak's decision in 1994 to divest its chemical business (which became Eastman Chemicals) to focus on digital technology was the opposite gamble, leaving the company extremely vulnerable to a situation in which digital technology did not take off, or in which it did not succeed in transforming itself, which turned out to be the case.

---

[148] Kahneman, *Thinking fast and slow.*

[149] Taleb, *The Black Swan*, p. 210.

AVENUE 3: DEVELOPING ADAPTABILITY

The idea behind adaptability is to be prepared to respond to changes in the environment without trying to anticipate them. Interest in this approach has grown considerably recently, with the notion of agility inspired by the software world. However, there are limitations to this approach: first, adaptation takes time. By the time the organization becomes aware of the changing environment, competitors may have already moved into the right places. In the companies I work with, I can always find someone who is aware of an ongoing disruption, but that doesn't mean that this individual awareness is translated to the executive level.

Second, the organization must be able to respond quickly. This is where all efforts are currently focused. But here we run into a contradiction inherent in large organizations: they succeed because they bring a notion of scale to their activities. You can't have scale and agility at the same time. Transforming yourself into an agile organization is largely illusory for a large organization.

Third, you can't adapt to every possible situation. For example, a car manufacturer can't predict whether its customers want a red, green, or blue car. Instead of producing a batch of each and risking unsold inventory, it can configure its production tool to determine the color only when customers place their orders. By being able to respond to unpredictable customer demand, he no longer must predict it. However, this only works because color selection is a relatively small set of possibilities. Beyond a certain number of options, the combinations become too numerous and the costs too high. The manufacturer cannot design a car on demand. In other words, adaptability works in situations of risk, where anticipation is based on a limited number of possibilities that are known a priori; it does not work to deal with uncertainty, where the number of possibilities is infinite and some of them are unexpected.

Fourth, adaptability reflects a form of passivity toward the environment. Yet research, particularly around the concept of effectuation, has shown that this is not how entrepreneurs and innovators think. They don't try to adapt to the world, they try to transform it. The world to which Starbucks should have adapted was one in which coffee consumption had been declining for twenty years. It should therefore have decided to focus on another drink. Instead, it made coffee popular again. Instead of adapting to this world by being agile, pioneers challenge existing assumptions. They change their environment. They don't simply adapt.

The cat that lands on its feet when you drop it upside down is a model of adaptation. But if you drop it from the top of a twenty-story tower, it will adapt perfectly, but it will end up dying. The ability to respond to events you can't predict in an environment you can't control is necessary, but it's not enough to thrive in an uncertain environment.

AVENUE 4: CREATE REAL OPTIONS

The theory of real options is based on the idea that a decision maker faced with an unknown future can bet simultaneously, but to a limited extent, on several possible futures. Let's take the example of a company facing an innovation in its environment. Three technologies (A, B, and C) are competing, and no one knows which one will win. The company is historically proficient in technology A, but not at all in B and C. If either B or C wins, there's a risk that the company will be completely shut out of the market. Hence what it can do is invest a small stake in a startup developing a B technology, and in a startup developing a C technology. If A wins, all is well, B and C disappear, and the company has lost its small stake, but the approach has saved it from having to invest as much as it did in A. If the full development of each technology cost $200 million, and the acquisition of a stake in each start-up cost, say, $20 million, then this approach cost 2 × $20 = $40 million (lost) instead of $400 million. It has therefore saved $360 million (not counting its investment in A, which occurs in both cases).

If, say, technology B wins, the company can increase its initial investment in start-up B and help it scale up. The initial investment of $20 million is an option that gives the possibility, but not the obligation, to invest in B later. It stays in the game without betting everything. This additional investment will be made once the risk of which technology will prevail (A, B, or C) has disappeared.

The real options approach is a powerful tool when there are several possible outcomes and it's not clear which one will prevail. However, it doesn't work well with uncertainty for several reasons: First, with uncertainty, future possibilities are very numerous and, above all, not always identifiable. In the example above, there are only three competing technologies. It's a closed universe and a very simple problem. But very often the future is much more complex: we would have to buy dozens, even hundreds of options to have a chance of winning, and even then, we wouldn't even be sure of success. The situation is even more complex: the company may *believe* there are only three competing technologies and ignore a fourth. This is common with innovation.

What's more, for an option to exist, it must be purchasable. But very often, in an uncertain situation like an emerging market, options don't exist and aren't available - there's nothing to buy. Economists describe this situation as follows: there is no market for entrepreneurial judgment, which is why companies are formed. It takes time for options to appear on the market and for the company to become aware of them. Moreover, the situation evolves with uncertainty. In fact, the real options approach implicitly assumes a static environment: you list the available options at the outset, select the ones you are interested in by buying them, wait to see which one wins, and then double your money. But in reality, everything is constantly evolving: the choices corresponding to certain options disappear (a molecule proves ineffective against the proposed treatment), but other possibilities appear (an Estonian start-up bursts onto the market). The choices themselves also evolve, because the entrepreneurs' job is to influence the environment so that the option they are working on eventually wins out. Real options theory ignores this dynamic aspect of uncertainty, which distorts scientific calculations.

Finally, real options theory assumes that options are independent of each other. More specifically, they are mutually exclusive and collectively exhaustive solutions. This means that if there are N options to consider, then N covers all possibilities, and that these possibilities have nothing in common; it's either A or B or C, but not A with a little bit of B. In reality, however, the options are mixed. For example, we imagine that the future of propulsion is the internal combustion engine or the electric motor, until the day comes when the hybrid engine arrives, which is a combination of the two.

Above all, it is impossible to enumerate the possibilities at any given moment; the nature of action in a situation of uncertainty is precisely to arrange the environment by composing a patchwork of possibilities that were not foreseen or possible at the outset. In the example above, we can imagine the emergence of new energy sources (fuel cells) or the production of very cheap oil from bacteria, which would render the original choice completely obsolete; the options initially considered would no longer make sense, and the problem would have to be completely rethought. This is a far cry from the simple, static, countable universe that real options theory requires to work. Finally, the theory is rooted in a paradigm of learning and risk (the future is countable and calculable in terms of probabilities). I delay my investment until I have more information, and I bet a small amount now that gives me the right to make that investment when I do. It is therefore of little use in uncertainty, because there are very few situations in which the options are few, perfectly identified, independent of each other, and invariant over time.

AVENUE 5: REINTRODUCE VOLATILITY

With the example of the turkey, we saw that the absence of volatility is a great danger: It leads us to think that our environment is linear, which makes the inevitable black swan even more costly. It's how we perceive the environment that matters, and the absence of explicit volatility, especially if it is prolonged, leads to the perception of a non-uncertain or linear environment. Volatility must therefore be deliberately introduced into the system to prevent it from falling asleep. You must create frequent small accidents. This is how nature learns: we resist germs because we are used to their contact. This is the principle of vaccination. Voluntarily introducing volatility into a system means taking small risks very often. Make small investments, try new approaches, multiply experiments so that the organization gets used to shocks and surprises, but without them having too much impact. This is the small wins approach: if it works, we capitalize by going for another small win; if it doesn't work, it's no big deal. We take small risks by aiming for small victories, at the risk of suffering small defeats. What we must avoid is an unnecessary dependence on dangerous predictions on a large scale.

AVENUE 6: ROBUST OPTIMIZATION

What can a cockroach and a professional tennis player teach us about resilience? A lot, according to a very serious article written in 2012 by Dylan Grice, then a financial analyst at Société Générale, a bank.[150] The oldest cockroach fossil is 350 million years old (humans: 3 million). It has survived no less than five mass extinctions. It can live without air for forty-five minutes, survive underwater for half an hour, withstand freezing temperatures and fifteen times more radiation than humans. It will eat virtually anything, including the glue on the back of postage stamps. And if it runs out of food, it can live for another month before starving to death. What strategy does it use to survive? It moves in the opposite direction of the air currents that signal an approaching predator. And that's it! It's simple, but spectacularly robust. Cockroaches prove

[150] Dylan Grice, "The Last Popular Delusions", Société Générale "Global Strategy" note, November 23, 2012.

that what's robust isn't necessarily optimal, that you don't have to try to be too smart for your environment, and that you can thrive on very simple principles. Like Fat Tony, a cockroach faced with a twisted question would avoid playing the game at all. It would accept that it isn't smart enough. Do cockroaches need a worldview, a noble purpose or a vision to survive? No, and it wouldn't help them. Don't either, it's often counterproductive.

What about tennis players? Professional players put the ball where they want it, at the speed they want it, with a precision and consistency that most players could never hope to achieve. The winner of a professional tennis match is the player who hits the most winning shots, but for most tennis players, the game is different. They're trying to make shots. They're trying to make points. But in the process, they make double faults, they go over the line, they hit the net. The winner of these regular games? The one who loses the fewest points! Professional tennis players win points, while amateurs lose points. They lose points because they try to score points that they can't score. We're just like them: we waste a lot of time and energy trying to be smarter than the others; we go to the limits of a world even though they're not clear and change abruptly. Optimization is not designed for an uncertain, nonlinear world. In the aftermath of the 2020 pandemic, the fragility of global supply chains, largely dependent on China, was exposed by the shortages that crippled production at many companies around the world. Rather than trying to be smart, it is often better to settle for not being stupid - optimizing in the face of uncertainty. Let's bet that companies will diversify their channels. They will be less efficient, but they will be more resilient.

AVENUE 7: MANAGING UNCERTAINTY SUBJECTIVELY

Uncertainty is not managed in the same way whether you're a banker, investor, entrepreneur, CEO of a large corporation, or an executive considering your personal future, which again underscores the role of identity. The need for anticipation is not the same depending on the goal being pursued. In some areas, less precise anticipation may be sufficient. For example, a bank making a loan to a company does not need to anticipate the company's economic performance in detail. It need only assume that the company will be solvent enough to repay the loan. Anticipating repayment is therefore less difficult than for an equity investor, whose profit depends on the company's ability to pay dividends, which is a higher performance requirement. A lender's need for anticipation is therefore less than that of an equity investor.

An investor can protect himself against uncertainty by diversifying his portfolio of holdings, an approach that venture capitalists in particular follow systematically: they know that most of the startups they invest in won't succeed, but they don't know which ones, and they obviously can't know, because they are developing in highly uncertain markets. The success of one will hopefully compensate for the failure of others. An entrepreneur can follow the same strategy by diversifying his activities, as mentioned above. The ideal situation is to have activities that are only weakly correlated and that share characteristics that allow economies of scope (e.g., the same marketing skills, the same production tools). The French Bic group is a good example of this approach: shavers, lighters, and pens share the fact that they are plastic objects that are complicated to manufacture but evolve largely independently. If lighters decline, for example because of a drop in tobacco consumption linked to the development of e-cigarettes, it's not certain that Bic will be able to do anything, but it will at least be left with the other two activities. An individual, on the other hand, will have to arbitrate between the uncertainty linked to his organization, as for someone who works for a newspaper today, and that linked to his professional life: consider joining a more dynamic sector. Some professions are more stable than others. In a way, being a doctor is very robust. You rarely become a millionaire as a doctor, but you can practice anywhere in the world as soon as you get off the plane. Other professions are dependent on the organization in which they are practiced, such as the technician who specializes in a machine developed in-house: his skills are not at all transferable to the outside world, and if a black swan hits the organization, it will be difficult to find a new job.

The big question posed by today's technological breakthroughs, such as artificial intelligence and robotics, is what skills you need to develop to manage your career in an uncertain world.

AVENUE 8: EXAMINE YOUR MENTAL MODELS

The uncertainty created by the changing world undermines our mental models. It makes our assumptions and beliefs obsolete. What was true is no longer true, and vice versa. What was impossible becomes possible, even essential. The risk is that we get stuck in models, some of which have become obsolete, but the difficulty is that we often discover them too late, after the crisis or the accident. The existence of uncertainty therefore requires a regular review of mental models, both on a personal and collective level. This examination boils down to the question: what do I (or we) believe that has become false? This is difficult because mental models, and our beliefs in general, are invisible. They are often taken for granted. Remember some of them: "The Germans will respect Belgium's neutrality", "Americans will never elect a raving lunatic like Trump", "Tesla will never succeed in making cars on a large scale", "a virus in a little-known Chinese city that kills old people doesn't threaten us".

Consider the invasion of Ukraine on February 24, 2022, which is another case of complete surprise for many experts. On February 17, a week before the invasion, Edward Luttwak, a respected strategy expert whom we have quoted several times, wrote on Twitter: "The latest IC [Intelligence Community] forecast: War is imminent, and Russian forces will rely on exceptionally intense artillery bombardment, including of Kiev. This implies a reckless gambler Putin, willing to make Ukrainians hate Russia and Russians forever. Neither is consistent with Putin's past record." There are three questionable mental models at work here: first, the belief that Putin would never act recklessly; second, that he would not want to make Ukrainians hate Russia forever; and third, that his past record is indicative of his future actions. We have discussed the latter, which is the immortality argument. "Reckless" is a judgment. Maybe Putin saw his operation differently, as something easy to do, a risk worth taking. And maybe he doesn't care what Ukrainians think about Russia and Russians. On the eve of the invasion, Luttwak was at it again. He wrote: "Once again, US intelligence has issued a warning of imminent invasion. I have disagreed with all previous warnings because the available Russian forces are far too small to control the largest country in Europe". The belief here was that if Russia attacked Ukraine, it would be to occupy it. We now know that Putin's idea was that a quick operation to seize Kiev would cause the government to flee, and Russia could complete the operation by installing a puppet regime in just a few days, without occupying the entire territory, and then go back home. Even the judgment of the best of experts can be distorted by false mental models.

A Future to Create: Thriving in Uncertainty

"Uncertainty sets us free."

Peter Bernstein

It's important to protect ourselves from uncertainty by trying to avoid undesirable futures, as this is a prerequisite for both individual and organizational survival. But we're not cockroaches, and simply surviving by avoiding absurd bets is not enough! What we need is to take advantage of the uncertainty that makes creative human action possible.

CREATIVE ACTION: ACTING LIKE AN ENTREPRENEUR

The pragmatic attitude of a world transformed by human action is that of entrepreneurship. As the economists Richard Cantillon and Frank Knight have observed, entrepreneurs are the economic agents who specialize in dealing with uncertainty. Uncertainty is their raw material. For a long time, the model of entrepreneurship was based on a paradigm of discovery. Entrepreneurs were the ones who discovered an opportunity and knew how to exploit it. Opportunity was therefore seen as pre-existing and having an objective reality. Yet, researchers have argued that opportunities can also be created. Entrepreneurs transform their environment through their actions. They create novelty in the form of products, services, organizations, and markets that did not exist before. Let's look at how this transformation is put into practice through a historical example: the creation of U-Haul, today the leading commercial vehicle rental network in the United States, with nearly 17,000 branches.[151]

---

[151] The U-Haul case and related quotes are taken from Stuart Read, Saras

The post-war period in the United States was marked by the return of demobilized soldiers who migrated to dynamic regions, especially in the West, in search of employment. This was a time when people were moving en masse, but there was no way to rent a truck to transport their belongings. One had to buy one, which was out of the question for most people, or hire a specialized company, which was very expensive. One could also buy a trailer, but that was a big purchase and would only be used once: what do you do with it after you'd used it? Leonard Shoen, himself a demobilized soldier, was faced with this problem. A handyman, he bought a used trailer cheaply and rebuilt it himself. His financial situation was precarious. As he puts it: "My savings were barely enough for a down payment on a house and furnishings, and I knew we'd be broke if I did that. So, we started a nomadic life, putting our stuff in a trailer and living between in-laws and parents for six months. I was a part-time hairdresser to make some money". He was surprised when his friends and family asked to borrow his trailer. Gradually, and with the help of his wife, he bought more trailers and started renting them out, gradually discovering the possibility of a commercial activity. He adds: "I bought the kind of trailers I thought I could rent at what I thought was a fair price. By the fall of 1945, I was so deeply involved in the project that it was 'make or break'". He had so little money that he moved his wife and young child to his in-laws' ranch in Ridgefield, Washington. In the fall of 1945, the Shoens began building their first trailers out of scrap metal purchased from the U.S. Navy. To advertise, they decided to paint the trailers bright orange with the evocative name U-Haul (you haul yourself) on the sides. With no funding, they had to use the family ranch garage as their first manufacturing and repair facility. Advertising was limited to phone book ads and the high visibility of bright orange trailers on the nation's roads-another first. They offered a discount to customers who agreed to find a dealer in the towns they moved to. Gradually, their dealer network grew. They also formed partnerships with service stations across the country. They supplied them with trailers, while they provided unused land and agreed to take over rental operations, further expanding his network without investment.

Here we can see that entrepreneurs are not solitary optimizing calculators external to the environment; on the contrary, they transform it with stakeholders (such as customers or service stations) who are also

---

Sarasvathy, Nick Dew, Robert Wiltbank, *Effectual Entrepreneurship* (Routledge; 2nd edition, 2016).

part of the environment. Most entrepreneurs don't start with a clear idea of what their market and offering will be. In fact, the Shoens didn't even realize they were entrepreneurs at first. They solved a problem they faced, nothing more. They applied a logic of control, modifying their environment to solve their problem. Of course, this modification was microscopic at first. But even then, they differed from thousands of demobilized soldiers who, faced with the same situation, simply worked around the problem. When the Shoens realized that others had the same problem, their entrepreneurial idea took shape. The logic of control, multiplied by the involvement of stakeholders - their first customers, the gas stations - was now applied to a much wider field and would lead, in just three years, to the creation of a huge company that would be the first to make one-way trailer rentals possible throughout the United States.

The Shoens did not focus on the predictable aspects of the future. They didn't study American internal migration, which had been developing since the 1930s, to anticipate a possible rental market. They did not analyze current rental companies to anticipate their potential supply in this context. They didn't decipher the weak signals that indicated the coming market. As a demobilized sailor, Shoen had no way of doing this. It didn't even occur to him. Instead, the Shoens focused on the aspects of the future they could control. The market they created was the result of that action. It was within their grasp: Shoen was a handyman, he knew where to find trailers and how to buy them at the right price, he knew how to find people who were interested, and so on. The controllable aspects were the resources at his disposal and the stakeholders willing to join him in his efforts (first customers, service stations, etc.). In essence, instead of focusing on the predictable aspects of a future they can't control, entrepreneurs focus on the controllable aspects of a future they don't have to predict. This approach, called effectuation[152], is not limited to entrepreneurship. As the sociologist Hans Joas observes: "Only when we recognize that certain means are available to us can we discover goals that had not previously appeared to us."[153]

The logic of entrepreneurs, then, is not to find a way to predict better, but to make prediction unnecessary. Uncertainty is resolved not by a particular technique, better access to information, or unique qualities, but

[152] For an introduction to effectuation, see Stuart Read, Saras Sarasvathy, Nick Dew, Robert Wiltbank, *Effectual Entrepreneurship.*
[153] Joas, *The Creativity of Action.*

by an approach that consists in creating the future. We are no longer in a "we need prediction, but it doesn't work" stalemate; we are now in a "prediction doesn't work, but that's okay because we don't need it" dynamics. This is a non-predictive strategy. It is possible to act under uncertainty without predicting and without being passive or reactive to events. For entrepreneurs, uncertainty is a raw material, the basis of their creative action, through which they transform their environment by creating new markets, organizations, products, and services. This creative dimension of decision making in the face of uncertainty is reflected in the fifth principle of effectuation, which states that the future is not written in advance, but results from what we do. This principle allows us to assert that entrepreneurs don't discover the future but co-create it through their decisions: the stream of future events is always (at least partially) indeterminate when a decision is made, and that decision, combined with those of millions of other actors, will necessarily modify that stream and thus the future. This shows how entrepreneurs do not choose among possible options but create the one they want. They take advantage of surprises rather than trying to avoid them. They do not seek to avoid uncertainty, but welcome the constant flow of new facts, a product of the complexity and richness of the world and a source of opportunity.

EFFECTUAL AND CAUSAL: THE TWO RATIONALITIES

We have seen that the dominant model of decision making (rational actor) assumes that a goal is chosen before finding the means to achieve it. These means are determined by examining the available information. This rationality is called causal. The name comes from the fact that for a given effect (goal), we look for the best possible causes (means). In marketing, we look for the most attractive segment; in human resources, we try to recruit the best profile for a well-defined position; in strategy, we try to achieve a certain market share, and so on. An example of causal reasoning is: "I want to get 10% of this market; what investment is necessary?" Causal rationality implies a logic of optimization (using as little means as possible) and emphasizes the importance of prior forecasting and analysis to avoid unpleasant surprises that will prevent the optimization sought. Of the four possible attitudes to the future, we identified above, causal logic corresponds to those that are predictive, i.e., plan and vision. With effectuation, we have seen that entrepreneurs use a radically opposite mode of reasoning. Rather than using goals to determine the resources needed to achieve them, effectuation uses available resources to determine possible goals. The term effectual comes from the fact that we imagine possible effects (goals) for given causes (available resources). An example of effectual thinking is: "I have $10,000 and a passion for sports. What business idea can I come up with?"

Effectual reasoning is relevant in uncertainty, where neither the products nor the corresponding markets exist at the time of their creation. In such a situation, causal rationality works poorly because it is difficult to define goals: you can't aim for a market share that doesn't exist, let alone sales, and the lack of objective information makes forecasting useless. In a situation of uncertainty, it's less about optimizing than about creating, and the two approaches are completely different. While the causal approach corresponds to a deliberate approach to strategy, setting clear goals that are stable over time, effective reasoning is non-deterministic and emergent. The notion of an ultimate goal almost completely disappears in favor of a series of goals presented as intermediate stages, set according to the means available at a given time. Causal and effectual logic are both part of human reasoning. One is not better than the other, and both are relevant in different situations. And yet most of our teaching is based on causal logic. Causal rationality is based on the paradigm of choice: the question of decision is framed in terms of a choice among several existing options. Effectual rationality is based on paradigm of creation: it's not so much problem solving as the creation of new possibilities from existing resources. This is the only approach that creates novelty.

The Mindset of the Decision-Maker in Uncertainty

"Convictions are more dangerous enemies of truth than lies."

Friedrich Nietzsche

U.S. President Lyndon Johnson used to ask: "And therefore?" at the end of a brilliant demonstration by one of his advisors. That's the question this chapter seeks to answer. We began this book by pointing out that, in an uncertain world, it is dangerous to predict, because to predict is to expose oneself, sooner or later, to catastrophe. This danger of prediction is the unsurpassable horizon of the contemporary decision maker. This is the starting point of Johnson's question. The correct formulation, then, is not "If I can't predict, what do you suggest instead?" because I don't suggest anything; I *can't* suggest anything. The correct question is, "Since I can't predict, what can I do to gain some control over events?" We've shown that in such an environment you can have two goals: to avoid certain futures and to create a future you desire. Creating a desired future means adopting an entrepreneurial mindset that uses uncertainty to change the environment to our advantage.

Using the elements of mindset summarized in the previous section, we can identify the principles that reflect the relevant attitude of the decision maker under uncertainty.

CONVERSATION RATHER THAN FORMALIZATION

Formalization freezes the problem at a given moment, while we manage "living", evolving systems that produce more and more facts. The result is that we act on a formal system that is necessarily out of date.

Moreover, there is no scientific evidence that an organization that systematically formalizes its strategy is more profitable than one that doesn't. Formalization tends to simplify the description, even though the system is complex. Conversation, on the other hand, maintains a continuous flow that considers changes in the situation, especially those resulting from our own actions. An important element in the success of conversation is learning to ask questions by practicing Socratic agnosticism. It forces us to ask questions rather than rush to provide answers. Socratic questioning is the generalist's weapon against the expert, the one who assures you that the Titanic is unsinkable, that Covid-19 is just the flu, that masks are useless, or that your project will be completed on time. The conversation must be held with all parties involved in the problem, illustrating the notion of technical democracy. Decisions can no longer be imposed; they must be negotiated. We are not "masters and owners of nature"; we must negotiate with it, and in this negotiation conversation is essential.

Conversation also has the effect of breaking down the separation between thought and action, whereby the analyst provides information to the decision-maker as a kind of weather service, without taking part in the decision-making process. On the contrary, in conversation, the analyst and the decision-maker constantly pass the ball back and forth, the former understanding the latter's stakes, which in turn enables him to better conduct his analysis and, in particular, to bring to his attention questions that didn't arise a priori. The effect of conversation is to put context back at the center of reflection and action, since decontextualization is the great sin of Cartesian thought. Conversation can use metaphors - the turkey, the U-2, Dr. John, etc. - as a vaccine against positivist automatisms. Again, this is a good defense for the generalist against the expert. The very notion of conversation creates equality among its participants and thus helps to break down Dr. John's arguments of authority ("I'm right because I'm an expert and it's complicated").

The conversation can only take place if the organization is able to generate cognitive diversity within itself. Diversity has been defended on moral grounds, but here we're talking about a defense on practical grounds: since the way we see the world reflects our individual and collective identity, we can't think about its complexity with a homogeneous social body, or we'll be in for some painful surprises. We therefore need to build *Cassandras*, i.e., institutional mechanisms that allow constructive dissent to be expressed.[154] It is the best protection against black swans.

Conversation also ensures that you're inside the system, not outside it. It has to happen, even with the "lower level" people, the ones we don't normally include in decision making. In an isotropic world, where the black swan is the small grain of sand we overlook, we can't know a priori who will be important. So we have to go "Byzantine" and - not out of duty, but with Montaigne's joy - rub shoulders with all the environments that matter, not just the most comfortable or those frequented by our clones, the Dr. Johns and the higher-ups. Strategic conversation considers the whole, not the top; it is democratic, not elitist; it is part of a flow, not an a priori calculation; it welcomes surprises, not avoids them. One condition for successful strategic conversation is to make assumptions and beliefs (mental models) explicit, and to revisit them regularly to test them and see if they are still valid. This systematic attitude of questioning assumptions can only be sustained if the organization is designed to constantly produce Cassandras who have the ability and institutional support to challenge them.

PARTICULAR CASES RATHER THAN GENERAL PRINCIPLES

The whole point of modeling thinking is to eliminate particular cases, to reduce everything to a single case. With uncertainty, it's exactly the opposite. It's the special cases, the unprecedented events, the black swans, that interest us because they have a major impact on our environment (safety, sales, etc.). Uncertainty is not the domain of calculation, it's the domain of judgment, the subjective, circumstantial assessment that allows us to form an opinion about what will happen. Similarly, we prefer a richness of description to axioms, unprovable propositions without which demonstration is impossible. Much of management thinking is based on rather fragile axioms. One of these is that one must predict in order to act. But as we've seen, this is not necessary: we can take transformative action without needing to predict. Nor is it necessary to have a clear goal, let alone a vision, to act. Many of those who have profoundly changed their environment have developed their vision only through action. In 1940, Churchill did not have a clear vision of Britain's future. He had developed a deep understanding of the situation and its dynamics, and he had a few firmly held beliefs. He correctly analyzed the immense American potential that

[154] This is the central argument of *Constructing Cassandra*.

could be unleashed. It is this deep understanding of the situation that must be developed, rather than investing in narrow and fragile predictions. Familiarity with cases and confrontation with reality require the development of *phronesis*. Proposed by Aristotle, phronesis is a practical wisdom that comes from an intimate familiarity with the contingencies and uncertainties of a particular social practice. It lies between *episteme*, abstract, universal knowledge - the realm of science and Cartesianism - and *techné*, the know-how associated with the practice of a particular craft. It represents a happy medium between two extremes between which management is constantly evolving: Cartesian abstraction and a set of decontextualized tools and techniques, such as classical strategic models. Unlike episteme, phronesis is not about what is true, but about what would be good to do in given circumstances, with goals for evaluation and prescription, and means for selection. It is the wisdom of judgment. For Aristotle, it is the most important of the intellectual virtues because it is necessary for the management of human affairs, including the management of episteme and techne, which cannot be managed by themselves.[155]

Serious consideration of the case is essential, for it is in the details that the key elements for action are to be found. In a world of black swans and unprecedented events, it is also in the details that we find the key factors that will bring about the sudden change in the environment. Cartesian, and later positivist, thinking has attempted to decontextualize and depersonalize analytical reasoning and decision making to the extreme, so that they are based solely on unquestionable principles and universal laws. Instead, we need to recontextualize the issues under consideration. For example, as we have seen, we cannot evaluate the options available to President Kennedy in 1962 with regards to Vietnam without understanding the political context of the time and the role played by the "loss" of China and the Korean War a few years earlier. We can't understand Nokia's situation and its gamble on mobile telephony in 1991 without understanding Finland's historical relationship with the USSR, its first trading partner.

THE CONTINGENT RATHER THAN THE TIMELESS

The positivist dream is to establish universal laws governing the evolution of the world. These laws exist for natural phenomena (planetary motion, chemical reactions, energy phenomena, etc.) or in

---

[155] Bent Flyvbjerg, Todd Landman, and Stanford Schram, eds, *Real Social Science: Applied Phronesis* (Cambridge University Press, 2012).

mathematics, but they don't exist in human systems. In a non-deterministic world, everything is contingent: what is could be otherwise. Empirical laws that can be observed over very long periods of time (such as the fact that elections are won in the center) are true until they become false. Nothing is ever truly timeless, nothing is eternal, neither empire nor enterprise. This contingency is put to good use by entrepreneurs trying to capitalize on it. We learn more from an incongruous event than from the umpteenth repetition of the same event. Many philosophers since Plato have tried to freeze time, to deny it, anchoring for a long time in philosophy the belief that fixity is a nobler and more dignified thing than change. On the contrary, time must be put back at the heart of human action, for it is time that brings about the source of change in the environment, by bringing in new facts. It is because of time that tomorrow will not be like yesterday, and that the environment is constantly evolving. This evolution does not take place linearly, progressively, but by leaps and bounds, i.e., by unprecedented events. Our thinking is shaped by continuity, but it's the discontinuous that really matters, the contingent, the unprecedented event; that's where the fortunes of people and companies are decided. We can, like entrepreneurs, take advantage of contingency and its surprises, take advantage of what we can't foresee; we can even try to provoke them, like those companies that go out into the field to discover things their models would never tell them, or develop the diversity of their cultural milieu.

IDENTITY RATHER THAN DATA

Contrary to the impersonal Cartesian view, the identity of the actors is at the heart of the action. The separation of mind and body has no biological basis. We make sense of our environment through our mental models (beliefs and values), and these models reflect our identity, whether individual or collective. This means that we always have a subjective approach to reality. Descartes would regret it, Montaigne would rejoice in it; it's inevitable, and rather than vainly trying to approach an illusory objective reality, it's better to acknowledge it and take advantage of it. This means getting involved in the process and revealing one's own interests in the work of anticipation: instead of calculating, supposedly objective predictors detached from the environment they study, we should prefer committed, subjective actors who risk their necks in their forecasts and whom we can therefore trust more. Someone who has something to lose if his prediction turns out to be wrong will be much more careful with predictive poison. Very often, decision-makers fail to understand their target because, as naive rationalists, they reject identity and the cultural dimension. Not only do they reject the impact of other people's culture, but they also reject the impact of their own culture on their analysis. For them, it's all about rationality, game theories, and supposedly logical behavior from a cautious distance, or worse, from a screen. But the world doesn't work that way.

The starting point is therefore the subject, not thinking à la Descartes, but acting à la Montaigne - individual or organization. Who I am, what I know and who I know. From there, the question becomes, "What can I do with that?" or "What do I want to do with that?" This immediately raises the question of values - what are my preferences? - and ethics - what is acceptable to do? What is the appropriate action? In fact, the social systems that are the object of our action are governed by the values of the actors who make them up. They are not objects with mechanisms. It's these values that we need to understand, without necessarily agreeing with them, in order to act on the system. And, as we've emphasized, you must put yourself in the equation. The decision maker cannot view the environment as an external object, like a chemist mixing products and observing their reactions. The decision maker is part of the environment, part of the problem, if only because he or she has already made decisions that have affected that environment. It's probably no coincidence that Montaigne, out of modesty and with a casual air, constantly talks about himself, writing in the first person and observing himself in action, with the benevolence but also the necessary distance befitting a philosopher. He is a reflective actor, fully involved in the world around him.

CONTROL RATHER THAN PREDICTION

Uncertainty makes it difficult to predict the outcome of a decision. The dominant decision-making model is the relative comparison of the costs and benefits of an action, which can lead to a dead end because the latter cannot be estimated. It can be predicted, with all the risks that entails. Instead, we can use the entrepreneurial logic of considering actions under uncertainty in terms of affordable loss: betting what we are willing to lose. In this way, we develop a prudential approach to uncertainty, but here prudence does not consist in refusing to act; nor does it consist in delaying our decision in order to obtain more information; it consists in acting decisively but prudently, in the knowledge that what we risk losing by acting is affordable to us, but that we have much to gain by acting, even with little information; we control the downside because the upside is uncertain. Of course, what's affordable to one person may not be affordable to another. Once again, we find the subjective dimension of action; once again, it all starts with the actor. You must participate! Just as a country cannot be reduced to numbers, it cannot be evaluated without being deeply understood, and it cannot be understood from a distance. We cannot simply be "analysts" staring at our screens.

This importance of action - action that reveals parties (options), action that reveals preferences, creative action - gives a dimension of control: because I act on the environment, I am the "pilot in the plane": I can influence its evolution and transform it according to my wishes and interests. Because other actors also perceive this uncertainty, I don't know what the future will look like any more than they do, and they don't know any more than I do. There is no objective knowledge of the future. The solution is subjective: we build a "crazy quilt" by joining forces with other players to co-construct the future, rather than waiting for it to happen. Importantly, it's not necessary to have a vision of the ultimate state you want to get to in order to transform the world. Again, taking a cue from entrepreneurs, we can start with a simple idea and grow it over time. Prediction is no longer necessary, and so the fact that it's not possible is no longer a problem. Of course, this action is closely intertwined with the strategic conversation; the two are just two sides of the same coin. We'll develop what historian Marc Bloch called *methodological opportunism* in relation to the Wehrmacht's lightning advance in 1940. "German officers had no precise orders, only broad outlines, and they relied on surprise. They were expected to use their judgment in the field. They believed in action and the unexpected," Bloch observes, "while we believed in immobility and what was already done." In any place and at any time, judgment consists of asking three questions: "What is going on?", "What does it mean?" and "What can we do about it?" We're back to the Socratic agnosticism which, in the face of uncertainty, consists of asking questions again and again, making hypotheses, making things happen by acting, and then learning from what happens. An attitude that historian Ernest May summarizes by asking, "What is the theory of the case under consideration?"[156]

Conversation rather than formalization, particular cases rather than general principles, the contingent rather than the timeless, identity rather than data, control rather than prediction-these are five heuristics or

---

[156] Ernest R. May, *Strange Victory: Hitler's Conquest of France* (New York: I.B.Tauris, 2000), 458.

principles for acting in uncertainty, not just to protect against it, but above all to take advantage of it and enjoy it. There are undoubtedly others. The very nature of uncertainty makes it resistant to structured, finite models. Everyone can develop their own principles that can be effective, provided they respect the nature of uncertainty. After all, to put oneself in the equation is also to develop one's own principles of action based on an understanding of the nature of one's environment.

Developing a Culture of Uncertainty

"In the depths of Alexander's victories, we always find Aristotle."

Charles de Gaulle

We have observed that while the environments in which we operate are mostly characterized by uncertainty, most of the tools and concepts used in organizations are designed for risk. This epistemological mismatch has many consequences, some of them very serious, because our tools are ill-suited to the situations we encounter: we use a map of the Alps mountains to cross the Atlantic. And if that's the case, it's largely because our mental models are mismatched. We won't solve the problem by proposing new tools, but by changing the prevailing culture in our organizations. It's a cultural challenge. The source of this dominance lies in education. An analysis of the shortcomings of our educational system is beyond the scope of this book, and many authors have long tackled it, but on this basis, we can outline a few relevant avenues.

Abandon the predictive paradigm: From an early age, children are asked what they want to be when they grow up. An 8-year-old child born in 1967 is unlikely to answer with "data scientist", "social media consultant", or "Zumba instructor", because none of these existed in 1975. All they'll have is nurse, firefighter, veterinarian, maybe astronaut. This logic continues in higher education, for example, when recruiting candidates for top business schools. Each of them is expected to arrive with a well-defined career plan for the next ten years, while one of the essential functions of school is to enable them to build that plan by discovering new subjects and meeting new people. This institutional reality takes a variety of forms: the requirement for a business plan to finance a start-up, the financial forecasts that are indispensable for budgeting within an organization, the requirement that a presidential candidate present a detailed program for his or her mandate, and so on.

The forecasting paradigm also dominates professional studies. For example, the Chartered Financial Analyst (CFA) designation is a diploma issued by the CFA Institute, a prestigious private organization. It is a globally recognized standard, and obtaining this extremely difficult certification confers international professional recognition in the financial world. To date, approximately 120,000 professionals have obtained the CFA designation, and they are present at the highest levels of all international financial institutions. In other words, the CFA has a significant impact on the way global finance works. And yet, in its official training manual, the "CFA Program Curriculum", we read: "The oil industry is characterized by a high degree of predictability". Considering that the history of oil prices is littered with significant forecasting errors, as we have seen above, this statement is shockingly false. In fact, the oil industry is characterized by a very *low* level of predictability. It is most unfortunate that generations of elite financiers have been trained to believe otherwise. This is just one example of the negative impact of a false epistemology, with a particularly strong impact in an educational institution, which is a vector and accelerator for the spread of this false epistemology. It is imperative that we teach the unpredictable nature of the future.

Educate for the complex, not just the complicated: We train our children to solve complicated problems by analyzing them, that is, by breaking them down into subproblems. What's more, we only give them problems for which we know there is at most one solution. In this way, we give them the idea that there is nothing that can't be analyzed, if we give ourselves the means and the courage to break down what needs to be broken down. And yet, for Charles de Gaulle, the primary role of education is to give future leaders "the capacity for synthesis", the habit of thinking in general terms, the notion of the interrelationships of things that illuminate the highest levels of action, the ability to make choices that are not choices of detail to the detriment of the whole. The excess of technology with which we are so enamored obscures the vision of the whole.

Develop epistemic humility: Teaching tends to focus on well-formulated questions with only one solution, which we must find. With this positivist logic, we train experts to sit on a formal knowledge base that fits perfectly with Cartesian goals: not to be questioned. The result is excessive confidence in one's knowledge base. And yet, as we have seen, the expert's overconfidence explains the catastrophic predictions in disruptive situations, precisely because the disruption challenges this famous knowledge.

This type of teaching thus develops a form of epistemic arrogance, i.e. the haughty, presumptuous attitude of one who has no doubts about the accuracy and relevance of his or her knowledge. We train experts who are overconfident in their abilities and for whom expressing doubt in the face of the complexity of the world is a form of weakness. This is what Taleb means when he writes: "My biggest problem with the education system is precisely that it forces students to produce explanations of the subjects they study, and punishes them when they reserve judgment, when they murmur 'I don't know'."[157] The knowledge so dispensed in the classroom shapes Dr. Johns and can become an obstacle to understanding what's going on in real life. However, when faced with a complex system, nothing is more important than to reserve judgment, as Montaigne wisely observed four hundred years ago. This epistemic modesty is fruitful, it is wise, it should be taught, and above all, it should be socially valued.

Anchor ourselves in the future: our educational system, especially in France, trains people primarily in the knowledge of the past. Nothing is more symptomatic of this than the agrégation, a specialty that France shared with the now defunct Soviet Union. An extremely prestigious diploma, the agrégation consists of memorizing everything - literally everything written by the great people who preceded us on the question at hand - without developing any original thought in the process. We are educating what Taleb calls "idiot scholars", who are encyclopedically uneducated, who know everything and understand nothing, and who then educate our children. In a changing world, we should be training our elite to think new thoughts and to believe that we can change the world, because that's what they will be asked to do from the moment they take office. And that's exactly what Paul Valéry was talking about when he wrote about teaching: "[...] it is a question of making you ready to face what has never been".[158]

This positivist logic, which favors technical and scientific education because it is less prone to ambiguity, is not exclusive to France. Marc

[157] Taleb, *The Black Swan*.

[158] Berger, Massé, and Bourbon-Busset, *De la prospective*.

Andreessen, an Internet pioneer and now Silicon Valley guru, wrote an article on his blog in 2014 titled "Culture clash", in which he explained that the humanities are no longer at the forefront of today's cultural needs. He added: "For those who aren't deeply immersed in math and technology, it's going to get harder and harder to understand the world."[159] In this he reflects what Madsbjerg calls "the Silicon Valley mindset", according to which technology will solve any problem, whatever that problem may be, what we called scientism above. If the hammer can't drive the screw in, well, never mind, we'll build a bigger hammer, we can afford it. Nothing could be more illusory. Historian Michael Howard adds that historical inculturation, in particular, is one of the sources of disaster: "People, often of magisterial intelligence, usually trained in law, economics, or perhaps political science, have led their governments into disastrous miscalculations because they don't know the historical context, the cultural universe of the foreign societies with which they have to deal. This is an awareness for which no strategic or economic analysis, no crisis management or conflict resolution technique... can provide a substitute."[160] Ah, but history can't be measured, and it doesn't fit on a four-box graph.

Fortunately, not everyone in Silicon Valley subscribes to Marc Andreessen's credo, and many companies now turn to philosophers to help them understand the world.[161] Interestingly, Madsjberg notes that many of the leaders of major American companies are literary types, including in the high-tech sector. Ken Chenault, CEO of American Express from 2001 to 2018, studied history, as did Sam Palmisano, former CEO of IBM, and Brian Moynihan, current CEO of Bank of America; Hank Paulson, former Secretary of the Treasury, studied English; Michael Eisner, former CEO of Disney, studied English and theater; Carl Icahn, the famous investor, has a thesis in philosophy. Paul Graham, a key figure in Silicon Valley and founder of the YCombinator incubator, which has produced Dropbox, Reddit, and Airbnb, among other "unicorns", graduated from Cornell University with a Bachelor of Arts degree before earning a Ph.D. in computer science from Harvard. He also studied painting at the Rhode Island School of Design and the Florence Academy of Fine Arts. And the list goes on. In a 2011 article for the Wall Street Journal, Norman Augustine, former CEO of

---

159 Quoted in Madsbjerg, *Sensemaking*, p. 27.

160 Michael Howard, *The Lessons of History* (Yale University Press, 1992).

161 Michael J. Coren, "Silicon Valley executives are hiring philosophers to teach them to question everything", Quartz, April 18, 2017.

Lockheed Martin, a defense and aerospace conglomerate, argued for a stronger humanities foundation in primary and secondary education. This is a far cry from the simplistic views of Marc Andreessen. Alan G. Lafley, CEO of Procter & Gamble until 2016, who himself had a degree in history before earning an MBA, advised young people who want to succeed in business to study literature or the arts. He explained it this way: "By studying the arts, sciences, humanities, social sciences, and languages, the mind develops a mental dexterity that opens the person to new ideas, which is a key to success in an ever-changing environment". Indeed, before World War II, de Gaulle wrote: "The true school of command is that of general culture. It enables the mind to exercise itself with order, to distinguish in things the essential from the incidental, [...] to rise to the level where the whole appears without prejudice to the nuances. There was no illustrious captain who did not have a taste and a feeling for the heritage and the human spirit. In the depths of Alexander's victories, we always find Aristotle..."

As long as our educational system continues to produce a majority of Dr. Johns and is organized so that they are the ones who reach the heights of political and economic power, we will remain fragile in the face of uncertainty, and disasters will continue. The shift from linear to nonlinear thinking, which welcomes uncertainty as an opportunity, as luck, as the opening of possibilities, won't happen simply by changing management tools. It requires a change in attitude, a profound change in culture. We must give up what we've invested in all these years of education and career. It's not easy. But the stakes are high. Forecasting, even if it can't always be avoided, makes our organizations fragile. The difficulty is that it often works because most of the time our environments behave in a linear fashion. Its non-linear nature rarely comes to the fore, and it's this rarity that makes it dangerous, because over time the mind has become accustomed to linearity. But when it does emerge, it does so brutally, with disastrous consequences. The world is becoming more uncertain, and the surprises are coming faster and faster. Long gone are the days when we could tell ourselves that with a little luck, we'd make it. Embracing uncertainty is certainly difficult, but it is now essential if we are to face what has never been but may be.

About the Author

Philippe Silberzahn is a professor at emlyon business school (France). His work focuses on how organizations deal with disruptions and situations of radical uncertainty. As a keynote speaker, management trainer and consultant, he works with the leadership teams of large organizations engaged in transformation efforts when faced with disruptions in their markets. He is the author of several books and numerous articles on these topics. He has over twenty years of experience as an entrepreneur and CEO in the software industry.

Printed in Poland
by Amazon Fulfillment
Poland Sp. z o.o., Wrocław

55648582R10114